HINDUISM

The Science of Self Realisation

Anupam Srivastava

Help and encouragement for young people to wake up to, recognize, unfold, and realize the spiritual dimension of their real personalities.

Copyright © 2024 by Anupam Srivastava

All rights reserved.

This book or any portion thereof may not be reproduced or used in any manner whatsoever without the express written permission of the respective writer of the respective content except for the use of brief quotations in a book review.

The writer of the respective work holds sole responsibility for the originality of the content and The Write Order is not responsible in any way whatsoever.

Printed in India

ISBN: 978-93-5776-960-0

First Printing, 2024

The Write Order

A division of Nasadiya Technologies Private Ltd.

Koramangala, Bengaluru

Karnataka-560029

THE WRITE ORDER PUBLICATIONS.

www.thewriteorder.com

Edited by Literary Connect

Typeset by MAP Systems, Bengaluru

Book Cover designed by Sankhasubhro Nath

Publishing Consultant - Priyanka Lal

Contents

Preface ix

Acknowledgement xiii

Foreword xv

1. Introduction 1

2. Strike the Balance 5

3. The Way Forward 9

4. Lord Krishna's Treatment To Arjuna Disease 21

5. Have You Counted Graces In Life? 53

6. What Is Dharma? 61

7. Signs Of A Spiritually Mature Person 77

8. The Science Of Spirituality, Religion And Rituals 83

9. The Nature Of The Self 97

10. The Spirituality & Self-Realization 103

11. The Path Of Spirituality 109

12. The Inner Equipment Of Experience 141

13. Self-Realization 161

14. Deepest Essence Of Vedanta 185

15. Vedic Philosophy And Approaches To Self-Realization 195

16. Spiritual Practice (साधना) For Self-Realization 207

17. Appendix 1 261

18. Appendix 2 265

19. About The Author 271

20. References 275

"Hinduism: The Science of Self-Realization presents Self-realization as simple and accessible, contrary to established notions. Anyone, regardless of their socio-economic background, age, gender, educational qualifications, prior scriptural knowledge, intellectual ability, or knowledge of the Sanskrit language, can realize their true and real selves. This book is a sincere effort to assist sincere seekers in investigating and realizing that they already possess all the skills and abilities required for spiritual practice or Self-realization. They do not have to learn these skills anew, but rather learn to invoke them. Perhaps they are unaware that they have already been invoking and employing these skills and abilities numerous times in their lives. It's just that they may not be conscious of having done so."

Preface

'Hinduism: The Science of Self-Realization' is a book written with a specific purpose: to present the idea of spirituality and religion, its purpose, and its usefulness in the day-to-day lives of readers, particularly the youth of India, comprising a fifth of the world's youth population and the Indian diaspora around the globe. This book does not aim to be a repository of knowledge but rather a guide to introduce and clarify the theme, unveiling its scientific and logical foundations. It is written with the intention of sparking the readers' interest in the subject and encouraging them to break free from the misconceptions and ignorance surrounding it.

Self-realization is a topic discussed in religious and spiritual discourses, often leaving individuals perplexed as to its meaning or significance. Even after delving into philosophical scriptures, one might emerge without a clear understanding. Instead, they may find themselves more bewildered, grappling with questions like, what is it? Is it real? Is it achievable? It can seem as complex as rocket science or as distant as a dream, discouraging people from delving deeper.

There appears to be a significant gap in spiritual and religious knowledge, especially among the younger generation. What little understanding people possess about religious themes often seems to be based on myths and inaccuracies. Not only are young people becoming increasingly critical of religious practices they witness, but they also find these practices illogical and irrational. At the same time, it's rare to find someone who can offer them a profound understanding of spirituality and religion as a Subjective Science of life, along with how the scientific ideas within can enhance their daily experiences.

Even those who engage in ritualistic and religious practices often do so to uphold family or community traditions or out of fear or blind faith. In today's materialistic and competitive world, the focus on improving the quality of living often overshadows the pursuit of a higher quality of life.

Religion, religious education, and spiritual ideas are crucial not only for better Self-understanding but also for enhancing our daily life experiences. From a societal perspective, religion and spirituality have historically provided a framework of values and social rules that bind people together and regulate individual and social behavior. This code of conduct also forms the foundation for the laws and rules of most countries.

Self-regulation and self-control help individuals insulate themselves from the social and psychological impacts of a fast-paced life. Spiritual and religious education offers a framework for leading a fulfilling life and can assist younger generations in becoming moral, disciplined, and responsible members of society. Spiritual education can enable individuals to enjoy more and achieve more without burning out in today's materialistic, competitive environment. Ironically, while this Subjective Science of life can help people become more resilient and steadfast in facing life's challenges, it's been observed that young people are distancing themselves from it.

Unfortunately, even without any knowledge of spirituality or prior spiritual practice, secularists and rationalists attempt to reform society, pretending to understand everything about spirituality and propagating the notion that religious and spiritual practices and experiences are all fraudulent. This misleads society, especially the younger generation, with serious personal, social, and psychological consequences. To the point where many young Hindus are now questioning the utility of spirituality. The absence of religious and spiritual education, both within families and in the state, is beginning to show its consequences in people's lives. Unfortunately, they remain unaware that engaging in informed and mindful spiritual practices can make them more resourceful and resilient in facing physical, social, psychological, financial, and other challenges with a smile.

The waning interest in spirituality and religion, coupled with religious illiteracy, has infected Hindu society, fostering blind faith, superstitions, and misconceptions about the role of religion in individuals' lives and society as a whole. These misconceptions are often peddled by so-called 'holy men,' many of whom lack genuine credentials. They thrive on the existing blind faith within society, unjustly tarnishing the reputation of true saints. Some individuals undertake spiritual practices based on the advice of these fraudulent holy men or those with no authority, wasting years on inappropriate religious practices.

Consequently, the majority of those practicing religion and spirituality do so according to their own individualistic ideas and understanding of what religion should be. Just as one does not prescribe medicine for oneself or represent oneself in court, undertaking spiritual practice based solely on one's own intellect proves ineffective. Spirituality is a science of life dealing with its subtle and subjective nature, requiring a careful study of scriptures under the guidance of a Self-realized and evolved teacher to be truly beneficial.

Secular education, juxtaposed against the unscientific face of prevalent religion, has pitted science against religion. Secular education has taken a prominent role in society, while sacred education has all but vanished, depriving generations of the inner strength and spiritual wealth it can offer. Within this context, the book presents an unconventional perspective on spirituality for young people, emphasizing the scientific nature of religion and spirituality.

Readers are encouraged to approach this book as a guide, redirecting their focus to the true nature and purpose of religion in life rather than treating it as a religious text. While it delves into various concepts, techniques, and teachings from the spiritual texts and holy books of the Sanatan tradition of Hinduism, it does not claim to be a religious text. Instead, it aims to elucidate the scientific and logical insights found in Sanatan scriptures, presenting them in a language that today's young generation can easily read, understand, and relate to their daily life experiences. This book offers encouragement, particularly with the profound message that Self-realization is simple and attainable, contrary to established notions. Anyone, regardless of their socio-economic background, age, gender, educational qualifications, prior scriptural knowledge, intellectual ability, or knowledge of the Sanskrit language, can achieve Self-realization. It aims to help readers recognize that they already possess the skills and abilities required for spiritual practice and self-realization; they need only learn to invoke them. Perhaps they are unaware that they have already invoked and employed these skills and abilities numerous times in their lives; they just haven't realized it.

In pursuit of this goal, some of the explanations may seem straightforward and simplistic. In conclusion, the author's intention is to assist and inspire young people, particularly Hindu youth, to awaken and explore the spiritual dimension of their personalities.

Acknowledgement

This book stands as a testament to the unwavering support, love, and encouragement of many incredible individuals who have been instrumental in shaping my thoughts and ideas through life enriching experiences I have had in my personal, professional, and Spiritual journey.

To my beloved family, whose patience, understanding, and belief in me never wavered. My sincere gratitude goes to my late Father Shri Prem Prakash Srivastava and my late uncle Shri Vidya Prakash, who sowed the seeds of spirituality in my bosom. This acknowledgement cannot be complete without mentioning the name of two excellent ladies, who laid the foundation of my life. My late mother Mrs Usha Srivastava and my late aunt Mrs Radha Srivastava, whose contribution in my life has been extremely valuable in shaping and blossoming my personality. I would particularly like to pay gratitude to my dear wife Kshama Srivastava for standing by me through the highs and lows of this writing journey. Her constant support has been my pillar of strength.

I want to take a moment here to express my heartfelt gratitude for the incredible support and contributions of all my friends, colleagues, students, and my countless clients for their encouragement and enthusiasm, which kept me motivated throughout. I am indebted to Dr Manoj Pradhan and Dr Sushil Dave in addition to all my co-spiritual seekers from Gita Study Class in Leicester, United Kingdom. Their belief in my abilities pushed me to strive for excellence. Thanks to them all for being my cheerleaders. Their unconditional support, guidance, and camaraderie have been invaluable. I am truly fortunate to have such amazing friends, colleagues, students and all my clients for giving me valuable life experiences.

In deep appreciation, I extend my heartfelt reverence and gratitude to Swami Chinmayananda Ji of Chinmaya Mission International, whose wisdom and teachings have guided me not only in writing this book but in shaping my perspective on life itself. His profound spiritual guidance, unmatched wisdom and his teachings have been a guiding light, illuminating the path that led to the creation of this book. I am profoundly grateful for his inspirational influence on my journey as an author.

To all those whose names I may not have mentioned but whose contributions were significant, thank you for your help, feedback, and inspiration. However, one name which needs a special mention is Shri Atul Rameshwara Dayal, whose selfless help and commitment to take this book to all luminaries and illustrious spiritual masters for seeking their contribution for this book is indeed commendable. He has taken upon himself to ensure that this book is launched with a big bang. We all can learn from his selfless Seva, for which I will always remain indebted. Finally, to the readers, it is your support and interest that truly bring life to these words. Thank you for embarking on this journey with me.

With heartfelt gratitude,
Anupam Srivastava

Foreword

Swami Yatindrananda Giri

|| श्री ||

अनन्त श्री   विभूषित परिब्राजकाचार्य, महामंडलेश्वर

पूज्य योगी यतीन्द्रानन्द गिरि
(श्री पंचदशनाम जूना अखाड़ा)

संस्थापक - जीवनदीप सेवा न्यास
संरक्षक - हिमालय परिवार एवं सिंधु दर्शन यात्रा समिति
पू॰ सदस्य - राष्ट्रीय परिषद् बी.जे.पी.

Date: 30-NOV-2023

The book 'HINDUISM: THE SCIENCE OF SELF-REALIZATION' by Shri Anupam Srivastava is an important contribution to one of the most relevant discourses of our times: Spirituality and religion. Its simplified explanation of spiritual concepts makes it a must read for everyone. This book will assist young people in discovering their spiritual awakening and, in the process, elevate their lives and of those around them.

My best wishes and blessings to the author, Shri Anupam Srivastav. –

Mahamandaleshwar
Swami Yatindranand Giri

जीवन दीप आश्रम नन्द विहार, रुड़की (हरिद्वार)
Mob +919412022156, 9897305061, Email: yogiyati@rediffmail.com

Swami Mukundananda

The full manifestation of the human potential can never happen without mastering the science of spirituality. The Bhagavad Gita calls it the 'king of sciences' and the 'supreme knowledge.'

In his book, Anupam Srivastava has meticulously elucidated the benefits of inculcating spiritual wisdom for wellbeing and happiness. He has made a strong case for harmoniously blending spirituality in our life alongside with a scientific attitude. His presentation is based on his decades long experience as an educationist, wellness coach, and his personal sadhana. His altruistic intention is to help the youth and Indian diaspora. The author's sincerity and intense belief in his message jumps out of every paragraph of his book.

Swami Mukundananda,
Author, Spiritual Teacher,
Founder of JKYog

Swami P.K. Aryam Ji

AARYAM INTERNATIONAL FOUNDATION

BENEDICTION

I am impressed with Anupam Srivastava's efforts in his book entitled Hinduism- The science of Self Realization, wherein he has made excellent efforts in helping his readers to effortlessly gain good and comprehensive insight in a concept so eluded and confusing. His presentation and writing style is impressive and captivating. to his readers, particularly young Hindus. His treatment of a complex topic of 'Self-realization' in his book read simple, realistic, and encouraging.

I particularly liked the way he presents the idea of lack of Self-realization as a disease to his readers and compares it with a diseased of the body and encourages his readers to consider the practical application of spiritual wisdom for improving the quality of their lives. The symptoms of this disease, as he puts it, are deluded sense of Self, which is riddled with negative emotions, including anger, contempt, disgust, dishonesty, fear, greed, guilt, jealousy, lust, nervousness, and many more in its varieties and combinations. So long as these symptoms are there, you cannot escape the miseries in life. No matter how many degrees and qualifications you may acquire, no matter how high you may climb the professional ladder, no matter how successful you may become in your business, no matter how much wealth, power, and fame you may earn, but you cannot escape the miseries of life. If you are happy the way your life is, Self-realization has nothing to offer you. His argument that as we take care of our diseased bodies, why can't we take the same attitude improve the quality of our live by embracing Spiritual wisdom.

In his book, Anupam Srivastava seems genuine in his intentions to help young people and all others to gain a better understanding of the concept and has pedantically expounded the advantages of contentment, success Spiritual Wisdom as contained in Vedanta. He has argued strongly and affably in favour of spirituality in our lives with a logical and scientific temperament. He seems to have amalgamated his decades long experience as a educationalist, spiritual seeker and his personal sadhana in writing this book with a genuine intention to help the youth and Indian diaspora. Anupam Srivastava's earnestness and strong faith in his writing springs out this book.

07/01/2024

Param Pragya Jagadguru
Prof. Pushpendra kumar Aaryam
Chief, Aaryam International Foundation (India, Mauritius & Switzerland)
Head : Bhagawan Shankar Ashram, Mussoorie (Uttarakhand)

Aaryam State, Bhagwan Shankar Aashray, Naag Mandir Road, Kyatkuli Bhatta, MUSSOORIE, Distt. Dehradun - Pin - 248179 - U.K. - INDIA
www.aaryam.org | email - aaaryam@outlook.com | +91 9891646565/66/67

Swami Dipankar

In our modern-day Indian context, everyone is surrounded by some problems or the other in their lives. It can be a social or family problem. Society is formed by family. So, the question is who will help us all liberate ourselves from these challenges. Therefore, I have been wandering around with a smile on my face, a saffron rob on the body in the streets, cities, and many provinces, begging for Hindu society to unite as one entity. As a Sanyasi, I have not been making this call to society for my own personal peace, but for doing a duty to society. A duty which will make the whole country one nation. It is this ascetic's dogma that I want to unite the Sanatani Hindu who are divided into castes in society. I as a young ascetic simply want the youth of this land to wake and rise.

I am thoroughly impressed with the similar efforts that Anupam Srivastava has made through his writing in his recent book called Hinduism-The Science of Self Realization. This book has come out in the most appropriate times. I have no doubt in my mind that this book will make the most important contribution to one of the most relevant discourses in our society today, that is Spirituality and religion. Its simplified explanation of spiritual concepts makes it a must read for everyone. This book will help the readers and young people in particular in discovering their spiritual awakening and, in the process, elevate their lives and of those around them.

I wish Mr Anupam Srivastava and his book all the very best and I sincerely pray that this book reaches the hands of all young people in India and helps them to wake up and Rise to their personal and national challenges.

Hon. Pujya Swami Dipankar
Dipankar Dhyan Foundation

Dr Ashish Gautam

DIVYA PREM SEWA MISSION (NYAS)
An organization that treats the wounds and heals the soul

Ref: DPSM/0124-14685   Date: 09/01/2024

‖ Greetings Message ‖

The masters of Kriya Yoga teach that spirituality is not just practiced on a meditation cushion. A spiritual person is constantly seeking opportunities to serve others, help others, and erase differences. We should learn to live for others. When we live for others, our hearts and minds are purified, and love and compassion flow more deeply. One who serves others seeks opportunities to help others.

From the perspective of Kriya Yoga, I have no doubt in my mind that this book will help the reader to embark on a profound journey into the essence of Hinduism. Anupam Srivastava's *'Hinduism: The Science of Self-Realization'* serves as a guiding light through the intricate depths of this ancient wisdom. Offering a compelling blend of spiritual insight and practical wisdom, this book intricately weaves together the timeless teachings of Hindu philosophy with a modern perspective, inviting readers to delve deeper into the understanding of the self and the universe. As you immerse yourself in these pages, prepare to embark on a transformative expedition toward self-discovery and enlightenment.

Certainly! This book provides and an excellent opportunity for young seekers to explore Hinduism as a pathway to understanding oneself in the present and shaping the future. Within these pages lie the keys to self-discovery, resilience, and an unwavering sense of purpose. It calls young seeker to discover the art of mindfulness, the wisdom of ancient practices, and the guidance to navigate life's complexities with clarity and grace. And to embrace the timeless knowledge of Hinduism to embark on a journey of growth, understanding, and fulfillment.

As a Kriya Yoga practitioner, I wish **Anupam Srivastava** and his latest book a great success. May God help his intensions to fructify with which this book is written.

आशीष

Dr. Ashish Gautam
Founder/ President
Divya Prem Sewa Mission
Haridwar, Uttarakhand (India)

Office: Divya Prem Sewa Mission Niyas, C-281, Shastri Nagar, Ghaziabad, U.P. Pin-2010002 Conetct - 09219692776
E-mail: divyaprem03@gmail.com, divya_prem03@hotmail.com, Website: www.divyaprem.org, www.divyaprem.co.in

Sri Arvind Guruji

अनुपम श्रीवास्तव याद में

अ - अनुपम अपने नाम को परिभाषित करते हुए, जीवन जीना सिखा रहे हैं।

नु - नुपुर की तरह हृदयों में बजते हुए, आत्म बोध करा रहे हैं।

प - परिवर्तनकारी ना ही चोगाधारी, आडंबर के विनाशकारी हैं।

म - मर्मज्ञ, कृतज्ञ, आध्यात्मिक विज्ञान से ओत-प्रोत ज्ञान में गीता धारी हैं।

श्री - श्री चिन्मयानंद जी के दिव्य ज्ञान से वैदिक दर्शन का मार्ग प्रशस्त किया।

वा - वास्तविक हिन्दू धर्म, आत्म बोध, आंतरिक शांति को हर स्तर पर सशक्त किया।

स् - स्वाध्याय को समझा, फिर समझाया, ज्ञान से ब्रह्म ज्ञान की अमृत धारा जारी है।

त - तर्क संगत विचारों की चादर ओढ़, आत्मविश्वास को बढ़ा कर अंधविश्वास पर चोट मारी है।

व - युवा जो पथ भ्रष्ट और आत्मघाती प्रवृत्ति वालों के लिए यह पुस्तक एक दर्पण है।

या - यातनाएं, मानसिक शारीरिक या हो आर्थिक, उनके लिए अनुपम का ये समर्पण है।

द - दया करेंगे दयानिधान अगर उन पाठकों का मिले साथ, तो हृदय परिवर्तन तय है।

में - मेरी भी प्रार्थना है परमात्मा से कि ये पुस्तक विश्व प्रसिद्ध हो, क्योंकि ये पूर्णत: आत्म ज्ञानमय है।

लेखन - श्री अरविंद नागर गुरुजी, आध्यात्मिक गुरु

Mr Atul Rameshwara Dayal

The path of spirituality is as easy as your spiritual journey. For centuries, the subject of self-realization has remained deeply mysterious, and the paths to attaining it have been arduous and challenging. The topic of self-realization shines in the dense language of profound texts, often distant from the understanding of common people. My Babuji Maharaj used to say that self-realization is very simple, yet we are attempting to lift the needle with a crane when we could easily pick it up with our hands.

Anupam Srivastava, in this book entitled Hinduism-the Science of Self Realization, has made a successful attempt to simplify the concept and the process of self-realization. He has used a language that is understandable to the common people. His book will pave the way for spirituality for the youth of India. I extend my best wishes to him for this wonderful creation.

ॐ पूर्णमदः पूर्णमिदं पूर्णात्पूर्णमुदच्यते । पूर्णस्य पूर्णमादाय पूर्णमेवावशिष्यते ॥

ॐ शान्तिः शान्तिः शान्तिः ॥

ओम! वह अनंत है, और यह (ब्रह्मांड) अनंत है। अनंत से अनंत की प्राप्ति होती है। (तब) अनंत (ब्रह्मांड) की अनंतता लेते हुए, वह अनंत के रूप में अकेला रहता है।

ओम! शांति! शांति! शांति!

Aum! That is infinite, and this (universe) is infinite. The infinite proceeds from the infinite. Taking the infinitude of the infinite, It remains as the infinite alone.

Aum! Peace! Peace! Peace!

-Isavasya & Brihadaranyaka Upanishad

Atul Rameshwara Dayal
Senior Journalist & Columnist

1

Introduction

India is the second-most populated country in the world, with 65% of its population below the age of 35 and an average age of 29 years. This demographic profile is projected to remain stable for the next three decades, extending until the year 2055. This provides India with an unprecedented opportunity for a demographic dividend, potentially spanning three to four decades of economic growth, prosperity, and intriguing possibilities for the future.

However, India's youthful population, while being a valuable asset, faces significant challenges. To fully harness the demographic dividend, it is essential for society and the nation to invest in human capacity building. This investment is crucial to helping young people participate effectively, productively, and confidently in India's rapidly evolving social, demographic, technological, and economic landscape.

A critical examination of India's education system is imperative. Teaching children the same curricula that have been employed for many decades is unlikely to yield different or improved results. Beyond traditional subjects like science, mathematics, and languages, India's education system urgently needs to incorporate professional, vocational, and life skills to enhance self-confidence and employability.

Regrettably, our approach to evaluating student performance often relies on memorization of set formulas and clever test-taking strategies, prioritizing reading, writing, and arithmetic. This approach must evolve towards a more holistic educational framework that includes scientific experimentation, technical skill development, and a focus on enhancing psychological resilience and spiritual well-being.

In the current social, economic, and political climate, particularly in urban India, students and young people find themselves under immense pressure to excel academically. They strive relentlessly to achieve higher grades in the 10th and 12th standards, with a particular emphasis on cracking competitive entrance examinations to secure better life prospects.

The pursuit of lucrative careers becomes all-consuming, leaving no stone unturned. Any perceived obstacle on the path to this objective generates significant fear and anxiety. The result, as we are all aware, is pervasive stress for everyone involved.

The constant fear of failure and the pressure of not disappointing teachers and parents erode self-confidence, reducing young individuals to low self-esteem. Much of their mental energy is consumed in managing these expectations, leaving little room for actual performance.

Academic institutions, including secondary schools, colleges, and esteemed institutions like IITs and IIMs, have been grappling with a disturbing issue: a rising number of student suicides within their campuses. The underlying cause of these tragic incidents is often attributed to the inability to cope with academic stress, peer pressure, and parental expectations.

Changing family structures, evolving social trends, and a breakdown in traditional support systems have created a void in meeting the physical, psychological, and social needs of children and young people in our country. This underscores the necessity for an alternative support system to address these needs.

According to government statistics, between 1993 and 2003, 27,990 students and young people took their own lives. This number increased to 28,913 in the following decade, from 2004 to 2008. Shockingly, this upward trend continued, with the number of suicides among 15–29-year-olds reaching 36,913 between 2009 and 2013 and surging to 46,554 between 2014 and 2018.

In 2019, the 18–30 age group accounted for 35.1 percent of suicides, while the 30-45 age group contributed 31.8 percent. Alarming as it is, the data reveals that at least one student in India commits suicide every hour. Between 1995 and 2019, over 1.7 lakh brilliant students took their own lives.

Data compiled by the National Crime Records Bureau (NCRB) indicates that, on average, one student in India commits suicide every hour, with around 28 such suicides reported daily. This number increased to 31 suicides per hour by 2020. In 2018, 10,159 students ended their lives, up from 9,905 in 2017 and 9,478 in 2016. The latest NCRB data for 2020 recorded 11,396 deaths of young people due to suicides, confirming the ongoing upward trend in suicide deaths among India's young population.

Numerous reports suggest that suicide rates in India are among the highest globally, with a significant proportion of adult suicide deaths occurring between the ages of 15 and 29. Studies have indicated alarmingly high rates of suicide ideation among medical students and in selected rural and urban areas.

Factors such as academic stress, prior abuse experiences, family expectations, strained relationships, unemployment, physical abuse, and family issues have all been significantly associated with suicidal behavior and ideation.

Another national cross-sectional study on suicidal ideation found a rate ratio of suicide deaths to suicide attempts and suicidality (suicidal ideation) to be 1:15:212. For every suicide death, there were 15 suicide attempts, but over 200 individuals reported feeling suicidal and entertaining such thoughts.

If we extrapolate this rate ratio to the 2020 figure of 11,396 suicide deaths among young people, it indicates an additional 170,940 suicide attempts and 24,15,952 young people who contemplated suicide in the same year. This staggering magnitude demonstrates that a substantial number of bright and talented students have reached the brink of hopelessness and despair.

These statistics reveal a distressing and alarming aspect of our demographic capital. Even those who did not resort to extreme measures are not in great shape; many suffer from Negative Affectivity. Negative Affectivity encompasses a range of negative emotions, including anger, contempt, disgust, fear, greed, guilt, jealousy, lust, nervousness, and more. It forms the foundation for the criminal and corrupt behavior witnessed in our society.

Inclusive education should not only encompass all sections of society but also incorporate a blend of secular and sacred education for our youth. Young people must be equipped with knowledge of their inner strengths, supported to experience and develop these strengths, and empowered to lead effective and productive lives.

Spirituality is the science of life, teaching the art of living while elevating the quality of life. Spiritual development is essential, especially for youth, to lead better, happier, and more harmonious lives free from tension, stress, fear, and anxiety. While secular education promises material well-being, the inclusion of spiritual education guarantees inner peace alongside material prosperity. Therefore, we must ask ourselves: how long should we delay the inclusion of sacred education in our system? The choice is clear and simple.

2

Strike the Balance

It is an unfortunate reality that in India, since its independence, we have often been presented with a choice between materialism and spiritualism, secularism and sacredness. However, what we often overlook is the historical fact that the state and its governance have frequently been guided by masters of spirituality and philosophy.

The socialist policies of the Indian administration were significantly influenced by three words: 'socialist,' 'secular,' and 'integrity,' which were added with the 42nd Constitution Amendment in 1976. Since then, there has been a strong political push to establish a secular character for India's socio-political framework. Consequently, India's educational policies have been swayed by secular, socialist, and leftist ideologies, often at the expense of sacred and philosophical education.

For the leftist ideology, societal betterment primarily involves combating societal moral failings. Therefore, left-leaning ideologies tend to focus their efforts on addressing issues like sexism, racism, intolerance, xenophobia, homophobia, and other societal ills. This emphasis on politics often overshadows India's philosophical ideologies.

Since leftist ideology is more concerned with reforming society than individuals, politics becomes the primary tool for societal improvement. As a result, character education has been marginalized in our education system.

Consequently, students in schools are taught to address social issues such as global warming and pollution. When they reach college, they are taught to combat economic inequality, religious and caste-based inequalities, and the alleged rape culture in society. Ironically, if there is indeed a perceived rape culture, it may be due to the lack of character education in our schools and homes.

Young people in India have become well-informed and skilled in pursuing materialistic goals but often lack human values and inner strengths to effectively navigate their personal, social, and psychological lives in a rapidly changing world. Money appears to be the sole pursuit to which many young people dedicate themselves wholeheartedly.

In contrast, Indian philosophical ideologies emphasize the moral improvement of the individual as the path to a better society. It encourages individuals to focus on their own weaknesses and flaws rather than external societal issues. These philosophies provide a framework for a fair and just society, placing greater emphasis on inner transformation.

Indian philosophical ideologies understand that societal change happens gradually, one person at a time. They do not advocate for fundamental societal transformation, especially in a society as inherently decent as India. Instead, they believe in improving society without fundamental upheaval.

Consequently, character development must be at the core of child-rearing and education, from primary school through university. Young people should be encouraged to become moral and religious individuals.

Only virtuous people are capable of freedom because freedom demands greater self-control. As society becomes more liberated, increased self-control becomes necessary. If most people cannot control themselves, the state, often through a more powerful government, will be compelled to do so.

Historically, schools and parents concentrated on character development through education. However, in recent decades, families and religious institutions, which have traditionally conveyed self-control, seem to be diminishing in the lives of many Indian children and young people.

We are now producing large numbers of Indians passionate about fixing state and societal problems but doing very little to fix their own character. This predicament is not unique to India but is a global issue.

The truth is that we cannot make society better unless we work towards making its people better. Consequently, addressing societal issues is crucial, but achieving lasting, positive transformation requires simultaneous efforts to morally transform each citizen.

It is undeniably evident that today's Indian society has suffered the consequences of extreme leftist ideological policies, both overt and covert. The time has come for India to undertake concerted efforts to educate its young citizens about self-control through moral, religious, and spiritual education.

This book is an attempt to assist and encourage young people to explore and awaken to the spiritual dimension of their personalities. If the youth of our country embrace and engage in spiritual education, regardless of their religion or faith system, India will be blessed with a dynamic, highly productive workforce characterized by Positive Affectivity. This, in turn, will greatly enhance the prospects of the 'demographic dividend' for our country.

3

The Way Forward

Within the context presented above, the question facing Indian society, therefore, is "Why are our young people so psychologically ill-prepared/trained to deal with and manage their mental conditions?" Academically and professionally, though, they might be bright, brilliant, and competent, but their performance problem and their inability to face and cope with life's personal, social, and psychological conflicts today indicates that they lack psychological resilience. They do not seem equipped with and/or trained to manage psychological challenges, conflicts and the stress resulting from life situations. It won't be too far out to suggest that they lack an insight into their own selves and their inner strengths. Wise people have always suggested that in order to meet the demands of the modern world, our students and young people require both Objective and Subjective Education and knowledge.

> The term 'Objective' refers to a secular education and the knowledge of the subjects such as maths, science, and history etc and 'Subjective' refers to a system of sacred education and knowledge of Self Unfoldment, which helps the students to become aware of and wake up to their own real personality and their inner strengths, which they already have.

Let us now investigate how this problem is caused. The cause of this problem lies in the belief that the ability to possess more worldly possessions (material wealth) guarantees happiness. From this belief follows the assumption that the ability to acquire material wealth comes from having an ability to earn more money; the possibility of earning more money comes from having a lucrative and plum job or being placed in a position of power, money, or fame; to place oneself in that position requires one to pass competitive examinations; and to be eligible for these examinations one must get as high grades as possible, but at least 90% or above. Only then one has a chance of being successful in life, thereby, happy.

Once such assumptions or notions get consolidated in the mind as a belief, the pressure begins to mount and progressively becomes intense. Such intensified beliefs, invariably, cause an illogical error in the minds of young people and more so in parents, teachers, schools, and society at large. This illogical cognitive error is a thought or a belief which says that students' performance reflects their own performance. If students fail or do not perform, it means they have failed as parents and professionals. Academic failing unfortunately gives rise to a dysfunctional assumption that you are intellectually weak or not intelligent at all. For most parents, who did not fare well academically in their own times, they now have a compelling urge to prove their intellectual prowess through the academic and professional success of their children. Meaning they want to relive their dreams through their children. They have a scheme for the young in their mind about how much grades they must get and what kinds of money-making streams they must aim for.

By hook or crook, the student must now live up to these expectations, frame by frame. There is an invisible straitjacket arrangement put in place for them, at home and at schools alike. Consequently, students have lost all their freedom and they cannot live their life anymore. All their actions and behaviors must align with the parents' and teachers' scheme of things, otherwise the hell will break loose. They are now walking on a tightrope of high expectations. They cannot afford to make mistakes and definitely not fail at any cost.

Students are, no doubt, academically intelligent and leave no stones unturned to learn their subjects. There are a lot of arrangements in place to ensure that they become proficient in their subjects of study. There are tuitions, coaching centers and institutions mushrooming in every nook and corner of the streets in every town and cities of the country. Parents have no dearth of money to spend on their extra coaching and tuitions; schools, colleges and institutions are fighting to be the best in the area and take pride in declaring that their students are succeeding and topping the competitive examinations so as to remain relevant and profitable.

However, there are no formal or informal arrangements in place in India, to systematically impart Spiritual (Subjective) Education to students and young people. India, a nation which has a brilliant and glorious past of being the source and the center for spiritual wisdom and had a lineage of countless spiritual masters who blessed this land with wisdom, and a well-established education system imparting education full of human values, seems to have suffered a memory loss in its desperate attempt to copy the western system of education in the name of modernisation. A land, where the Ganga of spiritual wisdom has been flowing since time immemorial, its children and young people are deprived and starved of the Knowledge of the Self (Atma Gyan - आत्मज्ञान).

Lord Chesterfield, an accomplished politician, and diplomat, known for his skilled oratory in the House of Lords, UK, guided his sons in his famous letters on oiling their mind for suppleness and flexibility; **Albert Einstein**, German-born physicist who developed the special and general theories of relativity, won the Nobel Prize for Physics in 1921 for his explanation of the photoelectric effect. He was well known for his views on religion when he said, "Science without religion is lame and religion without science is blind."; **Swami Vivekananda**, philosopher, thinker, religious and spiritual teacher, who interpreted Sanatan spiritual doctrine from a western perspective, emphasized on the need for combining spiritual education with material progress; **Mahatma Gandhi**, a well-known proponent of Swaraj (Self-governance), which on an individual level is vitally connected with the capacity for dispassionate Self-assessment, ceaseless Self-purification and growing Self-reliance; **Dalai Lama**, head monk of Tibetan Buddhism, emphasized on training one's mind to think differently, through meditation; **Matthieu Ricard**, French writer, photographer, translator and Buddhist monk, advocated on cultivating a benevolent mind, emotional balance, inner freedom, inner peace, and wisdom; **Swami Chinmayananda Saraswati**, of Chinmaya Mission International fame, a Hindu spiritual leader and a teacher was an ardent believer of and advocated for the training of the mind is the essence of education; and **S. N. Goenka**, a successful Indian businessman and vipassana meditation teacher, also emphasized that removing old conditionings from the mind and training the mind is the first step toward experiencing true happiness.

These personalities of the recent past and our spiritual masters of the old have created a collective wisdom, which indicates beyond reasonable doubt that, the training of the mind, oiling of mind and manners, developing inner values, training the mind to think differently, through meditation, cultivating a benevolent mind, learning to be emotionally balanced, achieving inner freedom, peace, and wisdom and to be more equanimous, is (must be) the essence of real education.

We as a country, no doubt, are producing the best professionals who are competing in the world market. We do take pride, rightly so, in the fact that the CEOs of a few large international corporations in the world are Indians. Unfortunately, however, as a nation, we have most definitely failed in Man-making. This is largely because, none of the qualities mentioned above by the spiritual masters are part of our education system starting from primary school level all the way to PhD degree level in universities in our country.

While a small percentage of our youth achieve high positions of power, fame, and money through their own efforts, another small percentage excels in sports and extracurricular activities on a national and international level, the vast majority of our young demography is left to their own devices. The vast majority is still untapped. There is no wonder, therefore, that 45% of our corporate workforce and 4.5% citizen in India are clinically depressed as indicated in a recent report published in 2017 & 2018, conducted by ASSOCHAM and National Institute of Mental Health and Nero-Science (NIMHANS), Bangalore on behalf of WHO respectively.

Understandably, if the material achievements must remain life's main objective of our young in India, the journey towards this goal can still be made comfortable, comparatively easier, stressless, more realistic, and achievable, if we can train them to realize and gain insight into their spiritual (real) strengths and put them onto the path of enhancing their spiritual personalities. Spirituality is a science of life to help one to understand their inner personality. Having gained an insight into themselves, they will be in a much better position to carve out their real personality decorated with inner truths by widening the horizon of their awareness and consciousness beyond the material dimension of life, thereby, opening their mind to a wider perspective of life. It involves a process of identifying and getting rid of dysfunction perceptions, wrong concepts, beliefs and ideas and notions about the Self.

The final destination of all world religions and religious practices, therein, philosophically speaking, is to prepare one for the spiritual voyage eventually, but one doesn't have to be religious or belong to a particular creed to embark on spirituality. It rather works better if one's mind is not coloured by preconceived notions and ideas. Spirituality, in fact, is available to all who have an open mind and are desirous of venturing beyond the limits of impossibilities. It is beneficial and useful for people seeking spiritual awakening irrespective of whether one is a religious or secular person, one is living an ordinary life, or achievers in any area of life. It is useful for people living in monasteries or ashrams, at the same time, people living and working in a city or town or a village.

In short, spirituality is waking up to the idea that you are a spirit with a body, not a body with a spirit and becoming consciously aware of who you really are, your real essence. It requires one to wake up from the ordinary, everyday consciousness, to a wider consciousness and work on identifying and removing dysfunctional concepts about the Self.

There has never been a doubt that spiritual growth or maturity is essential for a better, happier, and more harmonious life, free of tension, stress, fear, and anxiety. While secular education can only promise the quality of material living, the Sacred (Spiritual) Education in addition to the secular, will most certainly guarantee a peaceful life, while one enjoys the good standards of material living.

The purpose of education in India, therefore, should be to develop good human beings capable of rational thought and action, possessing compassion and empathy, courage and resilience, scientific temperament, and creative imagination, with sound ethical anchorage and values. It must aim at producing engaged, productive, and contributing citizens for building an equitable, inclusive, and plural society as envisaged by our constitution, that India has always been.

Producing engaged, productive, and contributing citizens would require a system of education, which can help young people to be essentially active, alert, confident, enthusiastic, energetic, helpful, open-minded, and sociable. These typically are the distinguishing cyphers of a personality with Positive Affectivity, which results in better sleep, a decrease in stress, increase in longevity, healthier coping styles, more positive Self-qualities, and are more goal oriented.

Positive Affectivity describes a personality, which knows how to experience positive effects (emotions, sensations, and sentiments) of life situations and as a consequence have effective skills in interacting and negotiating their day-to-day transactions with others and with their surroundings. Therefore, a healthy educational system must support in building a solid moral foundation upon which young citizens can carve out a positive affective edifice.

Within the current socio-political and economical context, when we contact the world of objects, we experience either joy or sorrow. A series of such experiences constitute life. The material scientists have always believed that life could be made happier by improving the objects and situations in the outside world. With this idea in mind, they have put forth great efforts for many hundreds of years to create the present world of scientific marvels and achievements. Today, we live in considerable comfort. Yet we feel ever-increasing stress in life and little lasting happiness.

When our control on the outer nature far exceeds our control over our own inner nature, an imbalance is created. This imbalance is at the crux of our problems today. Philosophy and religion rehabilitate our inner selves and provide us with the equilibrium to make our lives more fulfilling. Without the rehabilitation of the human personality, a mere rearrangement and beautification of the external world is of little help in providing peace and happiness. To do so is as absurd as putting a sumptuous food in front of a person suffering from indigestion, with little taste for food.

Materialistic growth raises the standard of living, whereas spiritual growth and inner rehabilitation brings about Positive Affectivity, which improves the standard of life. Both, the standards of living and the standard of life, have to be equally developed in order for us to go through life with ease and cheer.

A comfortable voyage by a ship must necessarily have good depth and width of its keel for it to raise and maintain the height of its mast. Failing to maintain such a proportionate balance between the two will topple over the ship. Therefore, the keel must be deep and broad enough for the ship to remain stable regardless of the height of the mast. In the same way, if the standards of life are deep and broad, like the keel, it can support any height of the standards of living one wishes to raise.

So in life too, if the standard of living alone is raised at the expense of the standard of life, society slides downhill. Whenever the standard of life is well established, the society grows peaceful and wholesome.

Material prosperity, by itself, cannot give us happiness—if we have not developed a healthy inner personality. In the first stage of inner growth, we gain added fulfillment by practicing intelligent Self-restraint, as the scriptural teachings of the world tell us. We generally don't like the idea of self-control or discipline. The typical individual today considers discipline as a shackle on their freedom, so they avoid spiritual or religious practices. Then there are others who unintelligently follow the words of the scriptures and forcibly deny themselves all enjoyments. When a person practices such unintelligent Self-denial, they create for themselves mental suppressions.

If, with the help of the world's scriptures, we gain an intelligent understanding of the laws governing our personality, we will find our lives inspired with a nobler vision of life. As we progress in our inward expression, our baser tendencies drop off. This rejection of baser values, following an understanding of a higher vision, is called **Sublimation** (as opposed to suppression). Sublimation is the elimination of our dysfunctional values as a result of intelligent conviction. As we aspire and imbibe the higher values of life, our consciousness and awareness broaden, and the lower tendencies and values automatically disappear. Sublimation strengthens our inner selves.

Our personality is clogged with imperfections, just as a mass of cotton is mixed with impurities. To remove the impurities from the cotton, the cotton is carded, combed, and beaten so that the pure cotton separates from the heavier impurities. Similarly, to remove our negative tendencies, we learn the nobler values in life. As we assimilate them, our minds soar to higher realms of thought, leaving our negativities behind.

The basic knowledge of what is good and what is bad is known to us all. In spite of it, we often choose a path that is not beneficial to our well-being. The Vedantic masters analyzed the reason for such conduct and discovered that there are two paths in life. (1) The path of the pleasant (Preyas- प्रेयस्) and (2) the path of the good (Shreyas- श्रेयस्). We are confronted with choosing one of the two paths at every single moment of our lives. The path of the pleasant, as the name suggests, pleases, fascinates, and entices us to take it—now! In contrast, the path of the good may have some unpleasant aspects and hardships at first. The path of the pleasant, though provides immediate pleasure, it later ends up in disappointment and sorrow. The path of the good can be unpleasant at first, but later brings happiness and fulfillment.

The path of the pleasant is generally guided by the demands of the sense organs and aimed at fulfillment of temptations and sense gratifications; it is known to bring temporary and fleeting joys in the beginning but proves to be painful later on; it is more alluring and caters to the extroverted mind; it is known to be a path of devolution and is chosen by the majority for immediate sense gratification. Therefore, it is denounced by all world religions.

On the other hand, the path of the good is guided by the subtler intellect, the inner voice. It is unpleasant in the beginning but proves beneficial and provides lasting happiness later. It has a hidden beauty, which is perceived by the introverted mind only. This path is chosen only by a few courageous ones who are interested in self-evolution. Since this path is based on sound knowledge, it is recommended by all world religions.

Our struggle and strife in life, from cradle to coffin, is instinctively motivated by an irresistible desire to be happy, which is the goal of our every thought, word, and action. Whatever we do, irrespective of our position in life, we all are in search of eventual happiness. Only in full and absolute contentment all searching will end, and this supreme state of happiness is the goal of all life and the subject of all the scriptures of the world. In this light that the rishis classified all actions into the two categories, that is, with reference to their results. The fruits of action can be of two kinds: (1) those contributing to the ephemeral joys in life and (2) those leading to immortal bliss.

That is, efforts can either contribute to some immediate passing material gains, or they can contribute in the long run to our Self-nurturing and Self-purification.

Anyone can excel in accumulating wealth, through foul and fiendish methods, which unfortunately seems commonplace in our society. To the ignorant and sensuous this may appear as an inviting possibility and a convenient way to succeed. On the other hand, each of us has the choice to build our lives upon more enduring principles of life, such as honesty, piety, mercy, love, tolerance, and to live for the greater wealth of inner peace and joy.

The weak-minded try to gain immediate flickers of joy by choosing the path of the pleasant, and thus deny themselves the chance to enjoy more lasting happiness later. People interested in building their inner strength chose the path of the good, unmindful of any unpleasantness and material privations, ready to suffer in the course of their higher pursuits. They are the ones who emerge as mighty personalities who not only lead fulfilling lives themselves, but also inspire the rest of society towards a more peaceful and happy life.

In addition to the Objective Scientists (such as economists, politicians, and scientists), another category of scientists exists. They are called Subjective Scientists, who investigate the human personality and draw our attention to the divine center within each of us. These are the Rishis of old. The Objective Scientists strive to raise the standard of living, whereas the Subjective Scientists' efforts are directed at raising the standard of life. Scientific achievements have a worthy place in human society. It is only fanatic materialism and secularism, divorced from inner development, that is bad for us. Similarly, a fanatically religious approach, without material development, can lead us to the dark ages. The obvious solution is a harmonious blending of the sacred and the secular. This balance must be struck.

4

Lord Krishna's Treatment To Arjuna Disease

Today, most of our young people are highly intelligent and professionally competent. They are making all concerned in the society and the country very proud by proving their grit and marveling at achieving great successes and reaching new heights in their professional lives. However, the brut reality is that there is a seriously concerning high percentage of such bright, brilliant, and professionally competent young people in the country who are finding the battle of life unbearable. Either they refuse to face it or easily give up the battle.

Arjuna, the invincible Hero of the Mahabharata, found himself in this predicament when he saw the array of battalions ready to fight. He was the most skilled and capable Master Archer of his time, with unrivaled talent in the art of warfare. He was so skilled and confident in his trade that he could hit the target with his eyes closed. His arrows had the ability to pierce the source of the sound. He had never lost a war in his life. The mere prospect of facing him in battle would sap his opponents' confidence and strength.

After reviewing both armies arrayed on the battlefield and the prospect of fighting and killing his own nears and dears, the great hero Arjuna sets fire to and brings down the egoistic edifice of false valuations that he had built for himself as a magnificent dwelling place for his personality. The unintelligent reaction to this great challenge ultimately destroyed and shattered his entire within. He recognised such close relationships on both sides of the enemy lines. This sight, possibly for the first time, brought to his mind the full horrors of a monstrous war. Perhaps, as a warrior and a man of action, he did not fully comprehend the extent of sacrifice that society would be required to make until that point. Hundreds of thousands of warriors must be killed in this war in order for his ambition to be realized and Duryodhana's atrocities to be avenged.

Arjuna had a long history of mental repressions, which had resulted in a plethora of dynamic energies seeking a channel of expression. His mind became divided as a result of his egoistic assessment of himself as the greatest hero of his time, as well as his anxious desire for a successful conclusion to the war. The preoccupation of his mind, dreaming intensely about the eventual end of the war, caused a complete separation between his **'Objective Mind'** (Manas - मनस - the Mind) and the inner mind known as the **'Subjective Mind'** (Buddhi - बुद्धि - the Intellect).

In this state of mental confusion, when his emotions have been completely divorced from his intellect, the Objective-Mind runs wild and comes to some unintelligent conclusions without the guidance of its Subjective-Mind. Similarly, Arjuna's denials clearly show how he came to be in such a state of mental grief. He was desperate for victory, for the kingdom, and for pleasures for himself and his relatives. But the daunting prospect of facing off against the great and eminent warriors ready to fight crushed his hopes, wrenched his ambitions, and undermined his Self-confidence, and he gradually developed the well-known **'Arjuna-disease.'**

> The mind is nothing more than a constant stream of thoughts. Doubting and deciding are two distinct functional faculties of the mind. **The Mind (Doubting Faculty-Sanshyatmika-संशयात्मिका)** is the faculty that deals with every thought with a doubt to decide whether it is this or that, good or bad etc. The intellect, on the other hand, is the faculty that aids in determining and deciding **(Deciding Faculty - Nishchayatmika -निश्चयात्मिका)**.
>
> The mind is outward oriented and focuses on the world of gross objects, so it is called the **Objective Mind (the Mind - Manas - मनस)** and whereas the Intellect is inward oriented and focuses on the subtler aspects of the Self, so it is called the **Subjective Mind (the Intellect - Buddhi - बुद्धि)**. The analogy of a river can help us understand the relationship between these two mental faculties. The mind is nothing more than a constant flow of thoughts like water in a river, and the intellect is like the river's banks, which direct the flow of thoughts just as the river's banks direct the flow of water.

Though pitiful, it is amusing to watch Arjuna's intellectual and emotional exhaustion as expressed through his decision not to fight the war. In his effeminate lack of self-confidence, he moans, drops his bow, and collapses on his knees in total hysteria. This clearly shows that Arjuna has become a victim of the situation rather than being a master of it. Such an illogical conclusion causes him to lose confidence, and he feels almost helplessly tormented by a creeping sense of growing inner cowardice.

This unhealthy mental weakness saps his heroism, and he desperately tries to justify his cowardice, making it appear divine and angelic, and parading it as pity. Thus, he deliberately misinterprets the purpose of the war and assigns a low motive to the just war simply to justify his pacifist idea. This sudden love for peace appears to emanate from his ulcerated mind rather than his known strength.

Maharishi Ved Vyas, highly intellectual, philosopher, and the Subjective Scientist that he was, seemed to understand the plight of the average person and the challenges they faced in their day-to-day transactions of life. He appeared to have a thorough knowledge and understanding of human psychology, as he understood how difficult it is for a person of average intelligence to comprehend the subtle and subjective dimensions of human personality. One gets a sense of Maharishi Ved Vyas' intellectual height and might, as he was, that presents a comprehensive and detailed understanding of human personality in the Holy Gita. He did not write the Holy Gita as a standalone book of wisdom, but rather studied and conceived of the socio-political context of the time and how it affects the common man, within which he composed the Mahabharat epic and placed the book of wisdom, the Holy Gita, in the exact middle of the text.

The second chapter of the Holy Gita begins with an announcement from Sanjaya, who paints a complete picture of Arjuna's sad mental state of desperation with a few well-chosen words. His thoughts had become flooded with Negative Affectivity. The very expression indicates that Arjuna was not in command of the situation at the time, but rather the situation had Arjuna as its victim. To get over, ridden by life's circumstances, is to ensure disaster on all occasions. Only unintelligent thinking, which allows it to be dominated by circumstances, can be victimized by external events.

In such a neurotic state, Arjuna had become a slave to the outer challenges, indicating that the cracking of the inner personality had created deep fissures in the character of the great hero. Arjuna, the greatest archer of his time, has become so destitute within that he has come to weep like a simple maiden. This is where Lord Krishna begins his divine treatment of his patient, which includes an introduction to his Real Divine Personality and the characteristics of a spiritually mature person, all the way up to verse 53.

After hearing the incredible prospects of and benefits accrued to a Self-realized and spiritually mature person through the discourse thus far in the first 53 verses of chapter two of Bhagavad Gita, any person, even with the meekest desire, would be inquisitive and anxious to know the distinguishing characteristics of the one whose intellect has come to equipoise. He would ask obvious questions, as Arjuna did at the end of verse 53, who was amazed and fascinated by the description.

Here is one of the most perfect word-pictures of a spiritually mature person, as interpreted and commented on by Gurudev Swami Chinmayananda Saraswati of Chinmaya International Mission. The following section is Gurudev's commentary and interpretation of the last eighteen verses from his book, 'The Holy Gita.'

अर्जुन उवाच
स्थितप्रज्ञस्य का भाषा समाधिस्थस्य केशव।
स्थितधी: किं प्रभाषेत किमासीत व्रजेत किम् ॥५४॥

Arjun asked:

> "What O' Keshava, is the description of him who has steady Wisdom and who is merged in the Superconscious state? How does one of steady Wisdom speak, how does he sit, how does he walk?"

Chapter-II of Bhagavad Gita

Arjun is asking a forked question: (1) A description of the state of mind in a man-of-realization merged in the Self-experience, and (2) an explanation on how such an experience will prompt his actions in the world outside, when he emerges from that heavenly experience.

The hysterical, dejected, and bereaved hero of Bhagavad Gita's first chapter has forgotten his hysteria and has come to take an active interest in the discussion. As a practical man, he is concerned about whether he will be able to live so vigorously in the world outside after achieving this great goal of life through Buddhi Yoga (बुद्धि योग- Intellectual Investigation). In the final eighteen verses of Chapter 2 of the Bhagavad Gita, Lord Krishna elaborates on the signs and characteristics of the Spiritually Mature (Self-realized) person. We see a portrait of a liberated (Jivanmukta) person in these verses who lives, moves, and works in the physical world of things and beings. In response to Arjun's question, the Lord identifies the characteristics and attributes of a realized saint, which are attainable by all with sufficient effort. The etiology, antidote, and means of acquiring these attributes are woven into the final 18 verses.

श्रीभगवानुवाच

प्रजहाति यदा कामान्सर्वान्पार्थ मनोगतान् ।
आत्मन्येवात्मना तुष्ट: स्थितप्रज्ञस्तदोच्यते ॥५५॥

The blessed Lord said:

"When a man completely is satisfied in the Self by the Self, having cast off all the desires of the mind, and, then O Partha, he is said to be the one of steady-Wisdom."

Ved Vyas recommends **'the casting of all desires'** as the words that come from Lord Krishna's mouth in this verse. How does one cast off all desires? How are desires created? To fully comprehend the suggestive and accurate meaning impregnated in this statement of Ved Vyas, we must first understand the make-up of the inner equipment (अंत:करण) and its operation. Here is a beautiful and insightful description of how our ancient Subjective Scientists gained an in-depth understanding of the architectural composition of human personality and psychology while sitting on their seat of contemplation using only their meditative and intuitive abilities and without the aid of any modern scientific tools, technology, or laboratories.

A contaminated intellect (बुद्धि) veiled by ignorance (non-comprehension of the truth of the Self- आत्म) becomes a feeding ground for desires, and he who has relieved himself of this ignorance through Right Knowledge (Knowledge of the Self) gained in perception naturally becomes desireless. The Lord is negating the existence of the CAUSE by explaining the absence of the EFFECT here: (1) Where desires are not, ignorance has ended, and (2) where ignorance has ended, there will be no desires. In any case, the Knowledge of the Self has already been revealed.

When one thinks of oneself as the Ego (जीवात्मा - the deluded Self) conditioned by the Body (ज्ञानेन्द्रियां), Mind (संशयात्मिका), and Intellect (निश्चयात्मिका) equipment, one has a burning desire for sense-objects (demands of the body), a binding attachment with emotions (demands of the mind), and a jealous preference for one's pet ideas (demands of the intellect). However, when the deluded Self (Ego) is transcended, the Ego becomes one with the infinite, implying that when the ignorance of being an Ego has lifted itself like a mist and the finite Ego stands face to face with the Divine Reality within him. The man of Steady-Wisdom, self-satisfied in the Self, no longer has any desire or appetite for the meager objects of the body, mind, or intellect. He is transformed into the source of bliss himself.

Ved Vyas refers to such people as 'Men of Steady-Wisdom.' (SthitPragya - स्थितप्रज्ञ).

दु:खेष्वनुद्विग्नमना: सुखेषु विगतस्पृह: ।
वीतरागभयक्रोध: स्थितधीर्मुनिरुच्यते ॥७६॥

"He who in prosperity does not yearn for pleasures, whose mind is not moved by adversity, and who is free from anger, attachment, and fear is called a Sage of Steady-Wisdom."

Another characteristic of a Man of Steady-Wisdom (A sage- मुनि[1]) is his **equanimity in pleasure and pain.** If Lord Krishna regards man as an actor in the previous stanza, He regards him as an 'experiencer' in this stanza. A silent sage is described as a stable being whose heart is undisturbed in sorrow or joy, who is unattached, fearless, and free of

---

[1] *A Muni–मुनि is practitioner of spiritual techniques (साधक), who has acquired a mental and psychological competence of tranquility and equanimity of mind. Such a person could be anyone who is living, walking, and toiling amongst us and negotiating life's challenges every day. A spiritual seeker who has acquired such a competence, through a process of constant, daily, and forever meditation and reflection, is entitled 'Muni–मुनि.' He doesn't necessarily need to shave his head or wear an orange or white robe. In modern times, such a Muni can be found in any attire that he may choose to wear.*

anger. Though hundreds of ordinary man's emotions are not seen in a Perfect One, Lord Krishna insists on only three emotions that must be absent in an individual who is a master in all situations: (1) attachment (Raga- राग); (2) fear (Bhaya- भय); and (3) anger (Krodha- क्रोध).

Through our interactions with sense-objects, we can easily see how our attachments to things in the outside world cause us to suffer from perplexing fear-phobia. When a person develops a strong enough desire to form a deep attachment, they instinctively begin to entertain fears about not winning the object that is so deeply desired; and if it has been secured, they fear about the security of the same acquired object.

Similar to how attachment to an object can lead to anxiety rising in waves and disturbing the person, anger refers to that person's attitude against people who stand in his way of the object of his attachment. Thus, anger is nothing more than a feeling that develops within us as a result of our attachment to an object, towards a barrier that stands in our way of the object of our attachment. As a result, the level of anger experienced in a person's heart is directly correlated with how afraid they are of the barrier standing in their way of obtaining their object of love. Thus, anger is merely our attachment to an object that has been placed in our way of desire.

According to Bhagwan Adi Shankaracharya, a Man of Steady-Wisdom is not distressed by calamities such as: (1) Adhyatmika (अध्यात्मिका) - those arising from bodily disorders (2) Adhibhautika (आदिभौतिका) - those arising from external objects such as wild animals (3) Adhidaivika (आदिदैविका) - those arising from unforeseen situations like rains, storms, floods etc. When more pleasures are attained, the fire of desire in a Perfect One remains unaffected by the addition of fuel. A man of steady wisdom, a silent, serene sage (मुनि), is such a person.

य: सर्वत्रानभिस्नेहस्तत्तत्प्राप्य शुभाशुभम् ।

नाभिनन्दति न द्वेष्टि तस्य प्रज्ञा प्रतिष्ठिता ।।५७।।

"He who is everywhere without attachment, who neither enjoys nor hates on meeting with anything good or bad, his Wisdom is said to be fixed."

This verse identifies and emphasizes detachment as a trait of the Perfect One that serves as an antidote to attachment. The person who is established in Wisdom is described as being unattached and facing life head-on with complete composure and poise. In order to avoid misinterpreting, we must understand this verse's genuine meaning here and its significance. Simple physical separation from daily responsibilities is not an indication of true discrimination or of perfection. However, many stupid fanatics actually forgo their responsibilities and flee, believing that because they have attained complete detachment from the sensual world, they would succeed in achieving their 'Objective' amid the peace and quiet of the forest.

In the first chapter of Bhagavad Geeta, Arjuna had already declared that he would forgo his line of duty and his field of endeavor. The Pandava-Hero of his day wanted to achieve perfection and peace by withdrawing into quietude in this manner. In the second chapter, Lord Krishna began his talk on a somber note to warn Arjuna against adopting this fateful action.

Lord Krishna goes on to explain what is meant by the advice to detach, i.e., to give up all attachments. In order to face all of life's challenges, both the 'auspicious' (Shubha- शुभ) and the 'inauspicious' (Ashubha- अशुभ) have to be in perfect equilibrium without either any uncontrolled rejoicing on the auspicious or aversion for the inauspicious experiences. The detachment from the outside world must also be accompanied by a growing balance within us.

Physical separation alone is not the path to a perfect life since it is merely a miserable existence of perpetual flight from reality. Living in 'Attachment' is characterized as a form of worldly servitude. The perfect one is he who lives in the world with divine freedom and skilfully handles both the joys and the sufferings that life may bring him. The good and the evil are both there in life as we all experience it. Living constantly in self-control, avoiding evil, and working to accrue as much good as possible is not an intelligent way to live. The Perfect One experiences both the best and worst aspects of life with equal detachment because they are permanently rooted in the true and the eternal essence of the very Self.

In response to Arjuna's query about the behavioral patterns of a Perfect Master, Krishna says, "To him, everything is delightful." Without the taint of his mental states, he views things as they are. On such a Perfect One, all of the behaviorism's recognised rules in current psychology are useless.

यदा संहरते चायं कूर्मोऽङ्गानीव सर्वशः ।

इन्द्रियाणीन्द्रियार्थेभ्यस्तस्य प्रज्ञा प्रतिष्ठिता ॥७८॥

"When like a tortoise which withdraws its limbs from all sides, He withdraws his senses from the sense-objects, then his Wisdom becomes steady."

A Man of Steady-Wisdom has the unique ability to withdraw his senses from all the unsettling fields of objects after having been explained that a Perfect One: (1) is ever satisfied in the Self, (2) lives in perfect equanimity in pleasure and pain, and (3) has within him a complete absence of attachment to rejoicing or any aversion.

In this stanza, the metaphor of a tortoise (कूर्म) is used to explain what the withdrawal of senses signifies. A man of perfections can voluntarily retract all of his antennae that protrude from his five arches of knowledge, known as the sense organs (organs of perception, that is Eyes, Ears, Nose, Tongue, and Skin), just as a tortoise can instinctively withdraw all of its limbs into itself at the slightest sign of danger and feel comfortable inside.

As a result, five unique beams of the same awareness emerge from each human like antennae, giving him full knowledge of the outside world. These five avenues of knowledge expose him to the countless stimuli (Form, Shape, Sound, Smell, Taste, and Touch) from the outside world, which when they enter his consciousness, cause all the disturbances he experiences in his interactions with the outside world. For example, a blind person cannot be troubled by the beauty or ugliness of a scene, and a deaf person cannot be worried or agitated by the compliments or criticism coming his way if these sense organs are not functioning in that person. A sensory item that cannot be seen, heard, tasted, smelled, or felt cannot elicit any feelings of joy or sorrow in the body. In this instance, Lord Krishna reassures Arjuna that a Man of Steady-Wisdom is He who is able to readily withdraw his senses from any or all of their regions of activity.

The ability to remove one's senses from the fields of objects at will is known as **Pratyahara**[2] (प्रत्यहार) in the Yog-Shastra tradition. Yogi achieves this through breath control (**Pranayama**[3]-प्राणायाम). A devotee, via his bhakti, can see and hear only the forms and tales of his beloved Lord; therefore, this comes effortlessly to him. Again, this (**Uparati**[4] - उपरति) comes to a Vedantin (through the Knowledge of the Self) from his well-developed and sharpened discriminative faculty. He has no trouble understanding the futility of licking the crumbs of joy and happiness in the wayside ditches of sensuousness, while he is the Lord of the very store of bliss infinite in his Real Nature.

विषया विनिवर्तन्ते निराहारस्य देहिनः ।

रसवर्जं रसोऽप्यस्य परं दृष्ट्वा निवर्तते ॥७९॥

---

[2] *Pratyahara is the Yogic practice of turning the mind to introspection by voluntarily shutting out distractions provided by the senses.*

[3] *Pranayama is the practice of breath regulation. It's a main component of yoga, an exercise for physical and mental wellness. In Sanskrit, 'prana' means life energy and 'yama' means control. The practice of pranayama involves breathing exercises and patterns.*

[4] *Uparati, is a Sanskrit word and it literally means 'cessation, quietism, stopping worldly action.' It is an important concept in Advaita Vedanta (one of the six properties (Shath-Sampati) of a spiritual seeker) in pursuit of moksha and refers to the ability to achieve 'dispassion,' and 'discontinuation of sensuous activities.'*

> *"The objects of the senses turn away from the Self-disciplined man leaving the longing (behind), which too leaves him upon seeing the supreme."*

The senses of a guy who is ill and hence unable to consume sensual goods appear to be under control, yet the desire for him does not disappear as a result. How can the desire for sense items themselves come to an end? In a similar vein, Arjuna questions whether even in a Yogin, the ability to resist temptations from the sense world may just be momentary and that, in the presence of suitably tempting conditions, he would be enticed once more. This verse specifically addresses his skepticism.

This concept can be easily understood if we watch the flow of goods (Sensuous Objects) from the stores to the customers. Only those who have been courting (passionately thinking about and contemplating) the products and are thirsty to possess them are drawn to them. When bottles wander out to restock the drunks' sideboards, the wine vaults are depleted! Advocates, artists, surgeons, and poets are not drawn to smithy-made plows; instead, they must travel to the farmers' houses. Similarly sense-objects eventually entice people who are wooing them with intense cravings. However, avoid the person who abstains fully.

Even though one makes earnest efforts to achieve abstinence, his or her intense taste for the sense-objects nevertheless lingers in the back of his or her mind, making it challenging to totally erase the memory of their flavor. The Supreme Wisdom of Lord Krishna assures the seeker that these mental images of sensual lives that the Ego has previously led from the beginning of creation (life) to the present will all be completely erased or at the very least rendered ineffective, as roasted seeds, only when the seeker transcends the Ego and experiences the Self.

Since we are aware that the tragedies and objects of sadness that exist in one plane of consciousness do not exist in another, this is not too difficult to understand. When I woke up and realized how small I was in the grand scheme of things, the Kingship I experienced in my dreams did not even slightly increase my dignity. The entire kingly splendor in my dream-kingdom will not be hindered by my meager existence in my waking condition, either!

Similar to this, the Ego (the perceived notion of the Self), that is currently present during the states of waking, dreaming, and deep sleep, has accumulated a dung-heap of perceptions that are all entirely sensual. However, these are ineffective when the same Ego experiences the plane of God-Consciousness after transcending all three tiers.

यततो ह्यापि कौन्तेय पुरुषस्य विपश्चितः ।

इन्द्रियाणि प्रमाथीनि हरन्ति प्रसभं मनः ॥६०॥

"Though he may be determined (to control them), O son of Kunti, the tempestuous senses do violently carry away the mind of a wise man."

Lord Krishna is now outlining to Arjuna the practical means by which he should diligently toil, in order to reach the eminence of perfection as a Man of Steady-Wisdom. He has previously discussed the characteristics of a Perfect-Master and emphasized that He is the one who has complete control over his sense-appetites.

In this verse, Lord Krishna draws Arjuna's attention to a regular event that even the most highly evolved person can experience: a fall from the heights of tranquility and equanimity to the gutters of sensuality.

Here, we must understand an internal mechanism involving the interplay of the sense temptations of the body, mind, and the intellect. The ignorance of the Spiritual Reality functions within any individual in three distinct aspects: (1) Unactivity (Sattva[5]- सत्व), (2) Activity (Rajas[6]-

---

[5] *Sattva refers to a mental mood of God Consciousness, where all activities are performed without any sensuous, selfish motive, but in total surrender to God. Therefore, there is no need for any desire prompted activities (Unactivity).*

[6] *Rajas refers to a mental mood of partial God Consciousness and partial Ego, where personal glory and sensuous desires are fulfilled in the guise of good deeds, social welfare activities. Therefore, there are a lot of desire-prompted activities (Activity & Dynamism).*

रजस्), and (3) Inactivity (Tamas[7] - तमस्). When the Sattva aspect in us is molested by the 'veiling of the intellect' (avarana - आवरण) and the 'lack of tranquility' of the mind (vikshepa - विक्षेप), we come to experience the sorrows that are caused by their endless roaming through the sense-organs. Unless well-controlled, they will drag the mind to the field of the sense objects, and thus create a chaotic condition within, which is experienced as sorrow.

Therefore, it is a warning as well as an advice to the seeker in Arjuna that he should not, on any score, let his 'Objective-Mind'[8] (Sanshyatmika- संश्यात्मिका) take hold of and enslave his 'Subjective-Intellect' (Nishchayatmika- निश्चयात्मिका). Invariably, among those who are practicing religion, the common cause by which very many true seekers fall away from the path is the same all over the world. After a few years of practice, they no doubt come to live in a certain inexplicably inward joy. Then being overconfident and often even vainful of their progress, they relax in their hardships (Tapas- तपस्). Relaxed in their vigil, when returning to the field of the senses, the tempestuous senses violently snatch the mind away from the poise of perfect meditation!

There is an apt puranic legend in this context, specifically to highlight and indicate towards this fall from the path of meditation, even of those who have attained a substantial degree of heights on this path. Menaka, who was born during the churning of the ocean (समुद्र मंथन) by the devatas and asuras, was one of the most beautiful, innately talented, and intelligent apsaras (celestial fairy) in the world but she desired a family.

---

[7] *Tamas refers to a mental mood of a total lack of God Consciousness and fullness of egoistic desires, where all deeds are performed with pure selfish motive for the fulfillment of sensuous desires (Inactivity & Inertia).*

[8] *Objective-Mind (संश्यात्मिका) and the Subjective-Intellect (निश्चयात्मिका) are two distinct mental faculties of the Self, which are interchangeably used as mind and intellect. Objective-Mind (संश्यात्मिका) is the doubting or indecisive faculty, whereas Subjective-Intellect (निश्चयात्मिका) is the decisive faculty of the Self.*

Vishwamitra, one of the most respected and revered sages, scared the Gods, who feared that he might create another heaven - Indra, terrified by his powers, sent Menaka from heaven to earth to trap him and break his meditation. Menaka successfully incited and invoked Vishwamitra's lust and passion with her beauty, thereby stopping his meditation.

तानि सर्वाणि संयम्य युक्त आसीत मत्परः ।

वशे हि यस्येन्द्रियाणि तस्य प्रज्ञा प्रतिष्ठिता ॥६१॥

"Having restrained all his senses, He should sit resolute, intent on me; His Wisdom, whose senses are under control, is steady one."

Since the sense-organs are thus saboteurs in the Kingdom of the Spirit that bring the disastrous downfall of the Empire of the Soul, the *Sadhak* in Arjuna is warned again that as a seeker of self-perfection, he should constantly struggle to control his sense-organs and their mad lustful wanderings in their respective fields. The modern reader of psychology would object to this advice as he would doubt that Krishna here is advising and leading Arjuna to unnatural suppression of his senses.

According to the West and/or modern thinking, to control is to suppress. Therefore, suppression is considered psychologically unhealthy. But the Vedic theory is not pointing to any mental suppression at all, rather it is only advising an inward blossoming, an inner growth and development by which one's earlier fields of sense enjoyments drop out, to make room for the perception of a newer field of ampler joys and more satisfying bliss. What is advised here is a dual process of (1) not only a withdrawal from the unhealthy gutters of sensuousness, but (2) simultaneously adopting a healthy technique of regular, constant, and consistent (नित्यम्, निरन्तरम्, चिरम्) attempt, with unabated enthusiasm, at focusing our attention on our Real and the Perfect-Self–The Supreme. The seeker here is advised to be steady in his awareness and wisdom.

The immoral impulses and unethical instincts that bring a man down to the level of a mere brute, are the result of endless lives (the duration of time in conscious awareness) spent among sensuous objects during infinite number of different manifestations, through which the embodied soul in each one of us had previously passed. It is humanly impossible for an individual to erase and transcend, in his lifetime, the thick coating of mental impressions gathered along his journey from life to life, from embodiment to embodiment. Naturally, this is the despair of all the promoters of ethics, the teachers of morality, and the masters of spirituality.

However, the Rishis of the old in their lived experience discovered for themselves a technique by which all these mental tendencies called vasanas could be eradicated. The technique is to expose the mind to the quiet atmosphere of meditation[9] upon the All-Perfect-Being is to heal the ulcers. By this process, the one who has come to gain a complete mastery over his sense organs is considered as the one who is steadfast in Wisdom' (मुनि).

The idea and a subtle suggestion here is that any chance of blossoming and flowering into full-blown spiritual beauty is not through the excessive use and the sheer power of the Will to control one' senses. He who has all of these sense-organs, of their own accord, lying tamely surrender at his feet, and who has come to rediscover the Infinite Perfection in himself, is called a Man-of-Perfection. His instruments-of-cognition (mind) and arches-of-knowledge (senses) remain intact and functioning. A Perfect One is he whose inner Satan has become, for the Sage in him, a tame Caliban[10] to run errands and serve faithfully.

---

[9] *Meditation is a technique where the seeker, through a regular, constant, and consistent attempt, with unabated enthusiasm, over a period of time, learns to withdraw his attention from the external world of sense objects, and draws his entire mental attention inward and focuses it on his Real and the Perfect-Self–The Supreme.*

[10] *Caliban - a character in Shakespeare's The Tempest, described as half-human native inhabitant of the island, who was enslaved by the character Prospero.*

ध्यायतो विषयान्पुंसः सङ्गस्तेषूपजायते ।
सङ्गात्संजायते कामः कामात्क्रोधोऽभिजायते ॥६२॥

"When man courts with the sense objects, it gives rise to 'attachment' for them; desires are born out of attachment, which are the fertile ground in which 'anger' germinates."

क्रोधाद्भवति सम्मोहः सम्मोहात्स्मृतिविभ्रमः ।
स्मृतिभ्रंशाद् बुद्धिनाशो बुद्धिनाशात्प्रणश्यति ॥६३॥

"From anger comes 'delusion,' which causes 'loss of memory'; this leads to the 'destruction of discrimination'; thereafter, he perishes."

From the verses 62 & 63 onward, in the next five beautiful verses, the attention of the seeker is drawn at the source of all evil in the case of the unsuccessful and the psychological theory of the fall of man from Godhood. It is important for the seeker to have full and complete understanding that he must try to conquer all of his **Indriyas** (senses) from all sides. Such a man, says lord Krishna, is a Man-of-Perfection as conceived in and contemplated upon, as explained in, and glorified by the spiritual books of the Hindus.

This section of the discourse also gives us a clear pattern of the autobiography of all seekers who have after a long period of practice come to wreck themselves upon the rocks of failure and disappointment. To a true Vedantic seeker, no fall is ever possible. However, there is no halfway house for such fallen victims; a slip for them means their destruction!! Therefore, the fallen as we already are, the ladder-of-fall must be thoroughly understood so that we shall know how to get back to our pristine glory and inward perfection.

The source of all evil starts from our own wrong thinking or due to false imaginations (false interpretations of life events). **Thought is creative; it can make us or mar us.** If rightly harnessed, it can be used for constructive purposes, if misused, it can destroy us. When we persistently court with a sense-object in our mind, the consistency of that thought creates within us an 'attachment' for the object of our thought. When more and more thoughts flow towards that object of attachment, they crystallize to form a burning desire for the possession and enjoyment of the object-of-attachment. The same force of the motion when directed towards the obstacles that threaten the fulfillment of our desires, is called anger (Krodha- क्रोध).

An intellect fumed with anger comes to experience delusion. The deluded intellect has no power of discrimination, because it loses all of the memories of the past. Anyone who is filled with anger is capable of doing acts while totally forgetting himself and his relationship with all others. Adi Shankaracharya says in this connection that a deluded fool who is in this mental condition might even fight with his own teachers and parents, while forgetting his indebtedness to these revered persons.

Thus, an individual, through wrong channels of thinking, becomes attached to an object; the attachment matures into a burning desire to possess that object. When an obstruction to possess that object-of-desire shoots him up into a fit of anger, the mental disturbance caused by his emotions deludes the intellect and makes the individual forget his sense of proportion, and his sense of relationship with things and beings around him. When thus a deluded intellect forgets its dignity of culture, it loses its discriminative capacity, which is called, in common parlance, 'conscience (Buddhi- बुद्धि).' Conscience is that differentiating knowledge to be enjoyed for sifting the good from the evil, which often forms a standard within us, to warn our mind against its lustful sensuousness and animalism. Once this 'conscience' is dulled, the man becomes a two-legged animal with no sense of proportion, and no ears for any subtle call within him than the howling urgent hungers of the flesh. Thereby, he is guaranteeing for himself a complete destruction inasmuch as such a bosom cannot come to perceive, or strive for higher, the nobler, and the Diviner.

The source of all evils is rooted in the contemplation of sense-objects. Now the meaning of deliverance (Liberation-मोक्ष) is described through the following verse.

रागद्वेषवियुक्तैस्तु विषयानिन्द्रियैश्चरन् ।
आत्मवश्यैर्विधेयात्मा प्रसादमधिगच्छति ॥६४॥

"*But the self-controlled man, free from both temptations and revulsion, with his senses under control, and even while moving among objects attains peace.*"

Though the sense objects are identified and described as the source of all evil, the implicit advice, most definitely, is not to run away from the world of objects. By doing so, nobody can assure for himself any inner peace, because the inner disturbance does not depend upon the presence or absence of the sense-objects in the outer world, but essentially upon the mind's agitation for procuring the desirable objects, or the getting rid of the undesirable ones.

Sense objects are inert and have no power whatsoever to repel or attract anyone towards them. It is my desire to acquire and possess them and constant contemplation over them, which lends them the power. For example, there is a lunatic who is whipping himself up and weeping in pain; his sorrows can be ended only when he is persuaded not to take the whip in his hand. He could be advised, even if he kept the whip in his hand, not to swing his arms in the fashion in which he is doing! Similarly, here the mind woos the objects and gets beaten up. Therefore, given here is advice that an individual who lives in self-control will no longer lend his own life's dynamism to an object to persecute him, through his own emotional dislike and like for that object.

The lunatic is immediately saved from the sorrows of the whip when he is taught not to wield the whip and strike himself. Similarly, when a mind is trained in these two aspects: (1) to live in self-control or (2) move among the sense-objects with neither an attachment for, nor an aversion to them, the disturbances and agitations in the mind caused by the sense-enchantments are all immediately brought under control. This condition of the mind is called 'Tranquility' or 'Peace.'

This is symbolically represented in the distribution of sweets after every Puja service and is called among the Hindus as Prasad or Bhog. The one who has, during the ritual, practiced perfect self-control and God contemplation comes to enjoy, as a result of his devotion and right actions, tranquility in the mind (शान्तिः), which is termed as Spiritual Grace or Divine Peace (Ishwara Prasad). Here, as far as Vedantin Student is concerned, Prasad is a mental purification. Such a mind, which feels in itself the least sense-disturbances, is considered as pure. The one who has learnt to live in self-control and has trained himself to live among sense-objects in a spirit of least attachment to, or aversion for them, has the least disturbance, because of the ineffectiveness of sense-objects upon him. Thereby, his mind automatically becomes increasingly calm and tranquil, and is considered as Pure (Prasad) for the purposes of the spiritual Life.

प्रसादे सर्वदुःखानां हानिरस्योपजायते ।

प्रसन्नचेतसो ह्याशु बुद्धिः पर्यवतिष्ठते ॥६५॥

"In that peace all pains are destroyed; for, the intellect of the tranquil-minded soon becomes steady."

Now the question is, "Why must one have peace of mind or what are the dividends of a tranquil mind?" Through this verse, Lord Krishna explains why one should develop and maintain tranquility of mind within himself. In tranquility, all sorrows are destroyed. Absence of sorrows is nothing but the definition of happiness. A peaceful mind is the significance of happiness. Peace is happiness, happiness is peace. Sorrow is nothing but a state of agitation in the mind, inasmuch as the least-agitated mind is a proof against all sorrows.

In order to clearly bring out the meaning that is implied in the phrase 'destruction of sorrows,' we will have to understand it as the 'Elimination of Vasanas (mental tendencies)' as mentioned earlier, Vasana granulations, upon giving a thick coating to the Subjective Mind, are the cause for its dilution which creates all sorrows for the imperfect ones; while the Perfect One transcends the Vasanas through the Buddhi-Yoga.

It is very well known that all the existing vasanas, within an individual who is facing life constantly, cannot be fully destroyed by him. The secret of doing so has been promised and explained here by Lord Krishna. Keeping the mind exposed to an atmosphere of tranquility (Prasad), consciously brought about through an intelligent life of self-control, is the secret whereby all the Vasanas can get eliminated.

नास्ति बुद्धिरयुक्तस्य न चायुक्तस्य भावना ।

न चाभावयतः शान्तिरशान्तस्य कुतः सुखम् ॥६६॥

"To the unstable there is no knowledge (of the Self); to the unstable there is no meditation; to the unstable there is no tranquilly; to the unstable there is no bliss."

This tranquility is extolled here by Lord Krishna. Lord Krishna explains as to why the quietude of the mind is so often and so insistently emphasized in the literature explaining the Hindu-technique of Self-perfection. The intellectual leisure necessary for cultural Self-development and the inner vigor required to regularly practice spiritual perfections—both of which a genuinely evolved person yearns for—cannot exist without a calm mind. There cannot be stability of intellectual application to life's challenges without tranquility. Without this self-evaluation of life and true observation with a clear discriminative analysis, we cannot have within us the required amount of Devotion (propelling force or inertia-Bhavana & Bhakti–भावना एवं भक्ति) to Self-knowledge. Without such a magnificent goal in front of us always inviting us into itself like a pole star, our existence will be a lost ship in an ocean that is getting nowhere and eventually flopping into some perilous rock.

The one who has no philosophical goal in life to strive and yearn for, will not know what the peace of mind is. To the one who is thus restless, where is happiness for them? To live in balance and sail safely on the uncertain waves of the ocean of life through both its smiling weather, and storming days, we must have a constant perception of the Real. Without a drummer, the dancer's footwork cannot be rhythmic and cannot keep a perfect time.

इन्द्रियाणां हि चरतां यन्मनोऽनुविधीयते ।

तदस्य हरति प्रज्ञां वायुर्नावमिवाम्भसि ॥६७॥

"Because the intellect, which trails behind the inquisitive senses, drags away his discrimination, like the wind carries away a boat on the sea."

Just as a ship with the sails up, and the helmsman dead would be completely at the mercy of the fitful storms and reckless waves, will not reach any definite harbor but get destroyed by the very tossing of the waves, life too gets capsized, and the individual is drowned if his mind is unanchored and left to be carried hither and thither by the uncertain buffets of passionate sense-organs. Therefore, the senses are to be controlled if man is to live a better and more purposeful life designed and planned for enduring success.

तस्माधस्य महाबाहो निगृहीतानि सर्वशः ।

इन्द्रियाणीन्द्रियार्थेभ्यस्तस्य प्रज्ञा प्रतिष्ठिता ॥६८॥

"Therefore, O Mighty-armed, those whose senses are entirely restrained from sense-objects have steady knowledge."

Lord Krishna is restating the same idea in this verse that has already been discussed in detail. That is, "If we demand from life something a little more enduring than tears, sobbing, sighs, and moans, then life in self-control alone is life worth living."

या निशासर्वभूतानां तस्यां जागर्ति संयमी ।
यस्यां जाग्रति भूतानि सा निशा पश्यतो मुने: ॥६९॥

"When everyone is awake, it is that which is night to all beings, in that the self-controlled man keeps awake; that which is night to the Sage (MUNI) who sees."

Through this verse Lord Krishna reiterates, in order to bring home to the seeker in Arjuna the idea that the world as experienced by an individual through the goggles of the body-mind-intellect is different from what is perceived through the open windows of spirituality. This verse's metaphorical language is so intricately detailed that the data-gathering modern intellect is unable to fully appreciate its poetic beauty.

The ignorant person never perceives the world as it is; he always throws his own mental colors on to the object and understands the imperfections within his mind to be a part and parcel of the object perceived. The world as viewed through a coloured glass pane must look coloured. The world looks 'as it is' when the coloring medium has been removed.

The body, the mind, and the intellect are the only three means through which the consciousness within us can recognise the world today. Naturally, we perceive the world as defective, not because it is so, but rather due to the ugliness of the media through which we view it. He is a mastermind when he is grounded in wisdom, opens his perceptional windows, and views the world with wisdom. When an electric engineer visits a city at nightfall when the city glows with lights, he quickly asks, "Is it AC or DC current?" While the same vision to an illiterate person is a wondrous sight and he only exclaims: "I have seen lights that need no wick or oil!" From the point of view of the illiterate, there is no electricity and no problem of AC or DC currents. The world that the engineer sees among the same lamps is not known by the unperceiving intellect of the illiterate; nor is the engineer awake to the world of the strange wonderment which the illiterate enjoys.

It is in this context, this verse says that, *"Which is night to all beings, in that the self-controlled man keeps awake; where all beings are awake, that is the night for the Sage (MUNI) who sees."* Here the attention of the seeker in the Arjuna is directed at this observation that the egocentric, finite mortal is asleep to the world-of-perception that is enjoyed by the Man of Steady-Wisdom; and the Perfect One cannot see and feel the thrills, besides the sobs which the egocentric person experiences in its selfish life of finite experiences.

आपूर्यमाणमचलप्रतिष्ठं समुद्रमापः प्रविशन्ति यद्वत् ।
तद्वत्कामा यं प्रविशन्ति सर्वे स शान्तिमाप्नोति न कामकामी ॥७०॥

"He achieves Peace into whom all desires enter, as waters enter the ocean, which filled from all sides, remains unaffected, but not the 'desirer of desires.'"

Lord Krishna is emphatically reminding the seeker in Arjuna again, in and through this verse, that only a wise and devoted seeker who has abandoned all desires and whose Wisdom is steady, can attain Moksha (Peace & Happiness), and not he who without renouncing cherishes desires.

For example, it is very well known that although millions of gallons of water reach the ocean through various rivers, the level of water in the ocean does not change even by a fraction. In the same way, even though an infinite number of sense-objects may pour in their stimuli and reach the mental zone of the Perfect One through his five sense-channels, they do not create any commotion or flux (desires) within his bosom.

A person who consistently maintains his own level of balance while being among sense objects and having his sense organs in constant contact with the item is referred to as a Man of Perfection or a True Saint. Such a person, according to Krishna, is the only one who can fully discover Moksha within him. In the Bhagavad Gita, Lord Krishna expresses his dissatisfaction with this accusation and expressly forbids the "desirers of desires" from experiencing any genuine serenity or joy.

The current belief in the material world is completely at odds with this concept. The materialists contend that one can achieve satisfaction and contentment by fanning their desires and gratifying as many of them as they can. The industrialization, mass production, and consumerism that underpin modern civilization aim to incite cravings. This attempt has now succeeded to such an extent that the average man has a million times more desires today than his forefathers ever entertained, a century ago. The financiers and the industrialists with the aid of modern scientific knowledge struggle hard to discover and satisfy new desires. To the extent that an individual has come to fulfill his newly created desires, he is taught by the day's civilization that he is happier than ever before.

On the other hand, great Indian thinkers of the past, perhaps through their experience, or through their more careful and exhaustive thinking, discovered that the joy created through satisfaction of desires can never be complete. They discovered that joy and happiness at any given time, is a quotient when the **'number of desires fulfilled'** (numerator) is divided by the **'total number of desires entertained'** (denominator) by the same individual at that time. This mathematical truth has been accepted by the modern preachers of secularism also but in their practical application, the old Rishis and the modern politicians seem to differ to a large extent.

The goal in the modern world is to raise the numerator, which is the 'number of desires fulfilled.' The Indian scriptural masters likewise lived in a milieu with a society of man. Their philosophical reflections focused on the social nature of man and increasing happiness in their community was also one of their goals. These Rishis of Religion, unlike the modern prophets of profit, did not think that trying to grow the numerator while also paying attention to the rate of increase of the denominator could lead to any discernible increase in joy. However, we are working very hard today to raise the 'number of desires fulfilled' while also attempting to limit 'the number of desires entertained.'

The scriptural conclusion, which appears to be a simple scientific truth, is that this situation cannot cause a tangible increase in the **'Quotient Of Happiness.'**

Herein, the Gita is only repeating what the Upanishadic Rishis never got tired of emphasizing in the scriptures of India. The 'desirer of desires' will never experience absolute peace (shanti). The man of peace and joy is only he who has achieved total mastery over his mind through the practice of detachment, preventing the sense objects of the outside world from inducing in him an endless number of yearnings or cravings. The things in the outside world cannot tease a guy by being there or not being there. Only when a man exposes himself unprotected and is wounded and crushed by his own attachments to sense items that are valued incorrectly (i.e., getting more and more sought-after goods will make him happier), can the outside world borrow its power to mistreat him.

In this verse, Lord Krishna is only giving a more elaborate and complete commentary upon the opening line of this chapter wherein He started the description of Man of Steady Wisdom. There, He stated, "A man is deemed to be the one of Steady-Knowledge when he entirely casts off all the desires from within his mind."

विहाय कामान्य: सर्वान्पुमांश्चरति नि:स्पृह: ।
निर्ममो निरहंकार: स शान्तिमधिगच्छति ॥७१॥

"Whoever gives up all cravings and walks around without longing or a sense of 'I-ness' or 'My-ness' achieves peace."

This verse is hinting at and indicating towards 'Sannyasa Yoga' (Renunciation- सन्यास योग). The word 'Sannyasa' is a highly misunderstood and redundant word for the modern-day person as he thinks and believes that Sannyasa means a 'Wandering Monk' who has abandoned his family and society in an attempt to fly away from all his responsibilities. Such a person, having shaved his head, wears an orange robe and wanders around in jungles. Such an act by a person is referred to as '**Sannyasa**' and he is referred to as a '**Sannyasin**.'

To the contrary, the Lord Krishna is advising on the Vedantic meaning and the definition of a true Sannyasa here that, "Sannyasa is a state of being wherein the Man-of-Perfection, having conquered the mental agitations that were created by the pairs-of-opposites, fights the battle of Life." Therefore, Sannyasa Yoga is essentially the renunciation of all desires and not necessarily renunciation of cardinal duties towards the Self, the family, and the society at large and associated responsibilities. Having renounced all desires, as discussed above, it is acceptable in Sanatan Tradition (Hinduism), if one chooses to be a Wandering Monk, wears an orange robe and shaves his head, but without renouncing all desire, it is not only hypocritical but a flight from the battle of Life.

This stanza explains the mental condition of the one who comes to discover Real Peace within himself. Such an individual renounces all desires and has no attachments or longings. The second line describes the condition of such an individual's intellect, and it asserts that it is without any sense of 'I-ness' or 'My-ness.' The Ego is the cause of the sense-attachments and longings. There are no longings or desires in the person, or at the very least, they are latent, wherever the Ego is not discernible, such as during sleep. The second line of this verse, therefore, claims the absence of the precise reason from which desires and agitation develop, if the first line of this verse describes a negation of the effects of ignorance.

The stanza's overall advice tells us that our own egotistical misperception and the ensuing hubris, which is exemplified by our never-ending demands for material goods and our infinite ambitions, are the root of all of our sorrows in the world.

Sannyasa, therefore, means sacrifice (of desires and attachments), and to live in the spirit of sacrifice after renouncing completely one's ego and its desires is true Sannyasa, wherein an individual comes to live in constant awareness of his fuller and ampler divinity. The general misunderstanding that to run away from life is Sannyasa, or to color the cloth is to become a true monk, has cast an irreparable slur on the philosophy of the Upanishads. Hinduism considers him alone to be a Sannyasin "who has learnt the art of living life in constant inspiration, which is gained through an intelligent renunciation of egocentric misconception."

Adi Shankaracharya explains this point of view in his commentary on this stanza. "That man of renunciation, who after completely giving up all desires, goes through life content with the bare necessities of life, who regards not even those things as his, which are required for mere bodily existence, who is not vain of his knowledge-such a Man of Steady Knowledge, who knows Brahman(ब्रह्म), achieves peace (Nirvana-निर्वाण), the cessation of all the suffering of mundane existence (Samsara - संसार). In essence, he turns into Brahman(ब्रह्म).

Knowing Brahman is becoming Brahman. Here the word knowing means Realization, which refers to a mental processing of the information (knowing-श्रवण), Reflecting over (मनन), and establishing the knowledge of the Real Self in the intellect (निदिध्यास्) through direct and the personal experience of the known. As soon as one comes to know the Real Self, their pre-existing egocentric Self effortlessly merges with and becomes one with the Real Self. For example, a river upon termination of its thousands of miles worth of constant and consistent efforts merges in and becomes one with the Ocean; the space in a pot, upon breaking of its walls, merges in the space outside of the pot and becomes one with it.

एषा ब्राह्मी स्थिति: पार्थ नैनां प्राप्य विमुह्यति ।

स्थित्वास्यामन्तकालेऽपि ब्रह्मनिर्वाणमृच्छति ॥७२॥

"That, O Son of Pritha, is the Brahmic-state. No one who achieves this is deluded. One achieves oneness with Brahman by being entrenched there, even at death."

Giving up all desires is the same as destroying all signs of one's Ego. Ego renunciation is not a life of dreary nothingness. Where the delusory Ego has ended, the state of full-Knowledge or Selfhood has dawned. To realize the Self in one's bosom is to realize at once the Self which is All-pervading and Eternal (Brahman-ब्रह्म).

Let us consider a couple more examples to understand this effortless transition of our limited Ego into the Supreme Self. It is exactly like the dispelling of darkness, upon the dawning of the light. Where there is light, the darkness disappears, and it cannot exist. The space inside a pot becomes one with the space outside the pot, when the walls of the pot are broken or removed. In the same way, when the limited Ego is dispelled or transcended with the help of the Knowledge of the Self, it merges into and becomes one with the Supreme Self.

When Ego has ended, the Consciousness is not known to be anything other than the Eternal, and as such the Knower of Truth in a brilliant experience of the Self becomes the Self, and therefore, this state of being is called Self-hood (brahman-sthithi- ब्रह्मस्थिति).

Even after coming to this realization, there is a chance that we will relapse into the ego's illusion and experience its world of flaws and suffering. To downplay this tragedy, it has been claimed that once one has experienced one's own Self, one can no longer relapse into one's previous delusions. The Self Realization experience need not occur in a person's formative years. It is sufficient to attain this Brahmic-State, as stated in the Vedantic literature, even in old age, nay, even in the final moments of this life, if a seeker can come to experience, even for a moment, this egoless state of tranquilly and poise, even a passing glimpse of the Selfhood.

The Upanishads describe the way as "Negation of the False and Assertion of the True." The same path in its practical application is designated here in the Gita, in Vyasa's original contribution as 'Karma Yoga.' To work without attachment, desires, egoism, and vanity, ever established in perfect equilibrium in both, success, and failures (duality), is to deny the Ego its entire field of activity, and unconsciously to assert the greater Truth, that is the Self. The technique of Karma Yoga from the Gita is, hence, very similar to Vedic technique of Meditation in terms of practice.

A Person of Steady Wisdom functions in the world with total freedom. Physically he demands nothing; emotionally he has no handicaps; intellectually he is always extremely brilliant because he has no hang-ups whatsoever. Such a person, functioning freely in the world as a master of all situations as well as of his own physical, mental, and intellectual equipment, is so contrary to all our expectations and experiences that a joe-blog with average intelligence will not be able to appreciate him unless, at least, a vague picture of such a person is presented to him. Only then will he see the full beauty of the one who is totally uninhibited, completely free, joyously living in the world, actively participating in the history making processes around him, serving everyone, while exhibiting infinite love, mercy, kindness, and forgiveness at all times; and uncompromisingly living his perfection in the midst of all worldly things.

In using thus, the first-person possessive noun, this scripture perhaps indicates that the Song Divine sung through the eighteen chapters of Bhagavad Gita is to be **'subjectively transcribed, lived, and personally experienced'** by each person in his/her own life.

The Srimad Bhagavad Gita stands out from the rest of the canon of religious literature due to the straightforward, useful, and timely manner in which it conveys the essence of Hindu way of Life. Sage Vyasa, through the mouth of Lord Krishna, masterfully brings the teachings of the Upanishads from secluded forests and tranquil mountains to our familiar world of agitations, chaos, and whirlwind activities. The Gita's teachings can be practiced in the midst of even the most harrowing of situations–a fratricidal war. Sri Krishna's teachings are not confined to the rare few, who are pure and devout seekers of Truth. It addresses all of us, complete with our confusions, delusions, and fear.

The Gita can guide us from our current pitiable condition to the most exalted state of supreme beatitude, and therein lies her glory.

5

Have You Counted Graces In Life?

"To be born as a human being is a sign of the Lord's grace. After this, to employ in life a deep discriminative understanding and to perceive the ultimate futility of all the ordinary mundane pursuits of life and thereby discover an enthusiasm to seek a nobler path of Self-redemption is still rarer. Manhood, burning desire for Liberation, the capacity to surrender completely to a Man of Wisdom–these things are rare indeed, and wherever they are found, they are due to the Lord's own grace."

जन्तूनां नरजन्म दुर्लभमतः पुंस्त्वं ततो विप्रता

तस्माद्वैदिकधर्ममार्गपरता विद्वत्त्वमस्मात्परम् ।

आत्मानात्मविवेचनं स्वनुभवो ब्रह्मात्मना संस्थितिः

मुक्तिर्नो शतजन्मकोटिसुकृतैः पुण्यैर्विना लभ्यते ॥२॥

"For all living creatures, a human birth is indeed rare; it is much more difficult to attain full manhood; rarer than this is a Sattvika attitude in life. Even after gaining all these rare chances, to have steadfastness on the path of spiritual activities as explained in the Vedika literature is still rarer; much more so, to have a correct knowledge of the deep significance of the scripture. Discrimination between the Real and the unreal, personal experience of spiritual glory and ultimately to get fully established in having consciousness that the Self in me is the Self in all–these come only later on and culminate in one's Liberation. This kind of a perfect Liberation cannot be had without merits earned in hundred crores of lives, lived intelligently."

-Vivekachudamani ||2||

Adi Sankaracharya, through this verse from Vivekachudamani, is emphasizing the difficulty of awakening ourselves to the real communion with the Divine in us. In fact, there are innumerable specimens of living creatures in the universe. Truth is the substratum of all and, therefore, the real nature of all creation, even the inert and insentient. In stone life too, Truth exhibits itself as Existence, but unfortunately, the stone is not aware of it. A little more evolved is plant life, which seems to be more aware of the world outside and so the plant compared to the stone is a higher evolved specimen in the world of beings. When we come to animal life, we find that different species exhibit different degrees of awareness not only of their external world of stimuli but also of their emotions and feelings.

Of them all, man seems to be the only living creature in the universe who is independent for his rational conquest and is the sacred being, which, through intellectual conviction, can gain a firm control over the emotion of the mind and apply this regulated and controlled energy for purposes of transcending psychological existence and thereby peep into the boundless realms of bliss and beauty, love, and perfection. It is in this sense that the Rishis considered man as the supreme being, while in this modern age, man is considered great since he has developed technology and can build machines. If one were to follow this argument, the monkey world would take it as a great insult when it hears a modern man declaring himself to be a descendent of the ape!

Adi Sankaracharya seems to emphasize that the spiritual text is meant only for evolved human beings since it explains and expounds a theory of spiritual perfection, which can be understood, practiced, pursued, and perfected only by men of certain mental caliber and moral character. Such perfect ones, who are ripe for a sudden and immediate spiritual Self-development, are always rare in the world at any given period of its history. Thus, the Acharya says, in this context, that to get a human birth is rare, having got a human birth to have a masculine temperament is still rarer. The use of the word 'Masculinity' here is gender-neutral and is used with a particular and specific reference to the qualities of the mind. With the body, no spiritual sadhana can be undertaken as explained in Vedanta. The main practices in Vedanta are reflection, and meditation, which are to be undertaken by a healthy mind and a keen intellect. So, it means that feminine qualities of mind and intellect are to be eschewed. A masculine inner personality, full of courage, discrimination, detachment, equilibrium, peace, and cheer, is the fittest instrument for a quick march to the goal indicated by Vedanta.

Understand it in this way. If the government is accepting applications for posts of a police officer and an engineer, quite understandably, required qualifications and competences for both these positions are very different and unique. Applicants with shorter heights will be rejected if it is less than the prescribed requirement. But a qualified and experienced applicant will be shortlisted for the post of engineer, even if he is short heighted. What is demanded of a police officer is a good physique and a body full of muscular strength, while an engineer requires intellectual qualities. An expansive chest and a pair of biceps are not needed to design a bridge or to plan a power project for the nation. What is meant is, qualifications are declared according to the functions required of the applicant. A seeker in Vedanta is expected to carry out daring intellectual flights to the unknown through a process of deep study, vigorous reflections, and tireless meditations. So here, when it is said that, according to the sastras, he must be a 'he-man,' it must necessarily mean that he/she should have a special quality of the head and heart. Therefore, the verse refuses none (male or female) that chance to study the scripture and seek through Vedanta one's Self-development, simply because one happens to have a feminine body.

Viprata (विप्रता): This is a term upon which the orthodoxy built up an absurd interpretation that Self-realization is available only to those who are, (by sheer accident of birth) worthy, or unworthy sons of Brahmanas. This misunderstanding has been glorified to the status of wisdom and the amount of devastation it has brought to Sanatan traditions looks almost irreparable now. As before, we must consider this qualification also as indicating a special quality of the head and heart.

Santosh (संतोष - contentment), Samadhan (समाधान - Spirit of Self-surrender) and Shanti (शांति - peace arising due to the right knowledge) are special qualities (Sattvika temperaments) of a well evolved man. Man in any generation, when observed closely, can be classified into three distinct categories—the animal-man, the man-man, and the Godman. He who is ever a victim of his gross instincts and a hopeless slave to his emotions and impulses is classified as an animal-man. When he has disciplined these instincts in himself, he is considered a full-grown, mature he-man. Such a Vipra (विप्र - wise person), meaning a man-man, has the necessary Viprata to strive rightly and grow steadily into the last stage of his evolution, the super manhood or godhood, when he becomes a Godman.

Vaidika Dharma Marg Parata (वैदिक धर्म मार्ग परता): When one has a human body along with the serener qualities of the heart and the Sattvika attitude of the intellect, one is indeed blessed with all the preliminaries for his evolution. But all these can run a waste if not properly harnessed and intelligently applied. So, Adi Sankaracharya declares that even after gaining all the above qualifications, rarer are those who will find the energy to apply themselves faithfully to the methods of integration as suggested in the literature of the Vedas.

Selfless karma (निष्काम कर्म), ritual (क्रियापद्धति), and practices of devotion (धर्मानुराग या धर्मनिष्ठा), Japa, puja and so on, alone can purify the inner personality and bring more and more integration to it. Concentration (ध्यान) increases through desireless actions and person who has greater concentration (Ekagrata-एकाग्रचित्त) necessarily has a finer Antahkaran (अंतःकरण- internal equipment). So, a steady concentration must be the initial attempt of all seekers, especially those on the path of knowledge.

Vidvattvam (विद्वत्त्वम् अस्मात्परम्): When such a man-man has developed a high power of concentration, he becomes fit for a profitable study and understanding of the scripture. But without the true knowledge of the 'Whys' and the 'Wherefores' of the techniques, he will not be able to keep up his enthusiasm for sadhana (practice) because of his limited understanding. Therefore, the study of the scripture is indicated here and the literature that shows the goal, is the Upanishads.

When a man-man, having developed his powers of concentration through selfless actions, studies the scriptures properly, he gains discrimination between Spirit and the Matter, the Real and the Unreal. Soon he comes to realize that the Self in him is the Self in all and ere long he gets established in his experience of Godhood.

Adi Sankaracharya, in enumerating these stages of Self-development, gives us in a nutshell the unwritten chapter in Darwin's half declared theory of evolution. Here we have all the various stages through which man consciously, by right living and Self-progress climbs on to the lap of the Lord, there to merge with Him, there to become Siva. This is called **Mukti**–the full and final Liberation of a mortal from all his limitations.

The last line is not a cry of pessimistic despair; it is the call of hope, urging man to wake up and act, to grow and achieve the highest gain. No reader of this verse should consider himself as standing low down in this upward procession. One who feels charmed by the call of Vedanta, who can appreciate its arguments, who feels a sympathetic understanding of the ideal indicated, is indeed at the fag-end of his transmigration, the product of an entire evolutionary past. If he makes use of his present chance with diligent and careful application, success is guaranteed to him by Vedanta. This is a call to man to throw off his lethargy, his dejections, his sentiments of Self-pity and to wake up to face life and through understanding, to grow fast to reach the goal–here and now.

दुर्लभं त्रयमेवैतद्देवानुग्रहहेतुकम् ।

मनुष्यत्वं मुमुक्षुत्वं महापुरूषसंश्रय: ॥३॥

> "Manhood, burning desire for Liberation, the capacity to surrender completely to a Man of Wisdom—these things are rare indeed, and wherever they are found, they are due to the Lord's own grace."
>
> *Vivekachudamani* ||3||

In the last verse, Adi Sankaracharya has told us the Human birth and necessary qualifications one must have for a vital and positive living which one can grow in one's inner evolution. In order to emphasize to the seeker the importance of the qualities which he should have when going to a great Man of Wisdom, seeking spiritual knowledge, these qualifications are stressed in this verse.

To be born as a human being is a sign of Lord's grace. After this, to employ in life a deep discriminative understanding and to perceive the ultimate futility of all the ordinary mundane pursuits of life and thereby discovering an enthusiasm to seek a nobler path of Self-redemption is still rare.

लब्ध्वा कथञ्चिन्नरजन्म दुर्लभं तत्रापि पुंस्त्वं श्रुतिपारदर्शनम् ।
यस्त्वात्ममुक्तौ न यतेत मूढधी: स ह्यात्महास्वं विनिहन्त्यसद्ग्रहात् ॥४॥

> "Is there a man, who having somehow gained a human embodiment and there having a masculine temperament and also a complete knowledge of the sacrifices, foolish enough not to strive hard for Self-realization? He verily commits suicide, clinging to things unreal."

This verse declares that having been born in a human form and possessed of the necessary masculine qualities of head and heart, when such an individual has also made a thorough study of the deep significance of scriptural techniques, if he has not the enthusiasm to walk the sacred path and reach the Divine Goal of Self-perfection, such an individual, alas, commits suicide. Having got such a rare chance in a million, if he is not indeed, committing hara-kiri and such a squanderer of human birth is very fittingly termed by Sankaracharya as a dull fool—mudhadhih (मूढधी:).

How does a person commit this senseless suicide? By his false attachments with the objects of the world, as he looks out from the parapets of his body and his mind, forgetting his own real nature, which is all pervading consciousness, he comes to misunderstand himself to be the matter envelopment (body, mind and the intellect), which are nothing but thought created encrustations around the divine in him, perceiving through the prism of the body, the mind and the intellect, he sees the Truth splashed and splintered into endless plurality and the objects give a delusory enchantment to the senses and the mind. To satisfy these urges of his body and his mind, the individual runs after the objects. Necessarily, such a deluded person, having misunderstood his real nature, becomes the 'samsarika' Egocenter, a victim of his own ignorance. This fall of the Self to be the selfish Ego is spiritual suicide.

There is no real suicide possible for the Atman. No danger can come to me simply because I dream the greatest of dangers, even though the dreamer in me suffers all the dangers of my dreams. The moment I wake up I realize that the dangers as well as the dreamer, who suffered them, were all my own mental creations only in an unsubstantial dreamworld. So, from the standpoint of Reality, there is no suicide. Adi Sankaracharya comes down to our level to help us discriminate between the Real and the Unreal, in and through our day-to-day life and it is in this sense that he says we commit suicide. It is not the destiny of the Self to suffer but it is a lot of the Ego, the Ego that thrives in this world to be the Sacred and the Divine.

6

What Is Dharma?

Dharma is one of the vaguest terms in our everyday language. Although there is no direct single-word translation in the world languages for dharma, it is usually interpreted as 'merit,' 'righteousness,' or 'religious and moral duties' governing individual conduct. In the Hindu and the Buddhist context, Dharma is considered an individual's duty fulfilled by observance of custom or law, the basic principles of cosmic or individual existence, including the divine law and conformity to one's duty and nature.

The word Dharma is derived from a verbal root 'dhar' (Dhri ऋ), meaning 'to hold' or 'uphold,' is thought to have been the main term used by Hinduism and Buddhism to describe their distinct visions of the good and well rewarded life.

Derived from the root 'dhar,' Dharma also means to uphold, sustain, support or the substratum. **"Something which unites the different features and elements of an object into a wholeness."** As indicated above, the word Dharma is typically interpreted as a religious code, righteousness, a code of morality, obligation, or acts of kindness. But none of these translations adequately represent the original Sanskrit term's unique sense. The definition that best captures this concept is **"Dharma is the law of being, that which determines what a thing or being is."**

For example, it is the Dharma of fire to burn, of the sun to shine, etc. Dharma, therefore, means not merely righteousness or goodness, a good deed, or duties but it indicates the essential nature of a thing, without which it cannot retain its independent existence. For example, a cold, dark sun is impossible, as heat and light are the Dharma of the sun; similarly, a hot and liquid ice doesn't exist, as solidity and extreme cold is its real nature. Without these essential qualities, these things cannot have an existence. In the same way, if you and I have to live as a truly dynamic person in the world, we can only do so by being faithful to our true and real nature. So, what essentially is the real nature of humans? Srimad Bhagavat Gita, Upanishads, and all the other spiritual Hindu texts, including Ramayana and Mahabharata, explain to us **'Our Dharma,'** that is our real nature.

A thing's Dharma is its innate law of existence. Without authentically upholding its own nature, a thing cannot continue to be itself. Its Dharma is **the nature or qualities that give something its unique identity**. Hinduism stresses on the 'Manava Dharma,' which means that a person must be true to their own inherent divinity and godliness. As a result, all of a person's efforts in life should be focused on upholding that dignity rather than passively slogging through life like a helpless animal.

Sacchidananda (सच्चिदानन्द) is said to be the real and divine nature of human beings. Breaking it down into individual syllables, we get the component parts of our real nature, that is, **Sat** (सत्- the Truth, the Reality), **Chit** (चित- Pure Consciousness) and **Ananda** (परमानन्द- the Absolute Bliss). **Love** (असीम प्रेम), **Peace** (प्रशान्ति) and **Bliss** (अनन्त एवं अक्षर आनन्द) are its essential qualities.

Sacchidananda , though is the destination of all recommended spiritual practices, is the means and the process of this destination too. One must have a sincere resolve to know the truth of their own Supreme Self, which is nothing but our own Pure Consciousness and the Life-Principle within each living being. Having known the nature of the Supreme Self, the limited Ego becomes one with it. One, who is thus realized, only has one experience, that is, absolute bliss, thereafter, one remains immersed in constant love, peace, and bliss.

All harmonized acts and efforts (कर्म), whether at the body (sensations), mind (emotions) or intellectual (ideas) level, resulting in maintaining and sustaining these essential qualities in the bosom, are considered righteous deeds (पुण्य कर्म), that is, **Dharam (धर्म)**. Any act or effort that is antagonistic to the essential nature are immoral deeds (पाप कर्म), essentially, that is **Adharma (अधर्म)**. Therefore, when one carefully analyzes their personal experiences, they will find that all positive experiences (i.e. positive emotions and feelings- स्वर्ग) are essentially caused by the positive thoughts about himself that he is entertaining, consciously, or subconsciously, in their mind. In the same way, all his negative experiences (i.e., negative emotions and feelings- नर्क) are essentially caused by his negative thoughts about the Self that he broods upon, in his mind.

This is the litmus test for each person to test whether this observation is true and/or correct for him or her. My emotions and feelings, that I experience on my mental level, are nothing but the reflection or the manifestation of the texture and the quality of my thoughts that I am entertaining at the present moment or have been courting with for some time.

In the same way, my actions, behaviors, the values, and the principles that I hold and promote, how I present myself in the society, my conduct with others, and all my transactions with the world outside, are necessarily fuelled and propelled by the texture and the quality of my thoughts.

Our Subjective Scientists have classified the texture and the quality of our thoughts in three categories i.e., Tamasic thoughts, Rajasic thoughts and the Sattvic thoughts.

Tamasic thoughts refers to a mental mood of a total lack of Pure Consciousness (God) and full-blown egoistic desires, where all deeds are performed with pure selfish motive for the fulfillment of my sensuous desires (inactivity & inertia). All I am concerned about is I, Me, Myself, and Mine. This is the lowest stage in my personal and/or spiritual developmental stage, where I have a total non-apprehension of my real nature.

For a better understanding of Tamasic desires, a parallel can be drawn with the physiological and safety needs as discussed by Maslow's hierarchy of needs in modern psychology. At this level of the hierarchy, an individual is rather concerned about and is motivated only to fulfill his basic needs of food, water, and warmth. Only when he is satisfied with his basic needs, he thinks about or is motivated by his safety and security needs.

Rajasic thoughts, on the other hand, refers to a mental mood with some degree of Pure Consciousness (God), and fully active Ego, where personal glory and sensuous desires are fulfilled in the guise of good deeds, social welfare activities to have a sense of personal glory and recognition. Therefore, there are a lot of desire-prompted activities (activity & dynamism). This is a stage where I have moved on a bit from I, Me, Myself, and Mine thinking and I want to have social recognition and verification of my good nature from external sources. This stage of personal development is akin to the psychological needs level of Maslow's hierarchy of needs where the individual is craving for satisfying his belongingness and love needs through forging intimate relationships and making friends. Thereafter, moving on to the Self-esteem need, I am motivated by gaining social prestige and accomplishments.

Sattvic thoughts refers to a mental mood of Pure Consciousness (God), where all activities are performed without any sensuous or selfish motives but are undertaken in the same way as we offer flowers, food, clothes etc., to the Deity of our worship in a mood of total surrender, reverence, and devotion to the God. Therefore, Sattvic activities are not prompted by selfish desires. There is no motivation, there is no altruistic desire, but one performs his role and the responsibilities, in any given situation, to the best of their abilities just because they must do their best for no reward or reprimand (unactivity). This is a stage of personal and/or spiritual growth and development, as per Maslow's hierarchy of needs, where the individual's greater amount of mental energy is now directed at Self-actualisation.

Self-actualisation needs are the highest level in Maslow's hierarchy of needs and motivation and refer to the realization of a person's full potential, Self-fulfillment, seeking personal growth and peak experiences. Maslow (1943) describes this level as the desire to accomplish everything that one can, to become the most that one can be. This stage of Self-development, in the spiritual domain, can be equated with a mental state of being in the Sattvic Mood, where the possibilities of Self-realization (आत्म-दर्शन) open up.

When an individual is operating at the Tamasic level, the majority of his cognitive activities (thoughts) are directed at undertaking activities solely for the fulfillment and the satisfaction of the needs pertaining to I, Me, and Myself. In other words, my decision to act or not to act is mostly motivated by *my* Selfish desires. Any hurdle or obstruction in the way of my needs, every time, results in (1) Attachment, (2) Fear, and (3) Anger.

At Rajasic level, having reached a certain level of selfish satisfaction, one begins to think about seeking personal glory and acknowledgement in the society through undertaking various charitable activities, apparently for the good of others, but primarily for social recognition, pride, and personal glorification. Their motivation is not necessarily for the welfare and well-being of others, but essentially seeking reward, award, appreciation, personal glory, and societal acknowledgement of their charity. Any hurdle or obstruction in the way of satisfaction of Rajasic desires results in (1) Attachment, (2) Fear, and (3) Anger.

These three prominent negative emotions of attachment, fear, and anger, particularly, in its various forms and combinations, are said to be the main culprits and fundamental cause for all our sufferings and miseries in life. These negative emotions (evils) are referred to as the Asura, Rakshasa, and the Danava in Hindu religious texts, Ghosts or Demons in Christianity and Satan in Islam. These Rakshasas, Ghosts, Evil forces, and Satan must be killed at any cost, to re-establish the reign of righteousness. Therefore, it is observed that whether it is Ramayana, Mahabharata, or any of our Puranic stories, they all have a common plot and a single theme of killing the evil forces in order to re-establish righteousness (Dharma).

All religious practices and ritualistic performances, prescribed in our religious and puranic texts, therefore, are essentially designed and recommended to help the seeker of the Truth or the devotee to learn the art of annihilating negative (Rajasic & Tamasic) thoughts and cultivating more and more positive (Sattvic) thoughts. At the Sattvic Mental level, the individual is not motivated either by the fulfillment of selfish desires or seeking personal glory. They mostly undertake desireless activities. All their activities (at body, mind, and intellectual level) in the world outside are dedicated purely to the activities themselves as these are good things to do. Such desireless activities (Sattvic Karma) are the same as the offerings we give to our deity during the course of our ritualistic worships. Since there is no selfish desire, there is no excitement or disappointment from the possible outcomes of my efforts. Consequently, the mind experiences and remains calm since there is neither any excitement for the winning or gaining nor any agitation for losing.

It is, therefore, advised and recommended that the sincere seeker must endeavor to achieve a Sattvic temperament of mind. Such tranquility of mind, so to speak, is an essential requirement, which makes an individual eligible to enter the gateway of Self-consciousness and with sustained efforts (Yoga) eventually to take a flight to the heights of Self-realization and to experience the glorious plane of the Pure Consciousness.

The path and the trajectory of personal and/or spiritual development and growth could be understood from a simile of a trajectory of a rocket, which is a vehicle for the satellite and fired with an intention to establish a satellite in space. The rocket is made up of various compartments of fuel and the satellite is stored in the top most compartment. When the rocket is fired from a launching station, it shoots up in space with the power generated by the burning of the fuel in it. This power gathers and generates a tremendous amount of throttle and gains supersonic speed which helps the rocket to move against the gravitational force. A sustained flight in the direction of the orbit, eventually helps the launch of the satellite in the orbit. Thereafter, the satellite, having reached its destination, floats in orbit effortlessly in space.

In this process, the fuel in the rocket is burning and dropping off one part of the rocket after another, while maintaining its speed, continuously burning its fuel, maintaining its force and the throttle. In the same way, a sincere seeker of the truth, burns the fuel of his unflinching resolve and determination (दृढ निश्चय, एवं संकल्प), with the fire of unshakable faith, commitment (श्रद्धा), and dedication (निष्ठा), begins the journey of his Self-Realization. With his single-pointed devotion (भक्ति), daily, constant, and forever meditation (नित्य, निरंतर, एवं चिरम् ध्यान), he first dislodges his Tamasic mood and moves up in the realm of Rajasic mood. Thereafter, continuing his daily, constant, and forever meditative efforts, he eventually gains for himself a Sattvic Mood. Sustained Sattvic mood over a period of time can be equated with the stage when the satellite is released in the orbit, whereafter it effortlessly floats in the orbit. In the same way, the ego-centric Self, drops off all its egocentric vestures (Tamasic, Rajasic and Sattvic consciousness) and becomes one with the pure Self-consciousness.

The Vedantic Theory

The Mind is Man. As the mind, so is the individual. If the mind is disturbed, so is the individual. If the mind is good, the person is good.

The mind, for the purposes of our study and understanding, may be considered as constituting of two distinct sides—one facing 'outside,' the world of stimuli that reach it from the objects of the world (outward oriented), and the other facing the 'within' which reacts to the stimuli received (inward oriented). The outer mind facing the objects is called the 'Objective Mind' and the inner mind is called the 'Subjective Mind.'

The individual is whole and healthy in whom the Objective Mind and Subjective Mind work in unison, and in moments of doubt, the Objective Mind readily comes under the disciplining influence of the Subjective Mind. But unfortunately, except for a rare few, the majority of us have minds that are split. This split (or separation) between the Subjective and the Objective aspect of our mind is mainly created by the layers of egocentric desires in the individual. The greater the gap between these two aspects of the mind, the greater the individual's inner confusion, the greater the egoism and higher the desires that the individual manifests in life.

At all times during our waking state, we experience the world of objects around us through the five 'gateways of knowledge,' the organs-of-perception. The innumerable stimuli, through our sense-organs (receptors), create impulses which reach the Objective Mind, and these impulses filter deep down to the subjective stratum through the intervening layers of individual egocentric desires. These impulses, once they reach a person's Subjective Mind, react with the existing impressions of his own past thoughts and actions, which are carefully stored away in the subjective layers, and express themselves through the five organs of action (effectors).

At every moment, man encounters different patterns of these stimuli, accumulating new impressions in the 'Subjective Mind.' Every set of impulses reaching it, not only adds to the existing layers of vasanas already in it, but also gets coloured by the quality of these vasanas hoarded within. When they are translated into action, the actions carry a flavor of the existing vasanas in the 'Subjective Mind.'

All of us live constantly, meeting a variety of experiences, and at each incident, we perceive, react with the perceived, and come to act in the outer fields. During this process, we unwittingly accumulate more and more dirt of new impressions in ourselves. The 'Subjective Mind' gets increasingly granulated by overlapping signatures of our past moments. These form, as it were, an impregnable wall between us and the Spiritual Divinity that shines eternally as pure Consciousness in all of us deep within the core of our personality.

The theory of Vedanta repeats that reduction and eventual purgation of vasanas is the means of volatilisation of the mind. When I look in the mirror and don't see my face, it's not because the mirror isn't reflecting the object in front of it, but because the reflected image is obscured by a thick layer of dust on the mirror. When I clean the mirror with a duster, the act of cleaning does not create the reflection of the face, but rather reveals the reflection that was already there. Similarly, man is not aware today of his divine spiritual nature because the 'Subjective Mind' reflecting it is thickly coated with the dull vasanas gathered by it during its egocentric, passionate existence in the world.

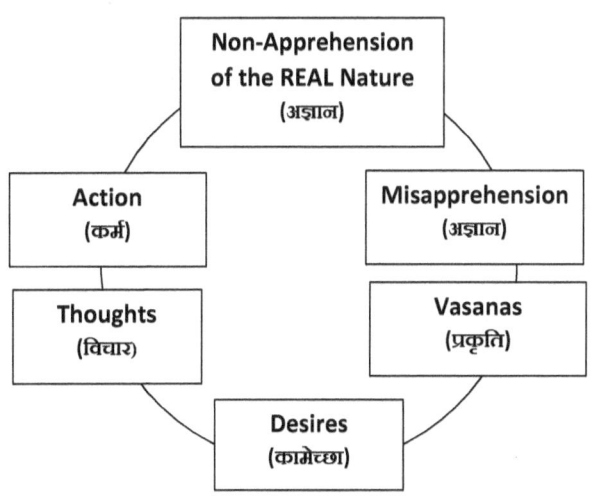

The **'Yoga'** mentioned in the Gita is to bring the subjective and objective aspects of the mind together in a happy marriage where the 'Objective Mind' is well-disciplined to act faithfully as per the guidance of the 'Subjective Mind.' This is accomplished only by the removal of the dividing factors-the-egocentric desires. The typical word used in the Gita to indicate this practical implication of Yoga is Self-explanatory Buddhi Yoga.

When the happy marriage between the subjective and the objective aspects of the mind has taken place, thereafter that equanimous **'Yogi'** (the practitioner) becomes skilled in action and with his 'Objective Mind,' he reacts intelligently and faithfully to the external stimuli; his actions become, as it were, a purgation of the already existing vasanas in his 'Subjective Mind.' Thus, through intelligent action, an individual can exhaust his existing impressions and ultimately redeem his 'Subjective Mind' from the granulations and make it clearer and more crystalline.

This idea has been emphasized by the great commentators like Adi Shankaracharya, who tirelessly repeat that selfless activity, performed in a spirit of egoless adoration and reverence to the Divine Ideal, would ultimately result in inner purification. This, according to Adi Shankaracharya, is the most unavoidable prerequisite before the 'Subjective Mind' can turn inward seeking to rediscover the sanctuary of the Self, the Spiritual Reality.

Spiritually speaking, the 'Subjective Mind' is thus a hidden weapon in man, serving as an outlet for the impressions that have accumulated in it. But the tragedy is that an average person, in his ignorance, misuses this dangerous weapon and brings about his own annihilation. He uses it as an 'Inlet' and creates, during his selfish activities performed with low motives, a new stock of mental impressions.

In order to exhaust them, nature provides new equipment (bodies), in which the same Ego comes to live, repeatedly, **life after life**[11]. The Gita's message is clear: actions should not be avoided, and the world of objects should not be denied. On the contrary, by making use of them intelligently, we must strive selflessly, and force the vary '**Samsara**[12]' to provide us with a field for exhausting our mental dirt, the vasana layers.

An unhealthy mind divided in itself, as has been explained earlier, becomes an easy prey to a host of psychological diseases. Because of its weakened constitution, it is easily infected by all contagions. Arjuna was a well-educated man, and the Mahabharata details reveal the environments in which he grew up. But for the entire Mahabharata, we would not appreciate Arjuna's mental condition so much, without which Krishna's message would have fallen flat upon the readers. As a result, the Gita is an intrinsic part of the entire Mahabharata, and without the Gita, the classic would have been a hotchpotch story devoid of pity and dignity, and the Gita would have been a mere philosopher's conundrum without the Mahabharata background. The story and the poem are an organic whole; without one, the other would be ineffective and empty.

Modern psychology goes on and on about the dreadful consequences of emotional suppression and repression. There are many times in our lives when we knowingly suppress many of our emotions; however, more often than not, we unconsciously suppress many of our feelings. Repressed emotions accumulate a tremendous amount of dynamic

---

[11] *Life is a series of experiences of joy and sorrow gathered during all waking moments. The expression, Life after Life, therefore, imply one experience after another experience lived during waking moments.*

[12] *Samsara refers to the cycle of birth, death, and rebirth, figuratively speaking, to which life in the material world is bound. It refers to cyclic states of awareness or consciousness i.e., Waking, Dreaming, and Deep Sleeping. Becoming consciously aware is called 'Birth' and dissolution of awareness (Deep Sleep) is called 'Death.' In between states, when you are neither sleep nor fully awake, such a dull state of awareness is called 'Dream.' Rising back to conscious awareness from deep sleep is called 'Re-birth.*

energy, which must find a way to express itself. Unless these energies are properly guided, they would boomerang back to destroy the very individual. Though there is no direct explanation for Arjuna's emotional repression, a careful reader of the story can easily conclude that the great hero, on the battlefield, succumbed to his repressed conditions and behaved as a victim of perfect mental disorder.

The causes of his emotional repressions are not difficult to find. A great hero, certain of his own strength, was destined to live among his Machiavellian cousins' unjust tyranny. At the same time, the great warrior and archer could not give vent to his nature because of the righteous policy of 'peace at all costs' of his eldest brother, Yudhishtra. These repressed emotions found a healthy field for expression in the severe tapasya which he performed during his life in exile in the jungle.

During the last years of their lives incognito, the Pandava family had to serve as menials in the palace of the Raja of Virata. The carping injustice and the cruel indignities of the situation caused, no doubt, a lot of repression in Arjuna's mind. But even these found a healthy outlet in the battle he had to fight against Duryodhana's forces, who had come to challenge the Virata-might.

When the Pandavas finally arrived in their native kingdom after a long and arduous journey, their tyrant cousin refused them not only their right to half of the territory, but also all terms of peace making.

Dhritarashtra, the shrewd, blind father of the Kauravas, most likely understood Arjuna's psychological state. Hence on the day previous to the war, he sent Sanjaya, his emissary, to Arjuna with a secret message. This message, full of mischievous import, sowed the seeds of dangerous ideas in the mind of Arjuna, directing his repressed energies into wrong channels, so that he became a hapless neurotic in the face of the great challenge. We shall read in the first chapter of Gita the very same argument and ideas repeated faithfully by Arjuna from the message he had received the previous day from his uncle.

On the fateful day when both the armies were getting into formation, Arjuna asks his charioteer, Lord Krishna, to drive the chariot to a point between the two forces, so that he may review the enemy lines. Larger in number, better equipped, more liberal in supplies and commanded by well-known personalities, the Kaurava formation, expanding itself like an 'eagle,' stood poised to swoop down upon the smaller army of the Pandavas. This was a sight that tested the Pandava hero's mental fortitude. Under the influence of the stimuli, his 'Objective-Mind' could not elicit any response from its 'Subjective-Mind,' because the disintegration of these two aspects was complete due to the intervening layers of his egocentric assumptions and desire-driven anxieties. The dynamic forces released in his mind due to the repression were not properly channelised, but were misdirected by the suggestions of Dhritarashtra's words, and therefore, the greatest hero of the times, Arjuna, suddenly became a despondent, bewildered, and a neurotic patient.

The 'Krishna-treatment' of this patient of psychological derangement was certainly a specific cure, inasmuch as, in the last chapter of Gita, we definitely hear Arjuna declaring that all his 'delusions have ended.' The rest of the story of how, having come into his own, he became a rejuvenated warrior of tremendous strength and valor, is quite well-known to all students of this great classic.

To a varying degree, every modern man is a victim of this 'Arjuna Disease' and the 'Krishna-cure' being specific, is available to all of us at all times in the philosophy of Gita.

Krishna indicates the two main lines of treatment in the second chapter, which is almost a summary of the entire Gita. One is a 'Treatment of Idealism' wherein Arjuna is directed to a greater Reality than his mind, ego, and intellect and thereby the divorce between the 'Subjective' and the 'Objective' aspects of his mind eliminated to some extent. In the second half of the same chapter, we shall read and come to understand how selfish activity will purge the existing Vasanas in the individual. Arjuna being a

Kshatriya, his mind was coloured by the impression of Rajasic activities (guna), and so he needed a battlefield to exhaust those impressions.

Thus, we find Krishna repeatedly goading his friend with the words, "Get up and fight." This does not necessarily imply that the Gita is a ruling-class propaganda text. It is a call to each one of us to get up and fight the battle of our own life, accordingly to our own Vasanas (Swadharma), so that we may exhaust them and thus gain inner purity.

The Psychological Theory

If the spiritual or religious literature is not very convincing for you, let us consider a modern psychological model, which provides a similar structure of the cause-and-effect relationship between our beliefs, thoughts, and behaviors. It is called Cognitive Behaviour Therapy (CBT Model).

Cognitive Behaviour Therapy (CBT) is a time-sensitive, structured, present-oriented psychotherapy that has been scientifically tested and found to be effective in more than 2,000 studies for the treatment of many different emotional problems and conditions. When used correctly, CBT can help individuals improve their lives and stay better.

CBT is based on the theory that the way individuals perceive a situation is more closely connected to their reaction than the situation itself. People's perceptions are often distorted and unhelpful, especially when they are perturbed. CBT helps people **identify** their distorted and dysfunctional thoughts (referred to as Tendencies in Vedantic Theory) causing distress and **evaluate** how realistic such thoughts are. Then they learn to change their cognitive distortions. When they think more logically and rationally, they feel better. The emphasis is also consistently on solving emotional problems and initiating lasting behavioral changes.

The cognitive model describes how people's thoughts and perceptions affect their feelings and behaviors. The cognitive model is at the core of Cognitive Behaviour Therapy, and it plays a critical role in helping therapists conceptualize and treat their clients' difficulties. However, it is worth noticing that in a CBT therapeutic process, the client approaches a therapist to seek help with a specific problem and the therapist helps them to resolve it.

CBT aims at identifying the dysfunctional thoughts, helping the client in identifying the cause of the dysfunction embedded in their early life experiences, that is, the distortion in their perception and helps them to discriminate between the distortion and the reality. Having realized the distortion, the client is, thereby, assisted in replacing their dysfunctional (negative) thoughts with functional (positive) thoughts. The client, who systematically follows the instructions of the therapist, stops experiencing the problem and consequently feels good and begins to enjoy his life again.

Having known a little bit about the CBT model and how our cognitive structure works, we can now say that distorted perception of reality is the fundamental cause of the most emotional problems faced and/or experienced by individuals in our society today. What are our modern-day problems facing our population, particularly, the young ones? These are stress, anxiety, depression, anger, jealousy, lust, temptations to be rich quicker, and the list continues. While they are trying to negotiate their life and trying to reach the desired materialistic goals, their abilities, their efforts, and their mental strength are all seriously hampered by the weakened psychological and emotional edifice causing the manifestation of these problems in the individual.

Both Psychological and the Vedantic theory are known to be effective treatments for the problems caused by illogical and irrational perceptions leading to dysfunctional thinking patterns. While the CBT offers an effective symptomatic treatment for the emotional problems, felt, experienced, and reported by the individual at a given time, it still remains limited in its scope. Having dealt with one problem at a point in time in life, there is no guarantee, however, that the individual will not face the same or similar problems in life again. The Vedantic treatment, on the other hand, not only helps the individual to remove the fundamental cause of the problems faced but offers a permanent solution by making systematic shifts in the cognitive arrangement by bringing the 'Subjective' and the 'Objective' aspects of the mind to work in unison.

CBT Model of Dysfunctional Thoughts

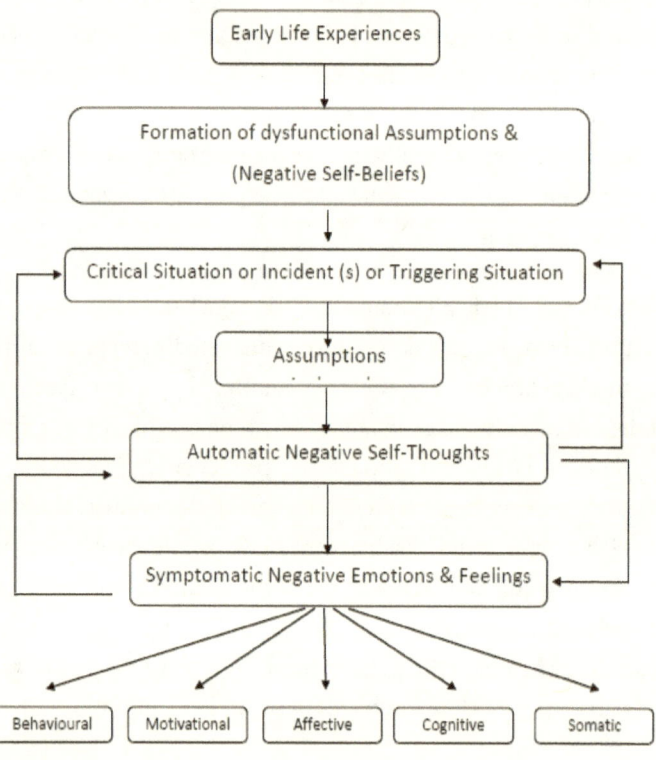

Figure: CBT Model demonstrating cause and effect relationship between Self-beliefs, Automatic Thoughts, Emotions and Feelings and resulting in dysfunctional thoughts, behaviors, and actions.

7

Signs Of A Spiritually Mature Person

A Spiritually Mature person is one whose personality has been imbedded and textured with the certain mental qualities, which allow him to remain calm, without getting excited in pleasure and agitated in sorrow. They courageously face all life situations without fear and positively respond to varied situations and transactions in life with confidence.

A Spiritually mature person is someone who has recognised and realized their real personality. They have gained equanimity in their perspective, and they view the world and the life situation from this vision. They have no confusion in their minds about 'the Good' and 'the Bad' of life. They are scientifically convinced that duality of experiences does not exist in reality, except in the minds, hence they do not waste their mental energy in getting excited in pleasures of the good and agitated in sorrows of the bad. They rather conserve and retain mental energy for the tasks in hand.

How would you recognise a spiritually mature person? What are the signs and symptoms of a spiritually mature person? How does he behave in the real world? Only way we can recognise a spiritually mature person, is by observing their behavior and conduct in day-to-day transactions within a family, out on the street, within an organization, and in the society at large.

1. They have a cognitive clarity, and they have sincerely taken a positive life position that "I am OK, so are you," instead of a common and widely held negative position, "I am OK, you are not OK." They don't have the compulsive urge of changing others around them. Rather, they keep their focus on changing themselves.

2. For this reason, they accept others as they are. They are comfortable with and remain unmoved in dealing with people who are different, have different values and personality traits.

3. They seldom experience conflict or stress since they believe that everyone is right in their own perspective.

4. They have learnt the art of "letting go." They do not hang on to or dwell on negative thoughts or experiences. They are not possessive of people, things, thoughts, or places.

5. They have become skilled in not hanging on to the past memories and worrying about the future. They have gained an intellectual clarity that **'the Past'** is a dead time and burial ground of memories, and they have no control, whatsoever, over it, at the same time, they also know that **'the Future'** is an unborn time. Rather than wasting their mental energy on the Past and the Future, they have learnt the art of staying in and enjoying the Present (the Life).

6. They do not have expectations from relationships. Relationships are not a business transaction for them. They give their best in relationships for the sake of giving. 'No Desire, No Disappointment,' is the thumb rule in their lives.

7. They have a very good clarity and understanding that whatever they do, they do it for their own sake. They are not deluded with the 'Atlas Syndrome.'

8. They take full ownership and responsibility for their words, actions, and thoughts (वक्तव्य, व्यवहार और विचार). Therefore, they do not blame other people, things, or situations, when things go wrong.

9. They have learnt to surrender all to the will of God and accept all as a Gift (Prasaad- प्रसाद) from God. This is a sign of their cognitive and intellectual clarity on their relationship with God.

10. There is no urge or a compulsive desire in them, whatsoever, to prove themselves or their intelligence to the world. They know they are. Therefore, they do neither get excited about their achievements nor do they get disappointed on failures, no matter how big or small these might be.

11. They do their best at all times without expecting any praise, reward, award, or accolade. They neither get dejected by nor do they ignore criticisms at the same time. They view all criticisms as valuable feedback and use it for their personal growth. They have a sense of gratitude for those who criticize them. They have learnt the art of building their house with the bricks people throw at them.

12. They are, reasonably and confidently, Self-aware; therefore, they seldom seek approval from others, nor do they feel the need to compare themselves with others. They know they are differently unique, so are others.

13. They are intelligent enough to differentiate and discriminate between their 'Needs' and 'Wants' and are courageous enough to let go of their wants.

14. They are reasonably at peace with themselves. They are seldom dissatisfied with or are in conflict with whatever they are, whatever they do, or whatever they have. They have acquired a unique sense of contentment with whatever comes their way and accept it as a Gift (Prasaad- प्रसाद) of God.

15. They have learned to be happy unconditionally. They do not seek happiness from material acquisition, preservation, and/or promotion. Nor do they have "only...if I have/be/do..." conditions to be happy.

A person who performs in the aforementioned ways effortlessly and naturally seems to have reached spiritual maturity. They have attained spiritual maturity simply by shifting their focus away from the 'Objective' dimension of life and focusing on the 'Subjective' dimension of life, away from the external sensory world of temptations and towards the inner world of contemplation on the Self.

The above behavioral portrayal of a spiritually mature person reads like a picture of an almost perfect person. Yes, indeed it is a glimpse of a near perfect person. While you read the above description, multiple questions must have sprung in your mind. Can someone have all these qualities? Is it for real? Is it possible for a normal everyday person to be like this in real life? It might seem like a 'Pie in the Sky,' so on and so forth. There must be a hundred such doubtful questions gurgling up in your mind.

There are millions of people, who have walked this earth and millions more are walking the earth right now, who have realized the supreme state of spiritual maturity. There is no doubt that millions more will walk this earth who will realize spiritual maturity in this lifetime, and you and I too could be one of these millions.

Bhagavan Sri Ram wasn't born as Lord Ram, but a son of Dashratha and Kausalya, Siddharth wasn't born as Gautam Buddha, but a son of Suddhodana of Kapilvastu, Jesus wasn't born as Jesus Christ or a Messiah but a son of Joseph from Nazareth, Mohammad Sahib wasn't born as a Prophet but in a poor but respectable family of the Quraysh tribe, Sankara wasn't born as Adi Shankaracharya but was born to Nambudiri Brahmin parents Shivguru and Aryamba in a village named Kaladi, Kerala, Guru Nanak was born at Rai Bhai Ki Talwandi (present day Nankana Sahib, Punjab, Pakistan) near Lahore to Kalyan Chand Das

Bedi, popularly shortened to Mehta Kalu and Mata Tripta. These are very well-known personalities that we know of. There are countless such personalities that we do not know about. There is an army of countless Self-realized or spiritually mature persons, in all sects, known as saints and sages. We know them as great people. All these great people were born as ordinary individuals as you and me. However, they evolved themselves to the greater heights of Self-realized and enlightened beings. All these people were born ordinary but through a process of Self-realization reached greater heights by their extraordinary zeal and efforts i.e., decision and resolve, commitment, and dedication and with single-point devotion. So can you and I!

Having removed significant dysfunctional assumptions or miscomprehension about oneself, they have a much calmer mind. Consequently, they conserve a lot of mental energy and put it to good use. With a tranquil mind, they are more likely to be successful in whatever they do, and they achieve more, without necessarily getting bogged down with the cataclysm of life. They are the most effective and efficient individuals, who live their lives artfully and with dexterity.

Such a person is described as spiritually mature person, the Bhagavad Gita calls him **Sthit Pragya (स्थितप्रज्ञ)**, a man of perfection, the Self-realized one, the one who has firmly established in the knowledge of the Self (the subject of all experiences). A Self-realized person is a dynamic, pulsating individual whose every moment of existence is dedicated to the service of humankind. He need not be retired from the community. We can view him right in the marketplace–downtown, in the midst of the calamitous, competitive world of temptations. Such a person, who keeps his composure and remains ever rooted in pure consciousness in the midst of turbulence of life, is called the One of steady wisdom (Sthit Pragya-स्थितप्रज्ञ). Such a spiritually mature hero is the subject matter and the protagonist of this book.

There are various tools, techniques, and processes available for the seeker of spirituality. A number of these tools and techniques are hinted at in this section. The next section of this book is going to expand on and decode the logical and scientific explanation of these various tools and techniques, which are available to us but within the garb of religious terminology. Almost all of which have now seemingly lost their real significance, philosophical import, and scientific suggestiveness due to our mechanical and mindless observance, called ritualism, in our day to life.

The following sections of the book are dedicated to presenting these tools and techniques with their significance and the real intent with which these were prescribed by our Subjective Scientists, for the very purpose of Self-realization.

8

The Science Of Spirituality, Religion And Rituals

Are spirituality, religion, and rituals exclusive or inclusive? Are these separate entities or intertwined?

After completing a certain degree of educational process through kindergarten onwards to primary and secondary school systems, a student gains the knowledge and begins to appreciate various subjects that he has been taught during the course of several years of systematic and ritualistic practice of going to schools. By the end of schooling, their intellect and mental temperament has developed enough to have an interest in and are reasonably clear in their mind as to what line of profession or career they would like to pursue in future.

They begin their personal investigation quietly and raise their awareness about various choices of career paths available to them to suit their temperament. They seek help, guidance, and support in deciding their future. They gather as much information to appreciate the glories and rewards available to them in various professional choices. The idea of their future profession or the career path begins to consolidate in their mind. Accordingly, they make a choice between arts, commerce, technology, and science etc., streams, based on their bent of mind and interest, to study various subjects specific to their chosen stream in greater detail at the graduate level. If their academic appetite is not yet satisfied and they wish to study further, they narrow down the focus of their study to a specific subject at the master's degree level. Having gained mastery over the subject, their intellect, supposedly, becomes refined and sharper in that particular subject.

When they go out in the competitive world outside to practice, they initially struggle to transfer their theoretical knowledge into practice. They struggle to transit away from the idealistic and academic environment of the university's classrooms into the pragmatic reality of the competitive world. They work under supervision and guidance of an experienced practitioner. During this phase, they need extra support and training to understand their job description better, they toil to become efficient and effective in their practice. Eventually, one day they find themselves to be significantly competent and independent as a practitioner over a period of time. Thereafter, they reach the glorious heights of professional achievements in their chosen careers.

A few, whose academic appetite still remains unquenched and generally are of investigative and inquisitive mind, enter into research and investigation and spend a few more years to become the doctor and the philosopher on the subject. They want to investigate the cause-and-effect relationship of a particular phenomenal observation that caught their attention during their higher studies or practice years.

This is a generic trajectory of academic progress an ignorant and illiterate child, who is totally unaware of numbers, alphabet, color, shapes, and sizes, takes through to becoming a competent professional. This journey takes him on an average 20-25 years of his youth and prime age, during this period he completely surrenders himself with absolute dedication and commitment in order to reach to a level of competence to earn money, often in abundance. With this monetary wealth, he is now capable of acquiring as many material possessions to live comfortably for the rest of their life. Securing a safe and comfortable future in abundance is one of the ultimate goals of the education system throughout the world.

Most of us spend almost quarter of our lives in worshiping 'the Dollars God' with a single pointedness, devotion, and complete surrender. Eventually, the money begins to manifest and keeps flowing through. The money helps us to raise the standards of our living, most certainly, however, it erodes the standard of our life. Despite enormous material wealth and all the comforts of life, we are not really happy. Are we?

You must be wondering why I have wasted so many words and space in describing the system of education in the world. Since most of us are very well acquainted with and have personal experience of the education system, it would be easier for us to comprehend the realm of spirituality, religion, and rituals, if I could draw a parallel here. It will also help us to understand whether spirituality, religion, and rituals are mutually exclusive or inclusive. Are these distinctly separate entities or if there is a degree of connectivity or relationship between these three?

We all, be it a parent, the society, or the government, firmly believe that education is a fundamental right and requirement for every child and have no difficulty in understanding that every child must go to nursery school as soon as they are eligible to do so and commence the journey of their educational development. This conviction is based on the established knowledge and the fact that the child's prospect and chances of material achievements, economic prosperity, and the quotient of happiness in life will be proportionately higher to the level of their academic achievements. This is the theory, the knowledge, and the belief, widely accepted in most societies in the world.

To ensure that every child in the world has the ability to acquire educational achievement, we have well established education systems and institutions in place in every nook and corner of every village, town, and cities in all countries of the world.

Every child who wishes to improve his or her chances and prospect of material achievements, economic prosperity, and the quotient of happiness in life, must sincerely go through the established system of education to gain the desired level of education to guarantee them corresponding level of material prosperity.

Material prosperity and the possible happiness in life is the promised land or the ultimate destination of the education system. The education system and institutions are the means to reach to the destination and the act of following the prescribed systems and the procedures to acquire the desired level of education and the qualification, as discussed above, is the process recommended to reach the promised land.

Just having the knowledge that education and professional qualification increases the chances of material achievements, economic prosperity, and the quotient of happiness in life, has no power, by itself, to take you to the promised land. Being aware of the education systems and institutions in place doesn't take one to the promised land either, or just doing your own things in the name of education, doesn't bring a qualification to you. All three in a synchronized fashion must be used i.e. (1) one must be convinced with the Knowledge as to why one must take up education, the enormous benefits will he accrue, (2) choosing the right and appropriate educational institution (the means) corresponding to the desired qualification, and (3) once the mind is convinced with the knowledge and the means, the required commitment to follow the recommended systems and procedures is an automatic result. This commitment in the heart of the student allows him to remain dedicated, diligent, sincere, and steadfast on the path to the desired destination or the promised land.

Educational arrangements are put in place in the world to give us knowledge of the material dimension of life and bring about materialistic prosperity and possible happiness. In the same way, the Spiritual arrangements are put in place by our Subjective Scientists to give us the knowledge of our inner world and the spiritual dimension of life and help us to gain spiritual prosperity to guarantee us a permanent happiness and liberation from all our miseries.

In parallel to the education system, Spirituality is the knowledge of the Self, our spiritual dimension, and the theory of the Spirit, and the science of the conscious principle. The Self Realization through spiritual maturity, that guarantees permanent happiness and liberation from all miseries, is the promised land or the destination of Spiritual Science. The Religions, the religious systems and institutions are the means to Self-realization through spiritual maturity and the prescribed ritualistic performances. The ritualistic performances e.g., Puja, Sadhanas, Paath, Abstinences of various description, Havan, Yagnas, and pilgrimages are prescribed rituals to acquire the desired level of spiritual acumen, the mental competences, skills, and abilities are the processes recommended to reach the promised land of Self-awareness and liberation from the miseries of life.

You must have often heard people claiming that they are not religious but spiritual. Some others would say that they are neither spiritual nor religious. While there are others who claim that they are atheist and don't believe in God. While I remain democratic in my attitude and have firm faith in people's entitlement of making individual choices in life, I am, however, of the view that to believe or not to believe in something, to like or dislike something, be aversive or possessive of something, the essential and the intelligent criterion has to be that one should have, at least, some degree of knowledge with authority on the subject in question. However, there seems confusion, lack of clarity and/ or understanding when it comes to the spiritual or religious dimension of life. Each person has their own arguments and justifications for their mindless pursuance or rejection of the religious practices.

The growing level of aversion to anything spiritual, religious, and ritualistic that people, particularly young people, display is concerning. It's not concerning just because I think or believe that people should be spiritual, religious, or ritualistic. None whatsoever. But merely for the reason that **'Spirituality, Religion and Rituals are scientific in nature and logically designed to improve the quality of our lives.'**

It is for this reason, I find it rather ironic that the modern secular societies in the world are structured heavily to pursue material growth and development, while the spiritual growth and development is left to chance. Towards the end of material development and growth, when we have managed to secure plentiful materialistic possessions, we are hardly satisfied with what we have acquired, let alone being in a position to enjoy our life. More worldly possessions we gather, the more we are blessed with stress, depression, anxieties, pains, fears, anger, and diseases. While we have devoted and dedicated all our lives in improving the quality of living, unfortunately, we have lost out on the quality of our lives.

Honestly speaking, I empathize with young people and do fully understand their aversion to religion or anything religious. The manner and the format in which the religion is presented to them, is so very difficult for their logical, rational mind and their scientific temperament to comprehend it, let alone accept it. Irrespective of the religious persuasion, if asked to explain, only a very few would be able to provide a decent and digestible, let alone logical and/or scientific, explanation to their religious practices and rituals, yet only a few would help them understand its relevance in their day-to-day life.

Can religion help them to study better? Can it help them to perform better in their examination? Can it help them to secure better life chances and better earning opportunities in life? Can it help them to be resilient to cope better with life's trials and tribulation? Can they make, maintain, and enjoy healthy and respectful relationships in life? Can they protect and insulate themselves from stress, anxiety, depression, fears and anger in their day-to-day life? Can they be wealthy, both materially and spiritually at the same time?

Fortunately, the unequivocal and a resounding answer is a **YES**.

For this, one must bring oneself to explore its real significance, understand its scientific, logical and suggestiveness, and dedicate oneself to seek clarity on the fundamental concepts; and with single pointedness and devotion. If one commits to grow and develop spiritually, then the above promises are a reality, otherwise God has always been gracious anyway. He blesses all and continues to do so irrespective of whether you believe in Him or not; or believe in yourself or not.

One of the common arguments presented by some is why should they believe in an entity called God which they can't even comprehend with their eyes. Seems like a reasonable argument. But my counter-argument, however, is that there are other such things that we can't see with our eyes, but we still believe in their existence. For example, our eyes are not capable of seeing the air or the gravitational force. Whether you believe in the existence of the gravitation or not, it doesn't really matter to the very nature of the gravitational force, it will bless the non-believer equally as it does to a believer, if he jumps from the 5th floor window. His body will hit the ground every time.

The sun blesses all with its light and warmth, irrespective of who you are. Be it a stone, plant, insect, animal, or a human, all are equally blessed by the warmth and the light of the sun. If you, however, lock yourself in a room with doors and windows shut and complain that you are not getting the warmth and the light, you can't really blame the sun, can you? Your experience in such a scenario will be absolutely correct if you believe that the sun is discriminating against you. However, if you are sincere in your wish to be blessed by the sun, all you have to do is to open the windows and the doors of the room or simply walk out in the open, and you will be instantly blessed by the heat and the warmth of the sun. All-natural phenomena work in this way. They make their resources available to all without favor or discrimination, without any expectation in return. In the same way whether we believe in God or not, it continues to bless us all. God's blessings can be multiplied many folds only if one is willing to make the right efforts in the right direction.

I don't think it is about whether I believe in God or not. I don't know how many can confidently claim that they know or understand God, let alone believing or disbelieving in His Existence. I think it's rather about making a simple and clear choice, whether you want to be in control of your life experiences, or you are happy that your life is being controlled by the hit-and-miss experiences. Whether the joys and sorrows of life are in your control, or you think and believe that you have no control whatsoever. It's rather about knowing how much control you can have in maximizing your joys and minimizing your sorrows.

The wise people from all denominations, through various spiritual scriptures, in no uncertain terms, have declared that **'Life is an accumulative experience of joys and sorrows.'** If the balance sheet of life has more joys and only far and few sorrows in between at a point in time in your life, one has heavenly experience and if the balance sheet shows an adverse account of more sorrows and less of joys, then one defines their experience of life as hell.

Our Spiritual Masters, the Subjective Scientists of the old, were very compassionate people, it seems, who out of their benevolence and kindness, dedicated all their efforts and energies in contemplation to investigate and understand the maze of our inner world over thousands of years. It must have been, I suppose, a very similar zeal with which our modern scientists pour their lives into investigating various worldly phenomena of the outer world, with an overall objective of making our lives comfortable and joyful. Our Subjective Scientists, in the same way, have not only gained an in-depth and comprehensive understanding of the inner world of subtleties but also evolved the science of life.

Therefore, whatever I do or don't do in the name of spiritual, religious, and/or rituals, it must be done with a very selfish desire to ensure that my life becomes enriched with joyful experiences and pleasures. Most people, particularly young people, who are critical and have aversion to spirituality, religion, or ritualism, generally give up all hopes in this aspect of life, because they never seem to arrive at or have known anyone who might have arrived at the promised land in their experience.

Consequently, they get disillusioned and disappointed with the prospects of any hope or help from spirituality, religion, or ritualism.

Most logical and rational people, who still have some faith left in them for whatever reasons, seemingly behave so very illogically and irrationally when it comes to their expectations and hopes from religious practices. They think, anticipate, and hope that just by reading a book, attending a discourse, performing certain rituals every now and then, pilgrimage to places of religious importance, chanting and reciting verses from the holy books will take them to the promised land. While the same people have spent 20-25 years systematically pursuing educational programmes to gain skills, abilities, and capacity to earn money and to acquire materialistic comforts. So, what makes them think that the spiritual growth and development journey should be any different?

Let us now revisit the similar description of the education system to hone into the relationship between Spirituality, Religion, and the Rituals. There is a well-established belief-system that money ensures a comfortable life. The chances of earning money are enhanced if one gains a qualification. Academic institutions are established to provide such qualifications. Those who wish to acquire capacity to earn money and aspire to put themselves in the position of comforts, will make all possible efforts to gain a place in these institutions and do all it takes to complete the educational programmes. Thereafter, the students conform to all established rituals in addition to attending academic institutions over a long period of time in order to gain the knowledge and the qualification, which they have come to believe will eventually improve their standard of living. They spend a good part of their life becoming competent to earn enough to have a comfortable life. Large percentage of those, who diligently follow the prescribed ritualistic practices of the Religion of Education, end up being blessed by 'the Dollar God.'

In the same way, Spirituality is the science and contains the theory of Life, which explains what life is and why and how one can live it intelligently and with dexterity, and live a misery-free life. Religions are the systems and the institutions of various tools and technologies, the methodology or the processes to learn the skills, abilities, and competences to live intelligently and work with dexterity, and how to make life a most enjoyable experience. The rituals are the prescriptions of various practices and the micro-systems to be followed diligently and must be systematically performed daily, consistently and over a period of time for acquiring the necessary skills to achieve the necessary mental conditions to enjoy the quality of Life.

Therefore, the question for us all to contemplate over is, can we be just either spiritual, religious, or ritualistic? In my personal opinion and experience, it can never be a matter of choice. All three must be seen, understood, and practiced as a synchronized whole. Let's consider an analogy of a journey and check it out for yourself whether you can reach your desired destination by undertaking just one aspect of it. To undertake a journey, one must have (1) a convincing and compelling reason to take the journey, the benefits of the journey, the knowledge of the destination, the route to take, mode of transport, knowledge of the traffic rules, being a safe and competent driver, gaining a driver's license etc.; (2) Having had the necessary the knowledge of the destination, acquiring a driver's license, finding out the safe and the quickest route to the destination and thereafter, choosing the means and the vehicle by which to travel, GPS navigation system or the Maps etc., to assist you during the journey and finally (3) one must perform the act of traveling.

Now you decide for yourself, which one of the three components alone is capable of taking you, comfortably in the shortest possible time, to the destination.

Spirituality is the science of the spirit within each one of us. The religions of the world refer to this spirit by various names e.g., the Soul, the Supreme Self, and the Life Principle etc. It is known as the Holy Spirit in Christianity, Allah in Islam, Aum and Brahma in Hinduism, Jinas in Jainism, Rab in Sikhism, Elohim in Judaism, Kami in Shintoism etc.

Life has two dimensions, that is, the material or comprehensible and the Spiritual or the incomprehensible. The material dimension includes our **body, mind, and the intellect (BMI)**. These are gross in nature and are comprehensible through our sense organs. The spiritual dimension includes our Soul, the Supreme Self, which is subtle in nature and cannot be comprehended through our sense organs.

However, there is interdependency between the two. The one cannot function without the presence of the other. The body, mind and the intellect are the instruments through which we contact and experience the world outside. Here by body, I mean all sense organs. The body is my physical identity, which helps me to gather sight, sound, smell, taste, and the touch. The mind is my emotional identity and doubting faculty, which deals with the stimuli captured by the body through the sense organs to determine whether it is good or bad, joyful or painful, and produces corresponding feelings and emotions in me accordingly. The intellect is the decisive faculty, which is a storehouse of all my past experiences and by using this data of the memories, it helps me to decide and reach a conclusion. Collectively, the body, mind, and the intellect, is my physical identity as a person and I refer to it as **'Myself.'**

At the same time, these instruments will be rendered ineffective if these are not enlivened by the Life Principle. Let us understand this relationship through an example of an electric equipment, let's say an electric bulb and electricity. The bulb is designed to produce light when the electricity passes through it, but it cannot produce light on its own. It must be connected to a source of electricity to manifest its potential. Though the power of electricity is totally responsible for the bulb to produce light, but without the bulb, the electricity has no capacity to manifest its power.

Same is the relationship between the material and the spirit. Our body (senses) perceives the sense objects, our mind feels the emotions and our intellect thinks the thoughts. The potency to the functions of the BMI is provided by the Spirit, the Soul, the Consciousness, the Supreme

Self, or the Supreme Reality, what we know as, the GOD. Our BMI is functional and enlivened by the presence of the Supreme Self. When the Supreme Self ceases to function within the BMI, we are wiped out from the face of this earth. We are dead!

Spirituality is the science of the spirit, the soul, the Supreme Self, and the Supreme Reality. Spirituality is the discipline to understand the nature of the Supreme Reality; its relationship with the BMI and how one can comprehend, know, and realize this incomprehensible subtle entity called the Supreme Reality-**the Self**.

You must have noticed in seminars, training, conferences, Self-help discourse, personality development and motivational speeches and such other places, a question is often asked, do you know **"Who are you?"** or you are asked to think and contemplate over, **"Who am I?"**

When you use the terms like 'I,' 'My,' and 'Myself,' have you ever stopped and thought about who and what are you talking about? Who are you referring to? You can try to answer this question now, before you proceed further in this book.

At your very best, after hours of contemplation, when you categorize all your answers to this question, you will find these answers fall in three categories, your physical, mental, or intellectual identities. You are either describing your body, its nature and qualities, or its relationship with other people in your life. For example, male or female, son of, daughter of, young and old, short or tall, fair or dark, student, employee, businessman, doctor, engineer, or a scientist etc.; or you may be describing your emotional state of being, for example, I am a happy person, I am content or satisfied, I am confident and energetic, I am depressed or elated or your likes and dislikes etc., or you might think about the ideas that you have about yourself, for example, I am a good person, I am a generous person, everybody loves me, or everybody hates me etc.

In a nutshell, you are describing your body, your mind, and/or your intellect. However, the question remains unanswered. When you say it is my body, my emotion, or my idea of myself, it must be obvious that you are someone other than your body, your emotions, and your idea of yourself. For example, when you own an object, let's say, a laptop. So, you will say that this is my laptop. This laptop belongs to me. You neither mean nor even vaguely imply that you are the laptop, do you? That means that you and the laptop are two separate entities.

In the same way, when you say that this is my body, my mind, or my intellect, you must be separate from these three. I must be something or someone other than my body, mind, and intellect. Who is this 'I' in me? Discovering that 'YOU' in you, finding the 'SELF' in yourself is the very objective and the purpose of the Subjective Science of Spirituality. The Science that helps to know, understand and realize '**Me**' in myself is called Spirituality.

9

The Nature Of The Self

The Self and the Supreme Self, being the subtle entity, is beyond the grasp of our sense organs. It can neither be seen by the eyes; can't be heard by the ears; nose can't smell it; tongue can't taste it, nor can it be touched. I cannot experience this 'Self' through my senses as I do experience other sense objects. Hence, its tangible qualities or nature cannot be defined or described but at best it can be indicated at. For this very reason, our Subjective Scientists have developed skills, techniques, and technologies, which are discussed and elaborated in our scriptures.

One of the main dangers, that one generally encounters, is that we try to understand this Subjective Science, if at all, and its subtle concepts in the backdrop of our conventional, almost negligible, knowledge and understanding of our religious and ritualistic ideas, that too, from its mythical and mystical version. Our limited and vague understanding of spirituality, for a good majority of us, comes from what has been handed down from one generation to the other, totally devoid of any logical, rational and/or scientific explanation to it. No one can dare ask a question, let alone challenge it.

If you wish, you can test it out. Ask a question to anyone, be it a grown-up, or a young person, **"What is the significance of Diwali and why do Hindus celebrate it?"** You will get two answers only to this question: (1) Bhagwan Ram came back to Ayodhya with Sita and Lakshman after killing Ravana, and (2) It signifies victory of Good over evil. This is where the answer will stop. Who wrote the story? Why did he write the story?

Is it really a story or a narration of history? What is the message the author is trying to convey through the narration? What is so significant that Hindus still celebrate the festival of Diwali for thousands of years? What is the use and relevance of this story in my Life?

This is really unfortunate that we have completely lost a rich tradition of education which was largely based on a Guru-Shishya Parampara. The teacher was a person, who has not only gained the knowledge from his Guru but has internalized that knowledge through direct and personal experience. Students' mental capacities were systematically developed to ensure that they had the ability to discriminate (Vivek-विवेक बुद्धि) between what was real, imperishable, and eternal, and what was not; ability to be dispassionate and give up on what was not real (वैराग्य); assisted them to develop mental qualities (Shath-Sampati- षट्सम्पति[13]) which would lead them to have a burning desire to know and liberate them from all miseries of life (मुमुक्षुत्व). Such students were considered worthy of knowledge of the Self. Such was the system of education where knowledge evolved through discussions, debates, questioning and answering and passed down the generations over centuries. The students were given authority not to settle for any answer to their enquiry unless they were fully satisfied and convinced with the answers from the Guru. They were also instructed not to accept answers unless these have passed the test of their direct and personal experience. Listen, reflect and practice (श्रवण, मनन, निदिध्यास) was the model of learning.

Asking questions and diving deep down to investigate the real imports of words and concepts doesn't seem to be our style of education and learning today. The best and most competent student is considered he who is an expert in memorizing information and offloading it on the examination paper and securing highest possible grades. Since India

---

[13] *Sam, Dam, Uparati, Titiksha, Kshama and Samadhan (सम, दम, उपरति, तितिक्षा, क्षमा, एवं समाधान) are the six mental properties students were required to gain through daily, constant, and forever practice, before they were considered worthy and capable (अधिकारी) of receiving the knowledge of the Self.*

became an independent country, for whatever wisdom prevailed at the time, we chose to prioritize and promote western system of education. Unfortunately, we chose what glittered like a gem over the real diamond. Consequently, we saw a major fall from the highest level of education down to mindlessness and fanaticism. We have divorced ourselves from philosophy of life and Spirituality since then. All we are getting out of it is a blind-faith and psychological dependence on an external supernatural entity called the God. We consider and believe God to be someone other than ourselves, sitting somewhere in the clouds, who will answer all our prayers and fulfill all our desires of life for joys and pleasures, someday, if he is so pleased.

Supreme Self (परमात्मा) and the Self (आत्मा) needs to be understood in its real context as these are discussed and detailed within various spiritual textbooks such as Vivekachudamani, Brahma Sutra, Upanishads, Bhagavad Gita and the likes. The **Supreme Self** is a name given to an entity we call God, and **the Self** is a noun used for referring to the mortal man, like you and me.

First and the foremost, the relationship between the two must be clarified whether these are two separate entities or these are the same thing but known by two different nouns. We will try to understand these with the help of a few examples. **The Supreme Self** is declared to be nothing but the purest form of the Self (you and Me) in almost all spiritual texts of Advaita philosophy. It is the form which will be a resultant when you and I have removed all physical, mental, and intellectual impurities from within our little Self. What does it mean? Consider **Supreme Self** to be a pure white, spotless, and clean piece of linen, for example. When the same pure white, spotless, and clean piece of linen is infested with impurities, dirt, and other foreign materials, it becomes dirty. Consider this dirty linen to be **the Self** (you and Me). With Self-effort, when the dirty piece of linen is washed, cleansed, and all impurities are removed, the dirty piece of linen regains its pristine glorious state of being i.e., pure, white, and clean again. This process of cleansing through **Self-effort** is called **Spiritual Practice (Sadhana-साधना)**. Through the Spiritual Sadhana, all that the little Self (you and Me) is trying to do is to regain our original state of being, as it was i.e., our pure, perfect and complete sense of Self (**Supreme Self**). This achievement of regaining one's own original pristine glory of the purest form is referred to as **Self-realization**. Now whether it was pure or dirty, in both states of its being, what remains common at all times, is the piece of linen. In the same way, the Self in its purest form is called **the Supreme Self** and the Supreme Self in its impure form is called **the Self**, that is you and me. Nonetheless, it is the same Self, which is within and without you and me.

The wise people, therefore, have concluded the above explanation in one simple statement that **"The man awakened to his own glory is God and the God forgetful of his own glory is Man."**

Let us now consider another example to gain a better comprehension. When we focus our attention on the space within a pot, we call it Pot-Space, which appears limited and small in volume as it is confined within the Pot. Though the Pot-Space, in fact, is the same limitless and expensive space, which is outside of the pot, but due to our ignorance we believe these two to be different from each other. In this case our vision is conditioned by the walls of the Pot, therefore, the space in the pot seems small and limited and different from the space outside of the pot. However, when the walls of the pot are broken, the Pot Space merges with and becomes one with the space outside the pot. In fact, the space, inside and out, was never two separate entities, but due to the conditioning of wall envelopment, it seemed different.

In the same way, Paramatma and the Jivatma are not two separate entities, but one. However, due to the envelopment of our body, the mind, and the intellect (BMI), the Supreme Self not only seems different from the little Self but feels low, limited, weak and incomplete too.

Since my body, mind and intellect doesn't have the capability to apprehend the Supreme Self beyond the limits of my senses, I become the victim of my non-apprehension. My Self-identity, therefore, is created through the feedback of my experiences, gathered since my birth through to the current day via the interplay of my BMI. Essentially, the Self-identity thus created is nothing more than my perceptions about myself. These perceptions are a collective evaluation of all my experiences, good, bad, or ugly, which are consolidated as beliefs in my bosom about myself. Invariably, most of us suffer with the negative Self-image, which remains buried deep down in our unconscious layers of our awareness. Subconsciously, I keep verifying these perceptions through subsequent experiences, which eventually get crystalised and consolidated as my Self-belief. Since I am totally unaware of any other source of all my experiences except my body, mind and intellect, I identify myself to be these instruments. Hence the notion, '**I am the body,**' '**I am the mind,**' and '**I am the Intellect.**' I believe myself not only low, limited, weak, and incomplete, but also identify with the limitations of my body, mind, and intellect. Consequently, I suffer and enjoy the pains and pleasures of these equipment respectively. This is the story of our lives, thereafter, the work on our autobiography of miserable, painful, and lustful life starts.

You can also say that the Supreme Self, due to my non-apprehension of its real nature, since it is veiled by the material envelopment of BMI, confusingly appears, and feels low, limited, weak, and incomplete. The deluded person with his low sense of the Self, which, otherwise in reality, is Supreme, Pristine, and Glorious, is called **the Being**, that is You and Me.

Spiritual Practice, therefore, essentially is nothing but to know and realize one's own real nature. Adi Shankaracharya has indicated at the nature of the Supreme Self in Vivekachudamani from verse 124 to 135, which is also enumerated in chapter 8 entitled '**Imperishable Brahman**' (अक्षरब्रह्म) in the Holy Bhagavad Gita to bring its personality, so to speak, within the awareness of the seeker to appreciate and comprehend it. The nature of the Supreme Self, as is indicated in most of our spiritual text is: (1) being the ancient (Purana), (2) Immutable and imperishable (Akshara-अक्षर), (3) all Pervading (Sarvavyapi-सर्वव्यापी), (4) the Complete (the Whole-पूर्ण), (5) the Pure (Shuddha-शुद्ध), (6) Self-effulgent (Swaprakashit-स्वप्रकाशित), (7) Self-born (Swambhu- स्वंभू), (8) Indestructible (Akshara-अक्षर), and (9) Inconceivable (Achintya-roopah-अचिंत रूप). We will explore these terms and the nature of the Self in the next section to follow.

Along with Adi Shankaracharya, all our spiritual text books such as Upanishads, Bhagavad Gita and the likes, promise that if one knows the nature of the Supreme Self, will be freed from all his personality encumbrances, and will attain liberation from all bondages.

The Philosophy goes further and declares that the knower of the Supreme Self becomes the Supreme Self.

Don't you think it is worth the efforts, if such great benefits are promised, to gain some comprehension of this unconceivable Self?

10

The Spirituality & Self-Realization

"The man awakened to his own glory is God and the God forgetful of his own glory is Man."

The Ultimate Goal of Spirituality

Self-realization is the ultimate goal of all spiritual practices. The word 'Self' in Self-realization remains elusive while the word 'realization' is reasonably understood. But the conjunction of the two presents the problem. Though everyone understands, at least intellectually, not many can really know what the 'Self' in Self-realization means. Fundamentally, all religious and spiritual practices are designed to understand the term and eventually to realize it.

One of the common problems, however, with almost all spiritual practices is that we try to understand these from the prism of our existing knowledge and perception of the religious and ritualistic practices that we have gained in our lives. It gives us a mystical and mythical notion of duality. One believes God to be an entity other than oneself. Since 'the God' is an all powerful supernatural entity, which runs and manages our lives, we, therefore, must pray and beg to 'that God' out there to fulfill our desires and make our life happier. We wait for our prayers to be answered. At times our prayers are answered and not on most occasions. Should God be temperamental or consistent?

To know God (Self) is to realize God (Self) and to realize God is to be God. The above statement, however, makes the job of a sincere seeker somewhat simpler to understand it intellectually that God is nothing but one's own Supreme Reality. With sincerity, commitment, dedication, single point devotion applied daily, regularly, and consistently over a period of time, it is possible for anyone to realize their true Self, their true nature, their own Supreme Reality. The very first pre-condition, therefore, is to 'know the Self' in this way. For this, one must have firm belief in the Advaita (Nonduality) philosophy of Vedanta and its proclamations that the Self within is one and the same as the Self without.

The Mahavakyas (singular–Mahavakyam, महावाक्यम्; plural–Mahavakyani, महावाक्यानि) are 'The Great Sayings' of the Upanishads, as characterized by the Advaita school of Vedanta with 'Maha' (महा) meaning great and 'Vakya' (वाक्य) meaning a sentence. These Mahavakyas are the codified essence of the knowledge of the Self, which our Subjective Scientists have realized over thousands of years of contemplation. These Mahavakyas are not only Vedic statements of our reality but also indicate towards the incremental evolutionary process of Self-awareness by the sincere student of spirituality. Following are the four Mahavakyas.

1. **Prajnanam Brahma (प्रज्ञानम् ब्रह्म):** Prajnana (प्रज्ञान) is Brahman (ब्रह्म) or Brahman is Prajnana. The Sanskrit word Prajna means consciousness. The consciousness is Brahman. This is the meaning of this Mahavakya 'Prajnanam Brahma.' It is Upadesa Vakya, that is, the statement of instruction or guidance. This Mahavakya is also known as Lakshana Vakya, the statement that depicts the nature of Brahman.

   Etymologically, 'Pra' means Supreme, and Jnana means Knowledge, wisdom, awareness or consciousness. Therefore, we may also take the meaning of this Mahavakya as the supreme knowledge is Brahman.

   Who am I? I am not the body. I am not the mind. I am not the intellect. If I keep negating like this, only consciousness will remain.

That consciousness is Brahman. This is also the meaning of this Mahavakya.

Prajnanam iti Brahman - wisdom is the Self. Prajnanam is an intuitive truth that can be verified/tested using logic. The Sat or Truth/Existent in the Sat-Chit-Ananda or truth-existence-consciousness-bliss, i.e., the Brahman/Atman/Self/Person, is determined by a higher function of the intellect.

A truly wise person is known as Prajna - who has attained Brahmanhood itself; thus, testifying to the Vedic Maha Vakya '**Prajnanam iti Brahman.**' The knowledge of Brahman is not intuition of Brahman but the Knowledge itself is Brahman.

2. **Tat Tvam Asi (तत् त्वम् असि):** Traditionally rendered as "That Thou Art" (that you are). This Mahavakya expounds on Jivatma Vichara (the individual soul), Brahma Vichara (the Supreme Self) and Jiva-Brahma Aikya Jnana, oneness of the two and respectively unfolds and decodes the three terms Tvam, Tat, and Asi. The **'Tvam'** refers to the essential nature of the individual soul, the **'Tat'** to the nature of the Supreme Brahman and the **'Asi'** affirms the oneness of Paramatma and the Jivatma.

Chandogya Upanishad of the Sama Veda, with **Tat** referring to **Sat**, 'the Existent,' alternatively translated as "That's how [thus] you are," with Tat referring to the very nature of all existence as permeated by the finest essence. As a result, this Mahavakya translates as 'That You Are,' 'That Thou Art,' or simply 'You Are That.' **'That'** indicates Brahman or the Supreme Being. **'You'** refers to 'you' as a seeker. "**You are that Brahman; the Supreme Being,**" is the indicated meaning of this Mahavakya and emphasizes on the fact that the Atma & Parmatma, the Self & the Supreme Self is one and the same as is the space in and outside of the Pot.

3. **Ayam Atma Brahma** (अयम् आत्मा ब्रह्म): Ayam Atma Brahma is the Mahavakya found in the Atharva Veda's Mandukya Upanishad. As other Mahavakyas, it also explains the Jiva-Brahma Aikya or the oneness of Brahman and Atman which is the basic tenet of Advaita philosophy. This Mahavakya is considered an Abhyasa Vakya or the statement of practice.

   This Mahavakya means "This Atman is Brahman." This refers to the individual soul or Jiva who has been conditioned by avidya or ignorance. Atman means Isvara or God conditioned by Maya or delusion created by the body, mind, and the intellect. The two words' implied meaning is 'the Jiva and Isvara without conditioning.' The meaning of the word 'Brahman' is the identity of the two words' indicated meaning or indirect meaning. The meaning of this Mahavakya can be understood by negating all of Jiva and Isvara conditioning to have the indicated meaning of nonduality. By contemplating the meaning that I am the nature of non-dual absolute as indicated, the forgotten real nature can be enjoyed. This Self is Brahman is a perception that confirms all other Mahavakyas.

4. **Aham Brahmāsmi** (अहम् ब्रह्मास्मि): "I am Brahman," or "I am Divine." This Mahavakya is from the Brihadaranyaka Upanishad of the Yajur Veda. In the beginning this world was only Brahman, and it knew only itself, thinking: "I am Brahman." As a result, it became the whole. If a man, therefore, knows himself to be the brahman in this way, he becomes the whole, the Brahman.

   Aham Brahmasmi then means "I am the Absolute" or "My identity is cosmic," but can also be translated as "You are part of God just like any other element."

   Adi Shankaracharya explains in his commentary on this passage that here Brahman is not the conditioned Brahman (saguna); that a transitory entity cannot be eternal; that knowledge about Brahman, the infinite all-pervading entity, has been enjoined; that knowledge of nonduality alone dispels ignorance; and that resemblance meditation is only an idea. He also says that the mantra is explained by the phrase Aham Brahmasmi.

"That 'Brahman' is infinite, and this 'universe' is infinite, the infinite proceeds from the infinite. Then taking the infinitude of the infinite 'universe,' it remains as the infinite 'Brahman' alone."

Nonduality and plurality, he explains, are contradictory only when applied to the Self, which is eternal and without parts, but not to the effects, which have parts. The 'Aham' in this memorable expression is not closed as a pure mental abstraction, but rather represents radical openness. Between Brahman and Aham-Brahma is the entire temporal universe, which the ignorant perceive as a separate entity (duality).

Infinite by nature, the Supreme Self is described here by the word Brahman (ever expanding; the ultimate reality); the word 'Asmi' denotes the identity of Aham and Brahman. Therefore, the meaning of the expression is, **"I am Brahman."**

These Mahavakyas, proclaimed by Rishis of various Upanishads from each of the Vedas, are independent of each other, but if seen together, they provide us a profound and logical order in which a shishya or the disciple is initiated and assisted by the teacher to evolve incrementally in his understanding and awareness of his own Supreme Reality. At first, when the teacher starts his teaching process, he helps the student with the knowledge of the Brahman and says that the knowledge of Brahman in itself is Brhman (Prajnanam Brahma, प्रज्ञानम् ब्रह्म). Having expounded over the essential nature of the individual Self and the Supreme Self, the teacher affirms the oneness of Paramatma and the Jivatma. He assures the disciple that **"You are that Brahman, the Supreme Being (Tat Tvam Asi - तत् त्वम् असि). You are that Supreme Reality I have been teaching you about."**

Having helped the student thus far, now the teacher takes the student in the realm of spiritual practice so as to help him to have the direct and personal experience of the essence of the Self. He helps the student to negate and reject the conditioning of the body, mind, and the intellect to help him comprehend the indicated meaning of nonduality. By contemplating over the meaning that I am the nature of nondual absoluteness, the student tries to experience the real nature of his own Self which has been forgotten by him. At this stage of contemplation, the student gains the insight that **'This Self within him is the Brahman itself'** (Ayam Atma Brahma - अयम् आत्मा ब्रह्म). The student, thereafter, continuing his contemplation and meditation, gains the direct and personal experience of the oneness of the Self within and without, he proclaims eventually that, **'I am Brahman' (Aham Brahmāsmi** - अहम् ब्रह्मास्मि). Such a state of awareness or realization is called Self-realization.

Now we know, what is the purpose of spiritual practice, Self-realization, and all ritualistic practices therein. Self-realization is a shift from dual identity of the Self (My Self & the Supreme Self are two separate entities) to oneness of the Self (My Self & the Supreme Self are one and the same), from the sense of limited Self to limitless Self, and from the ignorance of the Self to the Knowledge of the Self.

11

The Path Of Spirituality

For any worthwhile endeavor in life or any great purpose, there must be a good enough reason for an individual to make a choice and compelling enough reason to commit to it. Be it choosing your profession, career, buying a house, getting married to a person or changing your city or country. All such greater and important decisions of life are not possible unless the person is fully convinced, at least intellectually, with the proposition. Unless I am fully convinced with the glorious future in the offing, I will not move an inch in that direction. Even if I do not have concrete details of the prospect, however, only if I can vividly visualize the benefits and the glories of the proposition in my mind, that serves as a good enough propelling force for me to proceed in that direction.

In the same way, unless one understands the real purpose of spirituality and is not convinced with 'What will they get from spirituality? Why should they be spiritual? Where should they commence the journey from? What will be the final destination?' Unless they are fully convinced with the glorious future in the offing, no one will have any confidence or courage to march forward on the path of spirituality. A sincere seeker of spirituality must get all these questions answered before they contemplate their journey on this path.

When one marches forward on the path of spirituality, aiming at realizing the Self, generally encounters a number of hurdles on their way in the form of Self-doubt, lack of forbearance, inability to detach from existing habits and comforts, mental and intellectual challenges in discriminating between the material and spiritual dimension of one's personality and inability to control one's mind etc. Some of these challenges, amongst others, dissuade them away from the journey. Unfortunately, our existing religious and ritualistic practices and particularly the mindless and mechanical manner in which these are performed, demonstrated, and displayed, doesn't offer much hope to any sincere seeker of spirituality. There aren't many people available to children, young people, and the seekers of knowledge, who they can ask the questions to seek clarity on its logical and scientific nature.

Let us, therefore, investigate what pre-requisite qualifications and mental qualities must be gained to commence and sustain the march on this journey. There must be a technology and the technique for the sincere seeker to sustain their commitment, enthusiasm, and zeal on their way to the destination of Self-realization. It is the very same resolve, inner strength and the energy which sustains an athlete to win a race, while others give up before commencing the race.

Let us now consider an example of a treasure hunt. How the treasure hunter's activities can be a theme by which spiritual purpose, process and the technique can be explained and understood.

A treasure hunt can be successful only when the digger has the correct information on the place where the treasure is hidden. He must be fully convinced with the value, and the importance of the treasure in his life that he is about to embark on. He must have the propelling reasons for acquiring the treasure. He must also be enthusiastic and energetic enough to dig for and find the treasure. He must slowly and steadily, with hopeful patience and perseverance, continue digging and remove all obstacles that he might encounter on his way, till he reaches the goal of his seeking–the treasure trove. At last, when he comes to the rich vaults, he must be level-headed and calm enough not to lose his balance so that he is in a position to gather the treasure and make use of it.

Similarly, the infinitely rich treasure of Self-perfection that lies unseen beneath the outer layers of our matter envelopments in man's bosom is to be discovered as his own Self. The seeker must have the assiduity, industry, hope, and patience to search in the right place, in the right fashion, with unabated enthusiasm, in the face of even the most formidable obstacles, until he comes not only to see the treasure, but to gather it, possess it, and enjoy it as its sole proprietor. The seeker must not dig just anywhere; he must start his endeavor in the right direction as advised by those who know the truth as declared in the scriptures by our Subjective Scientists.

In the spiritual treasure hunt, the endeavor of digging is made with a number of tools, for example, the pickaxe of thought and the spade of discrimination. With these, we dig the earth and with a wheelbarrow of dispassion, remove the earth-the attachments with the body, mind, and intellect, which are the effects of the ignorance of the Self. This ignorance creates in us various misunderstandings, and it is these agitations of the mind and negative thoughts veils of the intellect that conceals the treasure Divine, the Self. The technique and the technology used in unveiling, unfolding, and recovering the treasure Divine, the Self from the earth of attachments is called Reflection and Meditation- Manana & Dhyana (मनन एवं ध्यान).

Reflection and Meditation prepare the mind for a single pointed application by bringing it to the state of least agitation. This is the condition of the mind and intellect for fit thought, the highest spiritual practice known to man. According to Adi Shankaracharya, this is the only path for complete and permanent Liberation from the chaotic confusion created by our ignorance of the underlying divinity in ourselves. Naturally, he points out the hollowness of all other methods and immaturity of all techniques which are, according to him, purified logic, soured reason, distorted vision, and false assertion compared with the perfect philosophy and detailed practicality of Vedanta.

In addition to the foregoing, the Self-effort is said to be the most important tool; in comparison to it, scriptural studies, and the ability to discourse on them are insufficient. Because of these considerations, it is logical to conclude that each seeker must strive with all sincerity and consistency in the right direction in order to realize in himself the eternal godhood of his spiritual nature.

We are to think of ourselves as a sick patient infected with a microbe of ignorance. All living beings are naturally healthy. Illness is the unnatural state of the body when it has deviated from its essential health for unknown reasons. Therefore, health is not to be created, but all our efforts should be to remove the cause that created the disease. A body rid of its disease germs comes to manifest full health and vigor. Similarly, ignorance (our unnatural state of being) creates in us all the maladjustments through which spiritual dynamism, divine glory, and supreme perfection (our natural state of being) are veiled from us.

No two patients with the same disease can be cured by taking the same dose of the same medicine. The same medicine can be used to cure the disease, but the dosage and application will vary depending on the degree of infection. Similarly, while Vedanta Sadhana is the same for all seekers, each seeker must apply it in his or her own unique way. Simply taking the medication does not guarantee a cure. It is determined by a number of other factors, the most important of which is Self-effort (Tapasya). The patient may be tempted to enjoy activities that his doctor has forbidden him from doing. But he must avoid them at all costs, or else the medicine may kill him rather than cure him.

So, the million-dollar questions are:

1. Why must one opt for Spirituality?

2. What is that secret ingredient which helps one to commence, walk, and sustain on an apparently treacherous path of spirituality?

3. How does one prepare oneself for the path of Spirituality?

1. **Why must one opt the Path of Spirituality?**

The path to a better society is almost always through individual moral development, that is each person has to battle with his or her own flaws and weaknesses. For this very reason, our old Indian philosophy, while providing a framework for a fair and just society and state, placed a greater emphasis on inner changes for carving out a robust and resolute individual personality.

Society changes with one person at a time and the change happens gradually rather than fundamentally changing the society. Society can be improved but should not be transformed, let alone fundamentally transformed. Towards this objective, each generation must work on the moral transformation of each citizen. Thus, character development must be at the core of child rearing and young people's education, and they must be encouraged to become moral and religious people.

There is not much to argue about the assertion that only a virtuous people are capable of freedom[14]. Freedom requires greater self-control. Therefore, if we aspire for a freer society, more self-control is necessary.

In the past, schools and parents concentrated on character building through education. Parents (Families) and religion, historically, have been the two primary conveyors of self-control. Unfortunately, the two primary conveyors seem ineffectual in the lives of millions of children and young people in our present-day society.

We are now producing vast numbers of citizens, who are passionate about fixing state, societal and global problems, while doing next to nothing about fixing their own character. The problem is that we cannot make a society better unless we make its people better.

---

[14] *True freedom, in the spiritual literature, is not to do what you want but is built on intelligent Self-restraint, which means that we have learnt to be truly independent and have developed a capability in us to stand apart from the influence of our perceptions, emotions, and thoughts.*

It can, therefore, be concluded that while fighting the societal evils in any decent and free society is necessary by battling with outside forces, it can only bring about a total, sustained and lasting transformation with positive outcomes only with the investment of sincere and committed efforts undertaken simultaneously on the moral transformation of each citizen.

It is undeniable that today's societies have suffered the consequences of extreme left ideological, overt, and covert policies. Materialism, greed, corruption, bribery, nepotism, disrespect for rules and laws, short-termism and immediate gratification, a shaky moral edifice, a life full of lust, quick fixes, and ready justification of wrongdoings have all eroded our nations' social, moral, and political character. It is time to get back to basics. Collective efforts must be made to educate all citizens, but especially our young citizens, to learn and gain self-control skills through moral and religious education.

This lack of self-control is responsible for most of our criminal activities, that we indulge ourselves in on a day-to-day basis. Our sense organs of perception continuously entice us and tickle our greed and lust to either acquire what we do not have or what we want to have more of, to be happier or constantly try to avert what we do not want, like or despise. Consequently, 100% of personal mental energy is consumed by such tireless efforts in either acquisition or aversion.

The path of spirituality provides one with inner strength to withstand Negative Affectivity. Negative Affectivity is a personality variable that involves the experience of negative emotions and poor Self-concept and subsumes a variety of negative emotions, including anger, contempt, jealousy, disgust, guilt, fear, nervousness, dishonesty, greed, lust and many more in its variety and combinations. Negative Affectivity is the viral infected foundation upon which the edifice of criminal and corrupt life is built. Spiritual development, therefore, is not only a medicinal antidote for Negative Affectivity, but also improves spiritual immunity and sustains spiritual health with Positive Affectivity instead and bestows one with the inner strength and the shield of self-control.

2. What is that secret ingredient to commence, walk, and sustain on an apparently treacherous Path of Spirituality?

The secret ingredient should reveal itself if we deal first with a few myths associated with spirituality in the beginning of this section as mentioned below:

Myth 1: The path of Spirituality is treacherous and difficult.

Myth 2: The path of Spirituality is available only to a selected and the blessed few.

Myth 3: The skills and abilities required for Spirituality are difficult to acquire.

Myth 4: Spirituality and religious activities are for the retired and the old.

Myth 5: Spirituality requires one to renounce family life and society.

Myth 6: Material and Spiritual life can't go hand in hand.

Myth 7: Amongst the various suggested paths i.e., the path of knowledge (ज्ञान योग), devotion (भक्ति योग), action (कर्म योग) or (राज योग), which is the most appropriate and profitable for spiritual development, growth, and maturity?

Myth 8: Walking the Path of Spirituality is not an option for the one who has lived materialistic life or a life of a criminal or the one who has no knowledge in this area.

These myths are common apprehensions, which most people in the Hindu society have, both within and outside of India. As has already been stated earlier, we look at spirituality from the prism of our existing experience and perception of religious practices and ritualistic performances all around us in society. Let's investigate each of these apprehensions and burst these myths one by one.

Myth 1: The path of Spirituality is treacherous and difficult

On the contrary, in fact, it is easy and simple. What is rather difficult is the decision to take the path. The moment you decide to take the path it becomes increasingly easier with every step one takes and every achievement one makes.

Such apprehensions though might feel real but are ill founded and baseless. The fact remains, however, that the prospect of learning any new skill that we wish to take up in life, always at first, appears impossible and difficult. Particularly when we compare ourselves with those people who are highly competent in that particular skill area. The very first negative effect of such a thinking is Self-negation. "I don't think I will ever be able to do so!" Such are the games our mind plays with us.

Now think of any skill that you are reasonably competent at today. Be it driving, rolling chapatis, baking a cake, a new language, performing yoga asana, weight lifting, building six-packs, sketching, painting or any skill, simple or complex, for that matter. Now if you go back in time to the day when this particular skill wasn't part of your thinking at all. You never thought of or felt the need to have this skill. Then came the day, for whatever reason, when you considered acquiring the skill for the very first time in your life. The prospect of learning the skill in question at that point in time, let alone becoming competent in it, must have felt daunting and impossible. But the fact remains that you decided, you took the plunge, and went ahead with your decision to learn. Consequently, now you are highly competent in the skill in question, which you thought was impossible for you.

For example, there was a day in your life, when you never felt the need to drive. Then came the day when you wanted to buy a car for whatever reason. You must, therefore, learn to drive. You had never driven a car in your life before and when you looked at the other drivers and their competence level, you must have had a degree of apprehension. You could not imagine yourself driving a car at that point in time. It wasn't possible for you to see yourself driving the same way as other drivers did. Hey!! Look at yourself now. You are as competent a driver as anyone else, which you thought you never would. Anything in life is impossible only for as long as you think and believe it is impossible. Conversely, this is equally true as well.

The reality is that we have competently learnt so many new, complex, and impossible things in life but we choose to ignore our own real tangible experiences for some unknown fears in our minds.

"The only way to find the limits of the possible is to go beyond them into the impossible," writes Sir Arthur C. Clarke[15].

It is insightful to note the four stages of the journey that one travels from being incompetent at one stage in life to being competent later on. Modern psychology provides a "Four Stages of Competence" learning model and tool to understand the psychological states that an individual goes through while learning a new skill, from incompetent to competent.

These four phases demonstrate that people are unaware of how little they know or are capable of when it comes to a particular skill. They are unaware of their own incompetence. When they recognise their own incompetence, they begin to learn and consciously apply a skill.

---

[15] *Sir Arthur Charles Clarke CBE FRAS was an English science-fiction writer, science writer, futurist, inventor, undersea explorer, and television series host. He co-wrote the screenplay for the 1968 film 2001: A Space Odyssey, widely regarded as one of the most influential films of all time.*

In English, there is a saying that goes, "When you know, you don't know... you begin to know." Eventually, the individual will learn to use the skill without even thinking about it; this is known as unconscious competence.

When they understand this model, parents, teachers, coaches, and trainers can learn to better recognise the learning needs of their students and develop learning objectives based on where they are in the learning curve.

The theory behind the four stages of competence was initially founded by Martin M. Broadwell back in 1969. The four stages of competence, also known as the four stages of learning, is a model based on the premise that learners are unaware of what or how much they know before a learning experience begins. Everyone starts out unconsciously incompetent, and as they learn, they progress through the following four psychological states until they reach unconscious competence.

1. **Unconscious Incompetence:** In unconscious incompetence stage, the learner isn't aware that a skill or knowledge gap exists.

2. **Conscious Incompetence:** In the conscious incompetence stage, the learner is aware of a skill or knowledge gap and understands the importance of acquiring the new skill. It's in this stage that learning can begin.

3. **Conscious Competence:** In the conscious competence stage, the learner knows how to use the skill or perform the task, but doing so requires practice, conscious thought, and hard work.

4. **Unconscious Competence:** In the final unconscious competence stage, the individual has enough experience with the skill that he or she can perform it so easily and they do it effortlessly and unconsciously.

Now, if you spare a few moments and reflect over any of your skills, you will be able to identify these phases clearly. One day in your life you were totally incompetent in a skill area and later on you were not only competent, but unconsciously competent in the same skill area. You are now proficient. You can do it with your eyes closed. This reflection must give you a strong sense of confidence that you are quite capable of learning any skill, only if you put your mind to it.

You might be apprehensive today about spiritual development, but all you have to do is to find the secret ingredient and one day you will be unconsciously competent in the arena of spirituality as well. Your own direct and personal experiences of the trajectory of learning new skills, in addition to the psychological explanation above, emphatically, encourages you to take up the call and commence your journey onto the path of Spirituality.

Myth 2: The path of Spirituality is available only for a selected or the blessed few

Yes, it might appear so, but in reality, it happens in the reverse sequence. Those who chose the path of spirituality, end up being the blessed ones. So far as **'being selected'** is concerned, the power to select and be blessed is invested in yourself and with each human being born on this earth. No one else is selecting and deciding for you. No one is specially or particularly predisposed to take up this path. Only you have to select yourself, decide to take up the path and you too will be similarly blessed as the few that you think of.

The central theme of various scriptural texts, including Upanishads, in a simplistic manner and in a comprehensible language is to help the young people and the new seekers to comprehend the idea and to encourage them to take these on board for their own benefits, i.e., a **fulfilling, successful and joyful life.**

The idea and the concept of Self-realization might feel like a '**Pie in the Sky**' particularly when we compare ourselves with the evolved souls. However, the fact remains that all the highly evolved souls, known to us from previous generations, were born ordinary like you and me but through a process of Self-realization reached greater heights by their extra-ordinary zeal and self-efforts. Self-effort, which includes things like **taking decisions and resolve, commitment, and dedication and with single-point devotion**, anyone can reach to the heights of Self-realization. This self-effort, in fact, is the cost one must pay for being blessed.

Spirituality is a humble call to all young people to end their mindless pursuits and desperate attempts at chasing after life, shake off all your ill-conceived notions about rituals, religion, and spirituality. Cast of all their blind and mindless practices of religion if they do any. Understand the true and real meaning and purpose of rituals, religions and spirituality and make the best use of these and reclaim all the love, peace, and happiness that you rightfully deserve. It gives one the hope that the result and the outcome of spiritual practices is not far away from them and not at a distant time in future. It is not going to give them anything **new** but will introduce them to their own treasure trove of inner strengths, that is, their **real Self** and draw their attention to the inner wealth that they already possess. The purpose of spirituality is to help them uncover and unfold their own reality. Such an achievement in spiritual literature is referred to as gaining what you already have (प्राप्तस्य प्राप्ति).

Myth 3: The skills and abilities required on the path of Spirituality are difficult to acquire

All of us know the process of shooting an arrow using a bow. Anyone has a good chance to shoot an arrow toward the bull's eye. If lucky, we might hit an arrow on the target board but not sure if we could hit the bull's eye, even with several attempts. But the master archer only needs one arrow to shoot straight into the bull's eye every time he is asked to.

In the same way, when you are spiritually mature, you are highly likely to be successful every time at anything you attempt at without getting stressed, frightened, frustrated, fearful, stressed or losing your peace of mind.

This is not a new path for you to tread on or a territory for you to charter. The skills and abilities required on this path are already available within you. You have used these skills and abilities hundreds of times before. It's just that you are not conscious of the mechanism and the technology with which you have been invoking the inner strengths within you. All you need to do is to become consciously aware of and learn the techniques to consistently invoke these blessings as and when you need them. This is where spirituality helps you to invoke your inner strengths at will, all the time.

If you have tasted success or achievement in your life, small or big, you couldn't have done so without the aid of a meditative mind (एकाग्र मन). Whatever idea or notion you may hold about meditation, it is but a technique to bring your mind to focus on a thought or a group of thoughts pertaining to a single theme, in the midst of all distractions created by your sense organs.

Let us now recall a time a couple of months prior to your final examination that you wanted to pass with a distinction. In order to achieve this objective of yours, let us review some of the sub-conscious mental processes you must have gone through.

(a) The desire to pass the examination with a distinction must be sufficiently intense in your mind, for you to have any chance to get the highest possible marks. Such an intensified or burning desire, in Sanskrit, is called **Mumukshutva** (मुमुक्षुत्व). This word actually means burning desire for Liberation (मोक्ष) in spiritual literature. Whether to liberate oneself from mediocrity in materialistic life or from the shackles of negativity in the spiritual dimension of life, the burning desire remains a common mental quality. Mumukshutva or the burning desire, therefore, is the very first qualification for a sincere seeker of spirituality too, the evidence of the seeds of which you have directly and personally experienced.

(b) When the burning desire to succeed or to achieve something in life intensifies in your mind, you automatically have a sense of discrimination in your mind. You instantly know what is good for you and what isn't, during this period prior to your final examination. You know that the best use of your time is to study, revise and rehearse rather than wasting time in other temptations of life. This power of discrimination (विवेक-शक्ति) of your mind between the good and the bad, beneficial, and detrimental, real, and unreal, fleeting, and permanent etc., is called **Vivek-Buddhi (विवेक बुद्धि)**, which is the second of the qualifications for a sincere seeker of spirituality too, the evidence of the seeds of which you have directly and personally experienced.

(c) This burning desire to perform well in your examination, leads you to prioritize and use your time wisely and effectively. Consequently, you now have a time table to make the best use of your time, where a vast amount of time is now allocated to your studies and revisions, reading, and practicing over and over again. You shock and surprise yourself as you start waking up early in the morning and keep studying till late at night. You are not at all bothered about what is for the breakfast, lunch, or dinner. You are not at all interested in who is coming in and leaving your house.

Birthday parties, clubbing, and outing, eating, and drinking, playing, and gaming, hanging out with friends, reading fashion magazine, watching favorite TV programmes, and keeping up with the jones' syndrome, chit-chats about movies and gossips about film stars, going to cinema etc., are all such activities now you put on the backburner. Rather they disappear from your life during these months of preparations. While all the above activities are still happening all around you, you remain oblivious and focused on one and the only thing, that is, your studies, revision, and practice from morning to night every day without a break.

Your mind remains preoccupied with the only thoughts of studies and examination from morning to night. You willingly and effortlessly give-up all above mentioned tempting and tantalizing activities, which were so very dear to you. This ability to become dispassionate and the ability to withdraw your attention, willingly and effortlessly, away from unhelpful activities and invest into what you consider good, is called **dispassion** in English and Vairagya (वैराग्य) in Sanskrit. Vairagya is an automatic result of a burning desire and discrimination, which is achieved effortlessly, when you bring your mind to focus on a bigger, better and the higher value or a purpose in life, the lower or invaluable pursuits automatically either disappear or are side-lined. You automatically develop a dispassion about them. **Vairagya**, therefore, is considered the third of the qualifications for a sincere seeker of spirituality too, the evidence of the seeds of which you have directly and personally experienced.

Here, I have demonstrated to you that you already have and used the skills of Meditation, Concentration, Discrimination and Dispassion in your life so many times. You have been invoking these skills, not just in educational fields, but in any other field of your interests. Be it sports or any of the extra-curricular activities that you sincerely committed yourself to, you were able to invoke these skills every time. It's just that you were not aware of these powers within you, and you didn't understand the mechanism of invoking these powers. Therefore, when you decide to take up the path of spirituality, you need not to learn anything new. All you have to do is **to commit yourself for spiritual development and invoke the burning desire in you.** The technique and the mechanism to invoke these powers, your own real nature, which are already lying dormant in you, will be effortlessly awakened. In spiritual literature such gains are referred to as "Getting what you already have (प्राप्तस्य प्राप्ति)."

Myth 4: Spirituality and religious activities are for the retired and the old

The most mindless, illogical, and idiotic idea that has been paddled by the left secular and communist thinking for decades and centuries is that spirituality and religious activities are for the later part of life e.g., old age, when you have nothing productive or better to do. By implication, it suggests that materialistic life and spirituality are mutually exclusive. Spirituality is suggested to be an additional extra activity in life, which one may cast their eye on, only if life's priorities permit. However, the evidence is suggesting otherwise. You have been invoking and using spiritual skill pertaining to the inner world for meeting all your materialistic goals and purposes. So how can it be exclusive? The bad news, however, is that the young population has fallen for it and have deprived themselves of enormous Positive Affectivity of spiritual science.

If you buy a TV set, for example, with all the latest features, functions, and technology, which you have never used before. The most intelligent thing will be to read the manual before you start using the set; Get yourself acquainted with various new features and functions, learn how best to connect the TV set with the sound system, if there is one and how best to configure your TV set to get the best out of its new features and functions. Once you do this common-sense thing, you are guaranteeing yourself the most enjoyable experience. On the other hand, will the intelligent thing be to disregard the manual until such time the TV set develops faults or is blown off completely and then you search for the manual?

A material object such as a TV set can be easily replaced with a new one if damaged. Human life, however, is the most precious gift and only a one-time allocation. There are no rehearsals or retakes. When must be the best time to understand life and the interplay of the life principle (the consciousness) with the body, mind, and intellect equipment? When should be the best time to read the manual of life? When these instruments are weak, damaged and almost inoperative towards the end of life (Old-age) or will it be intelligent to become master of these instruments at the beginning of life (Young-age)? When must one learn to drive a car? Before you start driving or after you have had numerous accidents and the car is badly damaged?

Our best performance in all productive and professional activities, including our successes, even in secular and materialistic life, require a mind which is calm and collected. Whatever one may understand and undertake spirituality to be, it is but a science of the inner personality, the inner world, and the most spiritual practices are designed, as a prerequisite, to learn to bring one's mind in control through the techniques of contemplation (Chintan - चिंतन), meditation, (Manan - मनन) and concentration (Dhyana - ध्यान). Spirituality is the science of life, which helps us to learn the art of intelligent living and raise the standard of life, alongside raising the standards of living.

Spiritual development, therefore, is essential for a better, happier, and more harmonious life, free of tension, stress, fear, and anxiety. While secular education can promise the quality of material living, spiritual education in addition to the secular, will most certainly guarantee a peaceful life, while one enjoys the good standards of material living. So, the obvious question facing us all is, for how long one should delay or postpone it. The choice, I suppose, is simple and clear.

Myth 5: Spirituality requires one to renounce family life and society

Renunciation (Sannyasa-सन्यास) is yet another word used in the religious and spiritual context, which has been grossly misconstrued. What we see and observe around us is that people are renouncing their family and leaving society to become a wandering monk. Such mistakes and errors are commonly committed by people when they just understand renunciation from its word meaning only and run with it. They miss the real import and significance of the word 'Sannyasa' or

'**Renunciation,**' which unfortunately, has been reduced to a mere word for the modern-day person as he thinks and believes that Sannyasa means a 'Wandering Monk' who has abandoned his family and society in an attempt to fly away from all his responsibilities. Such a person, having shaved his head, wears an orange robe and wanders around in jungles. Such an act by a person, we believe, is '**Sannyasa**' and the person is a '**Sannyasin.**'

On the contrary, the Vedantic meaning and the definition of a real sannyasa is that "Sannyasa is a state of being wherein the Man-of-Perfection, having conquered the mental agitations that were created by the pairs-of-opposites, fights the battle of Life." Therefore, **Sannyasa Yoga**, essentially, is the renunciation of all desires and not necessarily renunciation of cardinal duties towards the Self, the family, and the society at large and associated responsibilities. Having renounced all desires, it is acceptable in Sanatan tradition, if one chooses to be a wandering monk, wears an orange robe and shaves his head, but without renouncing all desire, it is not only hypocritical but **a flight from the battle of Life.**

This word Sannyasa refers to a mental condition of the one who comes to discover real peace within himself. Such an individual **renounces all desires** and has no attachments or longings. The condition of such an individual's intellect is without any sense of 'I-ness' or 'My-ness.' The Ego is the cause of the sense-attachments and longings. When the Ego is not visible, as when sleeping, the individual either does not have longings or desires, or they are dormant. As a result, sannyasa is a mental state in which the effects of 'ignorance' are negated, as well as the absence of the source of desires and agitation. Since it is believed in our scriptures that all our sufferings in the world are caused by our own egocentric misconception and the consequent arrogance, which is characterized by our ever-multiplying demands for wealth and endless desires.

Before you become even more confused and disillusioned by the prescription of '**Renouncing all Desires**' as suggested in our scriptures, let me provide you with clarification and bring your mind at ease. It must be sounding a bit confusing and contradictory as it seems that this book is encouraging you into spirituality to be able to achieve all your desires and be successful in life and at the same time, you have been asked to renounce all your desires. How is this possible at the same time?

The desires are mechanisms and schemes created by our mind to satisfy our sense appetites. In our delusion, our egocentric mind believes that by satisfying desires, it will be happy. Therefore, it remains constantly busy in running out to sense objects and keeps courting with them. All our mental energy is dissipated in desire satisfaction since there is a delusory scheme in place to make me happier. What we must learn and understand here is that no temporary material object can ever give us permanent peace and happiness. It is true that we do get a glimpse of temporary, fleeting joy and pleasure on acquisition of the object of our desires.

Spirituality, however, is not denying you any luxuries and comforts of life. It is rather, in its compassion, warning you to not be fooled by and chase after material possessions, believing these will make you happy. At their best all you can experience is a glimpse of real happiness in the form of temporary joys and pleasures. If the happiness was in the objects, then the object must give you permanent happiness at all times. But we know for sure that this is not the case. As soon as we possess the object of our desire, the charm, and the pleasure last only a few days and weeks and we start desiring for the next thing. Therefore, you are asked to give up desiring happiness from the temporary and fleeting material objects in life.

Another logic, to support this argument, comes from the Supreme Teacher of spirituality himself, the Lord Krishna, who was a king of an estate and had all the material objects of luxuries and comforts in his possession. So how can he ask you and me to not have material possessions? Won't it be hypocritical of him?

Therefore, what is being asked here is to give up desiring happiness from material objects, since it is nothing but delusional. Real and lasting happiness can only come from the real and permanent source, which is your own real nature, your own real Self, and your real personality, that is, the Supreme Self. That's where spirituality is asking you to divert your attention away from materialism and conserving your mental energy by reducing and terminating your mindless chase of material objects.

Sannyasa, therefore, means sacrifice (of desires and attachments), and to live in the spirit of sacrifice after renouncing completely one's Ego and its desires is true Sannyasa, wherein a person learns to live in constant awareness of his fuller and more ample divinity. The general misunderstanding that to run away from life is Sannyasa, or to color the cloth is to become a true monk, has cast an irreparable slur on the philosophy of the Upanishads. Sanatan tradition considers him alone to be a Sannyasin "who has learnt the art of intelligently living life in constant inspiration, which is gained through an intelligent renunciation of egocentric misconception."

Myth 6: Material and Spiritual life can't go hand in hand

This myth is as absurd as it can be. However, it is inappropriate to blame the modern man, who has lived through and through a materialistic life. In addition to this, he has the experience of religious practices and rituals, which have never been logically or scientifically explained to him. Hence, spirituality, religion, and ritualism, seem to him, not only one and the same thing but an additional extra and optional activity, which he may choose to take up, if at all, he has nothing better left to do in life.

If one thinks or believes that materialistic life cannot go hand in hand with spiritual life, such thinking can be easily and safely attributed to a lack of clarity and understanding of spirituality or confusing spirituality with something else.

Spirituality to life is as electricity is to an equipment, an engine is to a car. One cannot function effectively without the other. An electric bulb gives light only when the electricity passes through it. The electric bulb on its own cannot produce light, so can't electricity manifest its power without the bulb? Though electricity is not comprehensible to our eyes, yet it is the very cause for the light bulb to produce light. In the same way, though we cannot comprehend the Life Principle, the consciousness, or our own Supreme Self in us, which enlivens our body, mind, and the intellect equipment, yet it is the very cause and the reason for our body, mind, and the intellect to function in the world outside. The efficiency and the effectiveness of our body, mind, and the intellect directly depends on the efficiency and effectiveness of the subtle inner instruments.

Spirituality, therefore, is an art as well as a science of gaining understanding of the dynamics of these instruments and learning the art of keeping these instruments sharp and efficient at all times.

Therefore, for those who wish to live life to the fullest, be in total control of their lives, be insulated from the ups and downs, pins, and pricks of life, and aspire to be equanimous in the joys and sorrows of life, for them the material and the spiritual life must go hand in hand. For all others, life is already like a boat without the helmsman and the mast, directionless, tossed and turned by the waves, bumping into one rock after another, not sure if it will ever find a shore.

Myth 7: Amongst the various suggested paths i.e., the path of knowledge (ज्ञान योग), devotion (भक्ति योग), action (कर्म योग) or (राज योग), which is the most appropriate and profitable for spiritual development, growth, and maturity?

There is no one single or simple answer to this question if we are searching for the answer from amongst the established institutional structures in our society, in addition to religious practices. There are various schools of thoughts and institutional structure and practices already established for hundreds of years, who all are, almost in a competitive fashion, propagating and promoting their own specific modalities for spirituality.

General understanding amongst the followers of various paths is that all paths are equally relevant and important and will take you to the final destination. "All roads lead to Rome," as the saying goes. Such an understanding, by implication, suggests that one can choose either of the paths as per their mental temperament or preference, which will take them to their desired destination, i.e. Self-realization in the context of our discussion.

However, if you try to understand aetiologically within the context of spiritual literature, you will discover that these are not the paths as such, each one of which will independently lead you to your final destination. My personal experience, understanding and the view suggest that these are the mental and intellectual temperaments, inclusive of each other, connected in a cyclic order, as illustrated below in the diagram. Each one of these individually, though may bring some benefits to the practitioner, can never bring a total satisfaction. Such misunderstanding in the society since 7th sanctuary onwards has led people to different directions, in the belief that they would somehow someday reach the destination of Self-realization.

Unless you have all the required information on your chosen destination, whether it is a place you want to visit, or choosing a professional career, setting goals for your professional performance or targets or wanting to take up spirituality, how do you take such decisions? Unless you are fully convinced with knowledge gathered, there is no way any person with the slightest logical sense would be in a position to take a decision, let alone marching toward the destination. No one with a sane mind would be able to commit oneself to any idea unless they are mentally and intellectually convinced and sold on the idea. Only after you have realized and have the vivid visualization of the full glorious life and the benefits of the promised land, you would not be able to commit yourself to it.

For example, let's examine a situation to analyze mental processes one goes through, while taking a decision on important life choices. Let's say you are considering taking an entrance examination of a premier academic institute of engineering or medicine. What precedes the decision to choose the profession and take the entrance examination. It is most certainly the knowledge of the glorious future after becoming an engineer or a doctor, the potential of higher incomes, and the dreams of luxurious and comfortable life thereafter.

Once you are convinced of the bright future beyond reasonable doubt, the required devotion is an automatic outcome. You have no difficulty, whatsoever, now in committing yourself to a treacherous process of relentless hard work and slogging over the next few years. Self-efforts full of endless devotion day and night, not only to pass the entrance examination, but for the next few years of rigorous study, is a natural consequence and is available to you in abundance. You are now well poised to put forth all the work with dexterity and with a meditative mind, full of concentration and focus.

Cyclic Order or Spiritual Paths

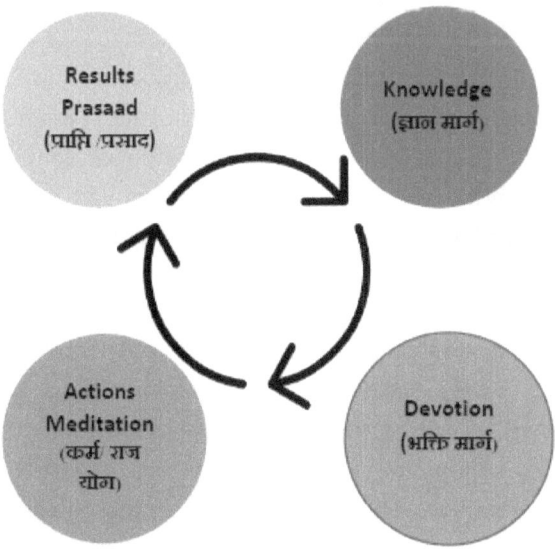

Unless your mind and intellect are fully convinced with the full knowledge and the glory of the Supreme Self **(Gyan Yog - ज्ञान योग)**, you cannot invoke the required devotion in your bosom **(Bhakti Yog - भक्ति योग)**. Without the propelling force of devotion, there will be no reason as well as no enthusiasm or energy invoked in you to bring yourself to put forth efforts and go through the pins and pricks of life **(Karma Yog - कर्म योग)**, let alone bring your mind to a meditative state to remain focused on the objective **(Raj Yog - राज योग)**.

The secret ingredient which helps one to commence, walk, and sustain on an apparently treacherous path of spiritual sadhana, therefore, is the same mental condition that of the treasure digger. Unless he is fully convinced with the possibility of finding the treasure trove and has faith in the information gathered, there is no likelihood that he will even contemplate, let alone take on the project of digging the ground a few feet down. It is the same faith, conviction in and commitment for the promised land that helps one to pursue the path of education. Both the treasure digger and the seeker of the education commit themselves to the required hardship and the sustained Self-efforts, only because both are fully aware of the glory of their respective promised lands and are convinced and committed to reach the desired destination at the end of their endeavors. This conviction invokes the necessary faith and devotion in their bosom which makes them commence, walk, and sustain on the chosen path to their desired destination, despite hardships. While on the path, it is the same faith, devotion and conviction which gives them enthusiasm and energy to encounter all the problems and challenges, willingly and smilingly, to withstand and forebear all the pins and pricks.

When an athlete's mind is intellectually convinced of the glory, fame, and the associated benefits of winning a Gold Medal at an international athletic meat, he remains motivated to practice his cardiovascular/respiratory endurance, stamina, strength, flexibility, power, coordination, agility, balance, and accuracy daily by running the distance and to ensure that he beats the previous records set by the winners of the races in the past. Such a **conviction in and commitment for the higher purpose** in life is the secret ingredient, which motivates and encourages one to practice daily, week after week, month after month until he gains the excellence in his competence and the absolute degree of confidence necessary to win the race until the judgment day.

In the same way, in the realm of the **higher spiritual purpose**; having gained the full and comprehensive **knowledge** and having convinced with the glories of Supreme Self and the process of Self-realization, leads one to have **faith** born out the knowledge of the supreme and a **conviction** in and the **commitment** for a glorious life of Self-realized person is the secret ingredient. These factors collectively are referred to as the **burning desire for liberation (Mumukshutva–मुमुक्षुत्व)** which is the first of the qualifications necessary to initiate one on the path of spiritual development. Your passion, commitment and dedication to the purpose will inculcate a **devotion** in you, which is a necessary mental condition of the seeker to sustain him on the path of spirituality. This devotion in the bosom of the seeker brings his mind to the required **meditative state of mind,** which helps him to remain focused with **single-pointed concentration and devotion**. Thereafter, what seemed treacherous in the beginning, by itself becomes a pleasant prospect and experience.

Myth 8: Walking the Path of Spirituality is not an option for the one who has lived a materialistic life or a life of a criminal or the one who has no knowledge in this area.

Most of those, who choose to walk the path of spirituality, have been materialistic in their outlook and have been suffering its natural consequences thereof, that is, the Negative Affectivity. Owing to varied circumstances of each individual, some choose it earlier in their lives, others incline towards it later in their lives and most never consider it. The issue is not as much about at what age in life one takes the path of

Spirituality, but more so about when one is blessed with the intensity of desire to liberate oneself from the shackles of miseries and pain. However, there is no compulsion or dictate issued by Vedanta to follow this path.

'मोक्षस्य कांक्षा यदि वै तवास्ति' (Vivekachudamani verse 82): This part of the verse is extremely potent and significant in response to this question as it indicates at the very democratic, and liberal nature of Sanatan tradition of Vedanta. There is a complete freedom and independence of choice. Only voluntary admission is permitted. Therefore, Adi Sankaracharya says through these words that this path is for you (only) if you indeed have a craving for Liberation from the miseries of life and when all your efforts in trying to be happy are redundant and nothing seems to work, and if you are desperate or keen enough to seek lasting happiness, only then you are invited to seek refuge in Spirituality. Otherwise, life is going on towards the doom's day anyway.

All prescriptions, advice, methods, modalities, techniques, and technologies are made available for only those who are willing and determined to walk the talk to redeem themselves from the Negative Affectivity of life.

It doesn't really matter what kind of animalistic life one might have lived before choosing the path. It doesn't really matter even if one has had a criminal life full of a demonic mind, behavior, and actions. It doesn't really matter what all kinds of **'Paap'** one might have committed in the past. The redemption from the miserable life is guaranteed to all those who have committed themselves to make a sustained effort over a period of time. Our literature is full of various examples and stories of those individuals who lived sensuous and materialistic lives but were redeemed eventually. The best example or an encouraging story, which most of us know, in this context, is that of the dacoit Ratnakar, who was not only just redeemed of his miseries but reached to the glorious heights of Self-evolution and Self-realization. To the extent that he gained the fame of Adikavi who was blessed to have written the epic poem called Ramayana and is famously known as Maharishi Valmiki.

The best answer to this myth has already been provided in an earlier section entitled '**Have you counted your Graces in Life.**' It is worth reiterating and repeating some extracts from that section here.

The call of Spirituality is not a cry of pessimistic despair; it is the call of hope, urging man to wake up and act, to grow and achieve the highest gain. One who feels charmed by the call of Vedanta, who can appreciate its arguments, who feels a sympathetic understanding of the ideal indicated, is indeed at the fag-end of his transmigration, the product of an entire evolutionary past. If he makes use of his present chance with diligent and careful application, success is guaranteed to him by Vedanta. This is a call to man to throw off his lethargy, his dejections, his sentiments of Self-pity and wake up to face life and through understanding, grow fast to reach the goal divine–here and now.

Adi Sankaracharya has told us that the Human birth, necessary qualifications and the importance of the qualities one must have for a vital and positive living which one can grow in one's inner evolution with sincere Self-effort. However, **to be born as a human being is a sign of Lord's grace.** After this, to employ in life a deep discriminative understanding and to perceive the ultimate futility of all the ordinary mundane pursuits of life and thereby discover an enthusiasm to seek a nobler path of Self-redemption is rarer grace still.

Having been born in a human form and possessed of the necessary masculine qualities of head and heart, when such an individual has not the enthusiasm to walk the sacred path and reach the divine goal of Self-perfection, such an individual, alas, commits suicide. Having got such a rare chance in a million, is he not indeed, committing hara-kiri and such a squanderer of human birth is very fittingly termed by Sankaracharya as a **dull fool (Mudhadhih मूढधीः).**

How does a person commit this senseless suicide? Shankaracharya is referring to man's mindless chase and running after the objects in the world outside to satisfy the sensual urge of his body and his mind, the intellect. Necessarily, such a deluded person, having misunderstood his real nature, becomes a victim of his own ignorance. This fall of the supreme Self to be the selfish Ego is spiritual suicide.

There is no real suicide possible for the Atman. So, from the standpoint of Reality, there is no suicide; but Adi Sankaracharya comes down to our level to help us discriminate between the Real and the unreal, in and through our day-to-day life and it is in this sense that he says that we commit suicide. It is not the destiny of the Self to suffer but it is a lot of the ego, the Ego that strives in this world to be the sacred and the divine.

So, there is plenty of encouragement for anyone, irrespective of their past, to commence the journey at any point in time in their life. It is never too late. Lord Krishna, in verse 72 at the end of chapter two of Holy Gita did say to Arjuna, स्थित्वास्यामन्तकालेऽपि ब्रह्मनिर्वाणमृच्छति, which means that the Self Realization experience need not occur in a person's formative years. It is sufficient to attain this Brahmic-State, as stated in the Vedantic literature, even in old age, nay, even in the final moments of this life, if a seeker can come to experience, even for a moment, this egoless state of tranquilly and poise, even a passing glimpse of the Selfhood.

3. How does one prepare oneself for the Path of Spiritual Development?

"The only way of finding the limits of the possible is by going beyond them into the impossible," says Sir Arthur C. Clarke.

By now it should be evidently clear that what seemed like a **No-Go area** for most people, what might have felt like a **'Pie in the Sky'** idea, spirituality, and Self-realization, in fact and in reality, is nothing like it.

It is impossible for only those who think it is impossible. For all others who are willing to go beyond the limits of possibilities, they end up venturing into the impossible.

It has already been convincingly demonstrated in this chapter that you already have the seeds of the secret ingredients in you. You have used it hundreds of times already in your life. But most people, including you, are not aware of these inner strengths. Even if you have some idea about it, you may not be aware of the techniques of invoking these powers within. One of the minor objectives of spirituality and spiritual practices is to gain mastery over the invocation techniques, so that you can summon these at any moment in your life.

All you need to do is to ignite the fire of **burning desire for liberation and Self-realization**. Rest is taken care of. However, while the skills, psychological and mental temperament required both for realization of material things and Self-realization remain the same, the Self and the Supreme Self, being the subtle entities, beyond the grasp of our organs of knowledge and perception, it does present an additional psychological and cognitive challenge to a man who has known nothing except his body, mind, and intellect. For him his only identity is what he has known and perceived through his senses. All his awareness and the knowledge of the world around him comes through the only equipment he knows, that is, his BMI.

Spirituality is a science of life which helps an inquisitive student to learn the techniques, the technology of knowing his Reality, his Real Identity and help him realize it. There is plenty of literature available in various languages. You will undoubtedly need the guidance of Self-realized masters though. This should, however, not be a show stopper for you. You do not need to worry about finding a Guru or wait for a Guru to initiate and induct you into the journey. The Guru will show up when you are ready for his guidance. The flower bud neither needs to worry about nor wander around in search of a butterfly, all that bud needs to do is to slowly and naturally blossom and open up into a flower and let its fragrance be released in the atmosphere. The fragrance of the flower will naturally attract the butterfly to pollinate and mature the flower into a fruit.

In the same way, when the fragrance of your inquisitiveness, passion, faith, and conviction rises up in your bosom, the Guru will show up. A Guru doesn't necessarily have to be a person in flesh and blood, it doesn't have to be a person alive today, it could be a book in the form of a translation or commentaries (भाष्य) on spiritual literature. Some suggestions may include, for example, translations or commentaries on Upanishads (उपनिषद्), Gita (गीता), Brahma Sutra (ब्रह्मसूत्र), Vivekachudamani (विवेकचूडामणि), Tattva Bodha (तत्वबोध), or Atma Bodh (आत्मबोध) etc., or a video recorded discourses by masters or in any other form. For sure, you don't have to go on a Guru hunting spree. A Self-realized Guru, no doubt is a most definite requisite in the path of Self-realization, but certainly not a prerequisite to start the journey.

Begin with acquainting yourself with the spiritual literature. As you begin to read upon the spiritual literature and as your knowledge grows to capture the value and the importance of Self-realization (ज्ञान, बहुमूल्यता, एवं महत्व), you will experience a clarity of vision and the faith (श्रद्धा) in Supreme Reality and the process of Self-realization. With increasing clarity in your mind, you will begin to develop a discriminative intellect (विवेक बुद्धि), which will help you to differentiate between the Real[16] and unreal, fleeting, and permanent, which is referred to as '**Nitya and Anitya Vivek**' in Sanskrit.

As you continue your focus on the higher spiritual values of life, you will find that you are developing a dispassion for the lower tendencies and

---

[16] *The word 'REAL' in spiritual literature refers to an entity which remains unchanged, unmodified, unaltered, neither has a beginning nor has an end, it remains as is during all times, past present and future. It remains unaffected by time and space. Therefore, the Supreme Self, Supreme Reality, the God, or Branham is the only reality, and everything else that is subject to our senses and perception are unreal.*

aspects in your personality, e.g., your negative and limiting thoughts, bad habits, addictive habits etc., which you consider are either unhelpful or only good for fleeting joys and pleasures. Slowly and gradually, you will begin to question your likes and dislikes, and be mindful of your thoughts, whether these are helpful or harmful. This kind of daily, constant, and forever (नित्य, निरन्तरम्, चिरम्) habit of reflecting over your thoughts in all waking moments is called **Mindful Meditation**, which one does with their eyes open. You will begin to negotiate and drop what you consider unhelpful and harmful things and thoughts one after another effortlessly. Growing awareness and realization that the sense objects, no doubt, make life comfortable, nonetheless, aren't the source of the real and lasting happiness, will result in a drop of your temptations for and clinging attachments with the sense objects (वैराग्य).

With each small success, your dedication, commitment, and devotion (निष्ठा, प्रतिबद्धता, वचनबद्धता एवं भक्ति) will strengthen. This will give you additional supply of enthusiasm and energy (उत्साह, व्यग्रता एवं ऊर्जा) to further your experimentation with attachment with things and beings. Your hopeful patience and perseverance, (धैर्य एवं दृढ संकल्प) will strengthen your resolve and keep you well directed and determined on your path. Consolidation of your conviction in the fleeting nature of sense objects in your mind, will, consequently, strengthen your dispassion for them. You will gain direct and personal experience and realization of the fact that the lasting peace and happiness is not in these objects. Therefore, your compelling desires for and mindlessly relenting after them will begin to slow down. If you continue to withstand and forebear all challenges smilingly (तितिक्षा) in this manner with Self-effort (अनवरत प्रयास), your mind will begin to experience a decline in the agitations in your mind caused by the relentless pursuit to acquire and preserve the sense objects. This results in a level-headedness and calmness of mind (आत्मसंवरण एवं प्रशान्ति). This tranquility of mind is the real treasure, a propitiatory gift (Prasaad - प्रसाद), which indeed is the precondition for the seeker of spirituality.

Only a mind which is calm and free from agitations, is capable of being in the state of meditation. Thus, you become qualified for spiritual practice.

As you get better at bringing your mind to a sustained tranquility and calmness, one begins to experience equanimity and equipoise. Thereafter, beautiful, and ugly, pleasant, and unpleasant, good, and bad will all be redundant for you. **All these binaries are the experiences of our body, mind, and intellect and not yours**. Such statements are really confusing, and I am sure a lot of my readers must be thinking as to how the experiences of our body, mind, and intellect are not ours?

We will try to understand that these are not the experiences of the Reality or the Self within me but the delusion or perception of reality. How is it possible? We will try to understand the dynamics of relationship between the Self and my equipment of experiences in the next section in more detail.

12

The Inner Equipment Of Experience

Spirituality and religion are the science of life, which attempt to bring about a transformation in our subjective inner lives. It teaches us the subjective dimension of our inner personality to help us master ourselves, to forge an unflinching tranquility, and to live an inspired life full of joys, irrespective of our outer circumstances. This is the intention and the core theme of all the scriptures of the world, and the spiritual practices as prescribed in Sanatan traditions.

With this purpose in mind, our Subjective Scientists examined life. They realized that life is a continuum of our moment-to-moment experiences. These experiences must necessarily be accepted as the units of life, just as each brick is a unit of a wall. The strength or weakness of a wall depends upon the quality and texture of the bricks that it is made up of. Similarly, the types and the kinds of experiences we have in life determine the nature of our life.

Equipment of Experience

Our experiences are a result of a transection of receiving and responding to a stimulus from the external world. The three fundamental factors, which constitute an experience must include:

1. An experiencer (the subject).

2. An object of experience (the object).

3. The connection between the two (the experiencing).

These three things are necessary constituents for an experience to occur, without which an experience cannot take place. Let us now consider a situation in our day-to-day life and examine how we gain experience.

"Karan (subject) receives an email message (object) containing the news of his grandmother's death, but he does not look at the content of the email. In this scenario, although the subject and the object are both present there, yet no experience of sorrow takes place since the subject and the object have not come in contact with each other. As soon as he reads the email, the subject and the object are now connected by his reading, thus becoming the connecting tie to complete the experience."

The body, the mind, and the intellect are the instruments of experience, through which the experiencer (subject) gains experience of the world outside. These are the same instruments available to us all to gain experiences of three different worlds through three different kinds of equipment:

1. We experience the world of objects, things, and beings through our body (senses).

2. We experience the world of emotions through our mind.

3. We experience the world of ideas and thoughts through our intellect.

If Karan can experience the world of objects through his body, the world of emotions through his mind and the world of ideas and thoughts through his intellect, then he must be different from his body, mind, and intellect. He must, therefore, be an entity different from these three instruments of experiences, though he has a very intimate relationship with these instruments. Karan becomes **a perceiver** of objects when he identifies with his body; Karan becomes **the feeler** of the emotions, when he identifies with his mind and when he identifies with his intellect, he is **a thinker** of his thoughts. However, Karan, the subject, is neither the field of experience, that is, the objects, emotions, and the thoughts

(OET) nor the equipment of experience (BMI). In short, if Karan is neither the OET, nor is he the BMI, he must be someone or something other than these two and an entity totally different from these.

So, who is the perceiver, feeler, and thinker in Karan? If you are asking such a question and if your thinking is pricking you with perplexity, you must congratulate yourself as you are becoming inquisitive to know about the very subject of study in spiritual science of life, which is the very subject of investigation in the spiritual literature.

The Self and the Supreme Self

The Life Principle by whose mere presence the intellect thinks, the mind feels, and the body perceives is the Supreme Reality (Brahman), the substratum for all experiences of the body, mind, and the intellect. This principle that lends its power, energy, or light, so to speak, to every being, according to Vedanta, the divine principle, AUM–also known as the Self (Atman), pure consciousness, or pure awareness. That by which Karan, you and I gain our experiences is one and the same everywhere.

In our day-to-day conversation, we all, every now and then, use various terms with reference to all pervading Supreme Reality. A few of us also have a good enough intellectual understanding of a few of these terms to hold a decent conversation and every now and then to win the arguments too. However, do you really understand the term 'Supreme Reality' or 'Supreme Self' with its various synonyms? Let's try to understand this concept from the following example from our Objective Knowledge.

Electricity runs through various electrical equipment and expresses itself differently in different equipment. Through a light bulb, it expresses itself as light, which illuminates your room; through a heater it produces heat to keep you warm; through a radio it expresses itself as sound and music; and through a fan it produces air and keeps you cool in the summer months. It is the same electricity everywhere, at all times. The heater, the bulb, the radio, and the fan are all different types of equipment, but they are able to function only because of one vitality alone–the electricity.

The Divine Principle, when it expresses itself through varied instruments of body, the mind, and the intellect is one yet manifests itself as many. Through the eyes it manifests as shapes and colors, with your ears as sounds, with your nose as smell, with your tongue as taste, and through your skin as touches and associated sensations. With your mind as feelings and emotions and with your intellect as your ideas and thoughts. One Conscious Principle is that holds the varied objects together in this universe, like a string which holds all the different flowers of various shapes and colors to form a beautiful garland. In the same way, the plant kingdom, animal kingdom and the human kingdoms–all are vitalised by this one Conscious Principle, facilitating all of them to gain their own unique experiences. Therefore, we can say that the Divine Principle in me is the very cause for my body, the mind, and intellect to function.

This Divine Principle is covered by a matter envelopment, which is constituted of the body, the mind and intellect. The mind and the intellect are the subtler forms of matter. BMI is inert and insentient, which has no power, whatsoever, to function on its own. The divine principle (the Self, the Spirit) is what enlivens and causes the equipment to function. In the same way, the Divine Principle, without the BMI equipment, cannot express itself on its own. It needs BMI equipment to express itself through. Therefore, it is the union of the two–the Spirit (Purusa) with matter (Prakriti)–that allows the manifestation of life as birth, activity, growth, decay, and death.

An electric bulb, by itself, cannot produce light. Electricity, by itself, has no way to express its power to produce light. Only when electricity is connected to a light bulb, electricity is able to express itself as light.

Similarly, the BMI equipment is inert. The Pure Self, by itself, has no expression. When the Pure Self pulsates through the BMI, the pure

Self manifests as Life. Pure consciousness, the Self, is the changeless substratum upon which all changes take place. The perceptions by the body are constantly changing. So are the emotions of the mind and the thoughts by the intellect. The reason we are able to notice these changes in our equipment and recognise these changes only because of the changeless entity, called the Pure Self or the Supreme Self. To understand the changeless, immutable, unmodifiable and the permanent nature of the Self, let us consider another example from our objective experiences.

Let's think about two people who are sitting in a closed compartment of a moving train. The first observation in this example is (1) they do not observe any change or movement with respect to each other, though in reality both of them are moving. However, when they look out the window, then they notice the movement of the train with reference to the stationary objects along the track. And the second observation is (2) so long as they are in the compartment of the moving train, they are experiencing all the effects e.g., jerks, shocks, and movements etc., generated by the movement of the train. However, if they stand outside of the compartment on the platform, none of the effects produced by the moving train will be experienced by them, while the train is still creating these effects.

Our ability to recognise the changes occurring in us, establishes the existence of a changeless entity, upon which these changes are taking place. This changeless entity is the Supreme Self. Based on the above description so far, we can conclude the nature of the Self as follow:

- The Self, by itself, is not able to express itself.

- The Self is the vitality Principle that invigorates matter.

- The Self is something different from the body, the mind, and the intellect.

- Because of the changeless Reality, the Self, we are able to recognise the changes occurring at our intellectual, mental, and physical levels.

Let's reflect on our own life span to help us to comprehend this concept that changes can only be experienced if there is substratum upon which these changes are taking place. For example, you can only see fast-moving images in a movie as a continuum only if there is a screen upon which the movie is being projected, without which you can't see the movement of images. When we review the changes in our body since our birth to the present day, we will have no difficulty, whatsoever, to remember clearly all the changes that our body has been going through. You might have a vague memory of yourself as a toddler, rather clearer memories when your body grew up into a boy or a girl, comparatively sharper memories of when you matured into a young person, thereafter into an adult person and so on and so forth until your present day.

Now the question for you to ponder over is, who is that person in you, who has been silently witnessing all these changes and growth in your body? Who is that witness who witnessed your childhood and your youth in the past and who is still witnessing you in the present? That silent witness in you and me has been identified by our Subjective Scientists as the Self in you and, which is the same Supreme Self outside of us.

Sometimes it could be confusing when you come across a variety of similar terms in spiritual literature, but various pronouns are used to refer to this Changeless Reality. These names are listed below, which are used throughout spiritual literature. You will come across many of these varied names used throughout this book too:

- Absolute

- Atman (Individual Self) the immanent aspect of Brahman (microcosmic)

- Aum

- Brahman (Supreme Self) in its transcendent aspect (macrocosmic)

- Consciousness Principle

- Life Principle

- Pure Awareness

- Pure Consciousness

- Pure Self

- Satchidananda (सच्विदानंद)

- Self (Atman)

- Spirit

- Supreme Reality

- Supreme Self (Brahman)

- The Truth

Locus of Happiness

Sat-cit-ananda (सच्विदानंद), is a Sanskrit conjunctive term used to describe the Supreme Reality which means **'existence-knowledge-bliss.'** SAT (सत्-Real) is that which doesn't not go through change or modification in all the three periods of time; that is, in the past, the present and the future.

SAT can be explained through an analogy relating the reality of mud to the reality of the pot made of mud. The SAT aspect of the mud pot is mud which existed before the mud pot was created, which exists now in the form of a pot, and which will remain after the pot is destroyed. In the same way, gold is the SAT aspect of all gold jewelry. Like the mud pot and the gold jewelry, all perishable things are made from a fundamental and permanent substance.

In the same way, the Brahman, the supreme Reality, is the fundamental substance of which the perishable world is made out of. This Supreme Reality was, is, and will remain whether or not the world exists. From the standpoint of existence and non-existence, the SAT is nothing but Brahman, a beginningless and endless existence at all times, which has never been non-existent.

CIT (चित्) refers to the pure Awareness or Consciousness. Now that we know that Brahman is ever existent (SAT), we must ask if Brahman is sentient or insentient. The word CIT reveals the aspect of Brahman, which, indeed, is Consciousness or Awareness itself. This consciousness exists in all states of experiences–waking, dreaming, and deep sleeping–illuminating everything that we experience. When we are not conscious of anything in our deep sleep, it even illuminates **'Nothing.'**

Having concluded that Brahman is existence (SAT) and Consciousness (CIT), we must still ask if this ever-existing Consciousness Principle is of the nature of happiness or sorrow. In response to such a question, the word ananda reveals the nature of Brahman, which, indeed, is bliss, fullness, and joy. **Anand, or bliss (आनन्द)**, is the experience gained when we are detached from BMI and are with our own Real Self as in deep sleep.

For example, when our desire for an object is fulfilled, the fleeting joy and happiness is that of being with our own Real Self. At that moment of desire fulfillment, we are totally satisfied with ourselves. At that moment, we do not want to be something else or have something else. Such a state of mind then experienced is called ananda, the fundamental nature of all beings.

We may think and believe that the fleeting joy and happiness experienced for the short while is produced by the object, but the object is only an instrument, which by itself, does not have the faculty of happiness or sorrow. However, the same object might have different appeals to different people or different appeal to the same person at different times.

For example, let's say you like a particular sweetmeat or a chocolate, which gives you a lot of pleasure every time. However, you might know someone else who doesn't like it at all. Secondly, while one or two pieces of sweetmeat can give you enormous joy and pleasure, the same sweetmeat, if consumed in a large quantity, could be a source of pain and suffering. We may start hating someone, whom we used to love immensely or the other way round. Evidently, it is quite obvious that **the locus of happiness or sorrow is not in the object.**

Rather, the locus of happiness is in ourselves, while in our mindless pursuits we keep on chasing the objects of desires to find happiness in them. Any external search, no matter how far and wide, for the sense objects is indeed a futile exercise and would only take us further away from the locus of happiness, that is ourselves. We need not be searching for happiness outside ourselves, we only need to realize our true nature, which is existence-knowledge-bliss.

Good and bad are the conceptual judgments of our intellect, pleasure and pain are our mental evaluations, and sweet and sour are the perceptions of our body. But when we are one with the Self, which lends life to all these equipment, we are not tainted by any of the experiences gained by these equipment. Established in the Self, one experiences the divinity that is present everywhere and at all times, one without a second.

The above analysis helps us to understand how our BMI creates experiences in us and how we experience the world around us. Only with a little intellectual reflection and analysis, we would not have much difficulty to understand that the locus of happiness is not in the objects but within our own Self. However, what is the mechanism within us which taints our experiences into a binary, which eventually becomes the cause of disquiet and constant agitation of the mind.

This hidden cause, which we fail to comprehend with the equipment of perception, is our **wrong evaluation of things and situations**. We generally evaluate all our situations in life in a binary fashion as discussed above. For example, win and lose, victory and defeat, profit and loss, or good and bad, pleasant, and unpleasant etc., are the binaries in which we evaluate all our experiences in life. Consequently, positive evaluation has Positive Affectivity and negative evaluation has Negative Affectivity. Sometimes we win and on other times we lose, sometimes we gain, sometimes we suffer loss. You can't win all the time as you can't lose all the time. Such is life. When Negative Affectivity increases in life, it feels like hell and when Positive Affectivity rises in life, we experience heaven.

However, we find ourselves in a constant commingle. We are constantly in fraught to win, gain, and have pleasant experiences, while pantingly trying to avert losses, dislikes, and unpleasant experiences. When things around me are happening as expected, I feel happy, if not then I am unhappy. Through this perpetual exertion, I have been tossed around, thrown up and down, I am hitting one rock after another like a boat in the sea without a helmsman and the mast. This is how each individual experiences life and writes their own autobiography.

Subtleties of Experience

No one would like or want to be trapped in life's conundrum and its capricious nature. Unfortunately, most of us are already there, like a share market stock graph goes up and down all the time. An intelligent man of perfection, however, would not like to have a whimsical life of uncertainty and constant fluctuation and change with no control over them. We have discussed in previous sections, as to how our experiences are created, which could be summarized and presented as an equation below.

Experience = Subject (Self) + BMI + Object

The world of objects, when comes in contact with our senses, plays out its follies owing to an unknown law, which we have little or no control over. However, we do have control over our reactions to our experiences. When our mind comes in contact with the objects observed, only then there could be any reaction created in our mind. Therefore, what is required of one is to train their mind to either stay away from or not to run after every object observed. Secondly, if we can train our mind so that it can produce positive reactions to any object observed under any circumstances, all our reactions will be positive. As already stated above, positive evaluation of the objects observed will have a Positive Affectivity, in the same way negative evaluation has Negative Affectivity. If we can train our mind to produce positive effects on the outer world of objects at all times, we will have a sustained happiness and peace in our experience. **Such a trained, poised, and balanced mind is capable of maintaining happiness irrespective of outer circumstances.** Even if outer circumstances are full of imperfections and sorrows, we would still be able to experience happiness and contentment.

What we need to understand, however, is how our experiences are converted into binary. What, in us, causes it to be tainted in binary fashion. It seems that we generally do not have much control over our reactions and responses to the situations we encounter daily in our lives. Our reactions and responses happen so swiftly and quickly in a fraction of a second, consequently the process feels automated and natural. This unknown cause within us determines the way we react and respond to things, beings, and situations. This unknown cause determines the way we behave in the world outside, the choices we make, our preferences, what we like or dislike etc. How we act in the world outside all seems natural. Over a period of time, these behavioral traits get consolidated in our mind as our personality. This evaluative judgment of my personality created by the BMI is called the Self-esteem. The Self-esteem experienced in the mind's eye is my Self-image i.e., Who, I believe, I am and What, I believe, my nature is like.

We never see, recognise, and experience the world *as it is*, but only as our mind and intellect interprets it. This happens due to an unknown factor called **mental filter** in psychology and which is referred to as **Vasana** in spiritual literature. However, there is a slight difference between the two. Mental filters are like coloured shades on my eyes, when installed, it not only changes the way how I perceive a thing thereafter but makes me selective in my perception too.

For example, let's say I hold a view that black cat crossing the road or if someone called you from behind when you were leaving the house is a bad omen. Not only will I be increasingly attentive to such happenings, but I will be selective to notice particularly corresponding negative experiences (bad Omen-अपशकुन) to confirm MY view. However, the fact of the matter is that in life the situations are happening at all times, which we evaluate and feel good at times and bad on others. The situations, things, and beings, which are in line with my expectations (अनुकूल), are experienced as good, comforting, and pleasant and the ones which are contrary to my expectations (प्रतिकूल) are experienced as bad, discomforting, and unpleasant. My filter, however, makes me notice only corresponding good or bad things and makes me filter out the rest. Over a period of time, such a filtered view is consolidated as a fact in my mind and becomes 'a belief.' Now I am convinced in my mind that something bad will happen if I see a black cat crossing the road or I will have negative results if someone calls me from behind when leaving home.

All my subsequent thoughts, behaviors, actions, reactions, and responses to the external stimuli are eventually channelised in this fashion and are coloured by such beliefs. The channelised fashion of thinking and behaving is called a **tendency.** This tendency in me is referred to as a **Vasana** in spiritual literature. These vasanas are like the dirt on the reflecting surface of the mirror of my mind, which reflects a distorted version of myself. My Self-esteem and the Self-image is nothing but a distorted version of my real Self, which is constructed from the bricks of these vasanas. Therefore, it can be concluded conclusively that most of us, at best, except those who are Self-realized, are the owners of a Distorted and Low-Self-Esteem. All our experiences, good, bad, or ugly, are conditioned by our Self-esteem. So, it should not be very difficult for us to understand when our scriptures assert that we do not see the world as it is. And consequently, I suffer its corresponding binary impact in the form of joy and agony, profit and loss, victory and defeat, respect, and insult and in its many permutations and combinations.

Let us now consider an example, which can help us to analyze, interpret and understand most of our day-to-day experiences based on the above theory.

You are a hard-working person, and you work 40-50 hours a week, 365 days of the year to earn your livelihood and to make your ends meet to support your family. Every now and then you also take up a few private assignments on the side to supplement your income. One day you saw the glimpse of the tail of a snake going under your bed. You are convinced that you have seen a snake under your bed in the bedroom. You know for sure it is there. From this point on, the most sensible thing for you would be to avoid the use of the bedroom, otherwise you run the risk of being bitten and dying. In such a situation, if an offer of one crore rupees is made to you in return for spending a night in the bedroom, would you accept the offer? Of course not! No amount of enticement can convince you to enter the bedroom, let alone spending a night there. While you toil all year round to earn perhaps just 10-20% of that money. God presented a situation for you to become rich and you are refusing it. Amazing, isn't it? But why do you do it? Because you are convinced and frightened that if you slept in the room, you will not be around the next morning to receive the bounty. The **fear of the snake** stops you risking your life. So long as the snake lives there, you will not enter the room. Would you?

Having so suffered over a number of days, weeks and months and almost permanently losing the use of a room in your house, one day you decide to invite an expert snake charmer to investigate the matter. Snake charmer goes in the room, looks under the bed and pulls out the snake on his fingers and shows it to you. It was, in fact, a rope that you mistook for a snake.

The moment you apprehend the rope, the snake disappears forever, so do your fears and anxiety. Snake was never there, but it existed in your mind and so long as it did, it caused fear and anxiety in you. All your subsequent behaviors and actions were dictated by the fear of snakes.

In the same way, all our perceptions of the world and the associated binary experiences, that we gain through our body, mind, and intellect, appear real to us, and cause all the miseries in our life. My evaluative assessment of myself, therefore, as a limited being, a mortal being, a being conditioned by my body, mind and intellect seems a reality to me. The body, mind and the intellect are the only means of my introduction that I know and have about myself. This perceived notion that I have of myself is, in fact, a distorted version of my real personality, my Real Self. However, since I do not know anything other than my distorted view, I am totally oblivious to my real personality, my Real Self. I do not have the foggiest idea that my real personality attributes are Purity, Perfection, and Completeness; a personality beyond modification and change in all periods of time, it is birthless, changeless, growthless, decay, deathless and beyond all mortal experiences. It cannot be altered, destroyed, or affected by anything. My real personality is such which doesn't get affected by joy and agony, pleasure and pain, profit and loss, victory and defeat, respect, and insult and in its many permutations and combinations. The moment we apprehend our real personality and the Real Self, all our miseries in life will disappear. The same way, as the snake and all its associated fears and anxieties disappear, upon apprehension of the rope.

Spirituality is necessarily a science of life which helps us to understand this distortion and delusion caused by our own senses, mind, and intellect, and helps us to demystify our delusion and recognise, apprehend and realize our real personality. **Recognising our own real personality and the Real Self is the only answer for all our miseries and to make our life happy, pleasant, and joyful, free from anger, fear, and guilt.** With Spiritual Sadhana, when one realizes his own real personality and their Real Self, and as one absorbs this view in their bosom and the idea of the new found reality gets ingrained in their personality, the real and immortal nature of peace, love and happiness blossom forth effortlessly and remains this way forever.

So, I must ask myself this question. Despite all my achievements, successes, fame, and wealth, that I have accumulated, am I satisfied with a life full of misery and Negative Affectivity? A life infested with the experiences of negative emotions and poor Self-concept riddled with negative emotions, including anger, contempt, disgust, dishonesty, fear, greed, guilt, jealousy, lust, nervousness, and many more in its variety and combinations. There couldn't be any doubt in any sane mind that the answer to this question could ever be a **'Yes.'** Moreover, the fact is that all creatures on earth, even a creature as small as a worm, does strive for happiness through all their efforts, let alone humans.

All our efforts, throughout life, are directed at and motivated by being happy. All our choices, preferences, likes and dislikes and actions, are invariably motivated by and aimed at being happy eventually. Spirituality, religion, and prescribed rituals, therein, are fundamentally designed to help the individual to achieve this very core demand.

In our materialistic life, however, we are constantly pouring all our mental energies into seeking sense pleasures and remain embroiled in satisfying one desire after another and hoping for a permanent happiness. How is it possible to have a permanent solution from temporary means? All it takes for the seeker of permanent happiness is to withdraw their attention from the world of sense objects and turn their attention onto their inner world of the real Self.

विषमविषयमार्गैगच्छेतोऽनच्छबुद्धेः

प्रतिपदमभियातो मृत्युरप्येष विद्धि ।

हितसुजनगुरूक्त्या गच्छतः स्वस्य युक्त्या

प्रभवति फलसिद्धिः सत्यमित्येव विद्धि ॥८१॥

Know that mortality soon overtakes a foolish man who walks the dangerous path of sense pleasures. Whereas one who sticks to the path of divinity, according to the instructions of a well-meaning and noble Guru, constantly walks the path-divine helped by one's own reasoning faculty, one achieves the end; know for certain this is true.

Vivekachudamani ||81||

In Vedanta, **meditation is the technique for gaining the final experience of Self-discovery**, but meditation can be successful only when the mind is not agitated by desires. In a sensuous life, one is never without some desire or the other. Thus, an individual cannot have success, both in the life of meditation and in the world of sensuousness. If one is fatigued after a long walk, one cannot recoup if one continues walking. A diabetic cannot bring his sugar level down, even by taking saline injection and metformin daily, if he is continuously consuming sugar.

The human mind is disintegrated because of its desires, and it cannot be brought back to its healthy integration without renouncing the very germs of its present disease. So, in Vedanta, great emphasis has been placed upon the necessity of avoiding the mind's running amok with its uncontrolled appetites. This idea is explained again in a very powerful style by Adi Sankaracharya, who crisply repeats what the Rishis have been continuously saying in the pages of the scriptures that the path of sensuousness leads straight to mortality while the path of divine leads to immortality[17] (मृत्युरप्येष विद्धि). Physiology also, in

---

[17] *Immortality in scriptural language, in contrast to its conventional understanding, refers to a state of being of a sincere yogi, who has come to Self-realization and identifies himself with the Self-effulgent Brahman (the Supreme Self), which is of the nature of Sanatan (Ancient), Adi (Beginningless), Anant (Endless), Nirvikaar (Unmodifiable), Imperishable (Undying), Ajanma (Unborn), Akshar (indestructible) etc. The one who is thus realized neither fears nor grieves over the mortality (Death) of the material dimension of life e.g., the Body, Mind, and Intellect.*

a much more limited sense of the word, declares that overindulgence impoverishes our vitality, bringing the physical structure to doom and death. In Vedanta, however, the term 'Death' connotes not only the condition of the body when life has ebbed out from it but includes the very principle of change and finitude.

Thus, sensuous activities with motives of pleasure and indulgence hardens the animal impressions in our minds and thereafter, thoughts begin to flow in that direction more and more powerfully. Such a stupid man becomes increasingly daring in his criminalities, until at last, he becomes irredeemable and slips down the ladder of evolution to be ultimately destroyed. On the other hand, the way up the evolutionary ladder is also open to man by climbing which he can slowly ascend to the very pinnacles of total fulfillment. This path has been beautifully described in the third line of the verse above 'हितसुजनगुरूक्तया गच्छत: स्वस्य युक्त्या,' which insists that he must follow the instructions given by reliable guides, the Gurus, on the path of Spirituality.

The Gurus must be well-meaning and worthy and not a mere gramophone record repeating what the shastras say but must be the men so well-established in their own experiences and so familiar with the path, that they can interpret it to different types of students belonging to different times and of different ages.

A student who has turned away from the tragic path of sensuousness and has stepped on to the glorious highway of the Divine, who is prepared to go forward under the guidance of a true teacher, with nothing but his independent discriminative reasoning to supply him with mental agility and strength, will surely reach his goal. In order to prove the vitality of these declarations, the last line of the verse ends with a powerful rejoinder, an emphatic assertion, '**Know this to be True** (सत्यमित्येव विद्धि).'

मोक्षस्य कांक्षा यदि वै तवास्ति त्यदातिदूराद्विषयान्निवषं यथा ।
पीयूषवत्तोषदयाक्षमाजर्वप्रशान्तिदान्तीर्भज नित्यमादरात् ॥८२॥

> *"If you have, indeed, a craving for Liberation, avoid sense objects from a distance, just as you avoid things known to be poisonous; and with respectful reverence, daily cultivate the nectarine virtues—contentment, forgiveness, straightforwardness, calmness and self-control."*
>
> Vivekachudamani ||82||

The overall purpose and objective of spiritual study and learning for a sincere seeker is thus to end their misunderstandings and sorrows in life. Therefore, Adi Sankaracharya in this verse is encouraging them for the development of noble qualities of head and heart which is yet another adjustment to be made by a student before a guaranteed success in Self-realization is assured to him. Having known a thing to be poisonous (पीयूषवत्), however thirsty you may be, you will not be tempted to drink it; so too, however tempting the sense object may look, an individual who seeks Liberation should totally renounce the idea that these objects contain even a trace of potency to supply happiness.

By withdrawing the sense organs from their respective fields of activities, we conserve a tremendous amount of mental energy which would otherwise be wasted. If this new found energy is not immediately harnessed to do special work, the chances are that we will spend this dynamism in mentally dreaming of sense indulgence. This brings about an ugly deformity in our personality. To remain physically inert but mentally sensuous develops a distorted personality, drained of all brilliance and beauty through suppressed desires and unseen mental dissipations. It is to avoid such dangerous consequences on the mental plane that we should have the guidance of the Teacher. Fresh fields have been discovered where the energy so conserved could be used up to raise smiling crops of beauty and profit.

We are told how an individual who has learnt to shun sense objects must immediately take up the constructive scheme of developing the positive qualities such as, contentment (तृप्ति), compassion (दया), forgiveness (क्षमा), straightforwardness (सत्यता एवं स्पष्टवादिता), calmness

(प्रशान्त), and self-control (आत्म-संयम् एवं आत्मसंवरण). When we analyze them, we find that each one of these qualities is, in itself, an attitude of the mind which will not suffer even the least disturbance in itself. As we diligently practice them, necessarily we will seek and establish our identity with our fellow beings and enjoy the intimate brotherhood of man and the divine fraternity of the soul. Most importantly we will gain a tranquil and peaceful mind plentiful of mental energy, which will help us in all our achievements be it in our materialistic life or our spiritual development.

However, there is no compulsion or dictate issued by Vedanta to follow this path. '**मोक्षस्य कांक्षा यदि वै तवास्ति**': This part of the verse is extremely potent and significant as it indicates at the very secular, democratic, and liberal nature of Sanatan tradition of Vedanta. There is complete freedom and independence of choice. Only voluntary admission is permitted. Therefore, Adi Sankaracharya says through these words that this path is for you if (only) you indeed have a craving for Liberation from the miseries of life, and when all your efforts in trying to be happy are redundant and nothing seems to work, and if you are desperate or keen enough to seek lasting happiness, only then you are invited to seek refuge in Spirituality. Otherwise, life is going on towards the doom's day anyway.

All such young people, who seek refuge in spirituality, are guaranteed to have a dynamic personality and will carry an attitude for whom **"There is nothing they cannot do"** and a life full of Positive Affectivity.

13

Self-Realization
Why, what, and how?

1. **Why Self-realization?**

This is an intelligent question. Any intelligent person must have such a question arising in their mind whenever there is a prospect or an expectation on them. Even if it is my own expectation or wish to pursue anything in life, I must ask such a question to myself. Being inquisitive and thinking **'Why'** is a sign of a logical and scientific mind. When I do something without knowing its purpose, it may not necessarily harm me, yet, at best, it is an unintelligent action based on blind faith. It's like shooting in the dark, hoping and believing that you might hit the target. Most of us behave like this in our day-to-day life. However, there is a difference between shooting a target with skill and without the skill. When one gains the know-how, necessary skills, and the art of archery, one can shoot the bull's eye at any time only with one arrow at their disposal. Rest of us, even if given hundreds of arrows, do not have much chance of even hitting the outer rings of the target, let alone the bull's eye.

Hoping that you would have read the previous sections in this book, I have no doubt in my mind that by now you have a good enough idea about the Self, Supreme-Self and Self-realization etc, at least intellectually. Even though we understand various spiritual concepts intellectually, we remain bewildered about them. Here we will revisit this theme and try to understand it with the help of an analogical story from my last book entitled, 'Why Young People Run Away from Religion.' This story is about a person who seemingly lost his memory following an accident, thereby, totally forgot who he really was and assumed a new personality and lived a miserable life corresponding to his new personality thereafter, that he believed it to be his real personality.

"An old beggar used to sit outside a gold mine entrance for many years, begging for alms from the miners. He had created a little shed made out of a plastic sheet and had a couple of bundles and parcels of a few old and torn off clothes as his possessions. He was mostly seen covered with multiple layers of torn off rags irrespective of the weather conditions. He not only looked disheveled, dirty, filthy, and unkempt but smelt disgusting too. No one in the mine or surrounding area knew who he was and where he came from. It seemed he was there since always. He himself did not know who he was and where he came from. He didn't even know what his name was. Everybody referred to him as 'Baba.' Often miners would feed him and give him money and sweets on occasions and festivals. He was a permanent fixture there and part of the scenery.

He knew the timings of both morning and evening shifts of the miners. He would be active and alert at these times and would diligently beg to each and every miner going in and out of the mine without fail. On other times of the day, he would be lazy and lethargic and sleep through the shifts.

One day, there came a fleet of posh black cars. A group of affluent and cultured men in expensive suits and ladies in expensive sarees, wearing gold jewelry, got out of those cars. They went straight to the beggar, collected him, and drove away. These cars took the beggar to a huge mansion in an affluent and posh area in the city. He was given a grand, warm welcome with an aarti-thali at the porch of this huge mansion. Once inside, he was given a good shower, clean and luxurious garments to wear. He was brought down to the main hall and was made to sit on a 20 feet long and beautifully curated dining table. Treasured China, sparkling crystals, and polished silverwares were giving a majestic feel to the arrangements. The beggar was made to sit on the head of the table. A most luxurious five course meal was served to him which he devoured with both his hands.

The next day, the family brought in the best doctors and specialists to check on his health and gave him the best treatment. Men, women, and children of the family would sit around him all day and help him to remember and recall, but the old man would not respond to any trick, technique, or treatment. Rather he was seen to be uncomfortable in this new environment. He found the behavior of these men, women, and children a little strange. He was used to humiliation, shame, disgrace, and disrespect. Every day he would keep asking and pleading to the family members to take him back to the mine. Days and weeks passed but there was no improvement in his mental condition. The old beggar was becoming increasingly impatient, eager to go back to his old spot.

However, after a couple of months, the beggar resigned to his fate and eventually settled down in the new environment. One day, when the family was having their breakfast downstairs, they heard a call from the old man's room. The beggar was calling the eldest son of the family by his name. The family had given up all hopes that the old man would ever recover. Since they knew who he was, they couldn't give up on him. No one could believe their ears. Leaving their breakfast, everyone rushed to the old man's room upstairs. As soon as the family members entered his room, he recognised them all. The whole family was jubilant and within no time, there was a festive environment in the family.

The old man's memory had come back, and he remembered that he was the head of the family and the owner of the very gold mine, where he begged. He recognised each person in the family and his real identity. He realized that he was the owner of the gold mine. He owned all the gold that was there in the mine. He was not just the owner of the Gold that had been excavated to date but also of all that Gold that was yet to be excavated from the mine.

The moment the beggar realized his **Real Identity**, as a Gold Mine Owner, his identity that he had assumed as a **beggar** evaporated into thin air and consequently, his begging behavior, Self-pity, and all his miseries disappeared with it. He did not have to make any effort to dispel his miseries. He had come out of his painful life in an instant, just in the blink of an eye. Even he did not have to make any additional efforts to accept, assume, and fit into his original personality. Instantly, he began to behave like a filthy rich man as though he never was a beggar. So, a man, who was originally a Rich Man turned into a beggar and the same man who was a beggar for years becomes a Rich Man again. In other words, it can be said that the beggar came out of the Rich Man and the beggar dissolved back into the Rich Man, like the salt melts into water.

Self-realization is exactly like this. One doesn't get anything new, just realizes what he really is. This transition from a deluded sense of Self to one's own real Self is a cognitive journey, which is nothing but a cumulative total of all the steps taken towards a destination. As our committed, dedicated, and sustained steps on the path in the right direction culminate in the destination, so does our journey of Self-realization. When someone realizes their Real Self, there would be no extra-ordinary mystical experience as such. There would be no blinding shower of lights or announcement from the sky or Vishnu's Vishwaroop emerging out of the clouds of mist etc. It is an incremental evolution of my cognition, my sense of being, my awareness which in fact is a seamless transition of the mental state of being of a mortal Self into an immortal Self, of a limited Self into limitless or Supreme Self, of a Nar (man) into Narayana (God). One begins to see, realize, accept, adopt, and absorb those personality attributes, which they never believed they had. The process of Self-realization is a process of gliding from one plane of consciousness into the higher plane of consciousness. Nothing more or less. As my awareness about my Real Self, my Real personality grows and assimilates in my bosom, my experiences in the world outside began to change. Things, being and situation began losing their potency to affect me negatively.

Now let's return to the question, **'Why Self-realization?'** Why do we suffer the agonies of life? A painful life is a disease caused by non-apprehension of the Real Self. All of us, except the Self-realized ones, are suffering with this disease. It would not be wrong to suggest that unfortunately this is a congenital disorder which we all are born with.

No one can escape it, certainly not from its symptoms. The symptoms of this disease are Negative Affectivity and a deluded sense of Self, which is riddled with negative emotions, including anger, contempt, disgust, dishonesty, fear, greed, guilt, jealousy, lust, nervousness, and many more in its varieties and combinations. So long as these symptoms are there, you cannot escape the miseries in life. No matter how many degrees and qualifications you may acquire, no matter how high you may climb the professional ladder, no matter how successful you may become in your business, no matter how much wealth, power, and fame you may earn, but you cannot escape the miseries of life. If you are happy the way your life is, Self-realization has nothing to offer you.

However, the spiritual path of Self-realization is for you (only) if you indeed have a craving for Liberation (मोक्ष) from the miseries of life and when all your efforts in trying to be happy are redundant, ineffective and nothing seems to work, and if you are desperate or keen enough to seek lasting happiness, only then you are invited to seek refuge in Spirituality. Otherwise, life is going on towards the doom's day anyway. As stated earlier, the Vedantic System of treatment is very secular, democratic, and liberal in nature. There is no compulsion whatsoever in Sanatan tradition of Vedanta. There is complete freedom and independence of choice. Only voluntary admission is permitted. Most of us, by default, have chosen to continue to suffer and live a miserable life. However, for all those who are desperate to liberate themselves from the clutches of miseries, Self-realization is the only answer.

Self-realization can be considered as the treatment modality for a miserable life offered by Vedanta not only to treat the disease and all its painful symptoms but also to re-establish your spiritual health as a direct by-product of the treatment which includes everlasting peace, love, and happiness. This proposition is not very dissimilar to a treatment that you may consider for treating a disease of your body. A disease, which gives you a lot of discomforts, pain, and agony, when it becomes unbearable you approach a doctor, who gives you a prescription for treatment. When you complete the treatment and take the medicine as prescribed by the doctor, the disease and all its symptoms disappear, and you become healthy again. Though you may think and believe that the doctor and the treatment has given your health back. But the fact remains that the doctor, the treatment, and the medicine did not create your health but removed the very germs that caused the disease and the symptoms thereof. The health, though, is the original state of your body, with treatment and medication, when the disease and its symptoms are removed, you regain your original health. Health is the original state of the body. The corruption was caused by the disease. When you remove the corruption, the body regains its original state of being. So, the answer to the question, "Why Self-realization?" is the same as "Why Medical Treatment?"

Now, the intent behind writing this book is to help young people and seekers of liberation to gain an insight into the bigger, better, and profound reasons and purposes inherent in our spiritual texts, religious practices, and ritualistic performances, that is to realize one's **Supreme Sense of Self**. Due to lack of the right information and knowledge, these may appear to be useless and ineffective. However, with sincerity and reverence, if one undertakes this journey, it will culminate at a destination where the beggar will eventually realize his True Identity; that of the owner of the gold mine, which he always was. One would realize that they had assumed themselves to be the beggar because they were neither aware nor did they apprehend their True Identity. The moment one realizes their True Identity, they will effortlessly assume, accept, and absorb to their True Divine Identity and their real nature. Their begging behavior and associated miseries will be sublimated effortlessly.

2. What does Self-realization mean?

The question, 'What Self-realization means?' has already been answered in various sections of this book, perhaps not directly. So, let's attempt at this question directly here and in our routine day to day language with the help of our modern-day vocabulary. This hyphenated word contains two independent words, that is, Self and Realization. We generally have no problem with '**Realization**,' which simply means to know. Implying getting to know something that I did not know before. But this is not the case with the word '**Self**.' Though this word is so commonly used, we assume that we know its meaning and its import. The expressions like myself, yourself, themselves, ourselves etc., are a few of its uses in common parlance. Perhaps we do know the dictionary meaning of the word, which refers to a person's own nature or qualities but when it comes to know its meaning within the context of Spirituality, we find ourselves confused, confounded, bewildered and perplexed.

If you are really interested in knowing what '**Self**' means or refers to within the spiritual context, try to answer a simple question, that is, **Who are you?** When trying to answer this question, please make sure none of your answers relates to or connected, directly or indirectly, with your body, mind, or intellect. I am assuming that you know by now that you are not the body, mind and/or intellect. You are someone or something other than these three. There is an unknown entity within us which sustains these three. That unknown factor is what we are trying to investigate or find. This means, the answers indicating your name, your title both personal and professional, your relationships with others, your height, weight, and complexion etc., and all such nouns and pronouns with reference to your body are to be excluded from your answers. Second, exclude all such answers which refer to your mental evaluation about yourself, that is your emotional being, your feelings, your emotional qualities and nature etc. For example, I am a happy go lucky person, I am stressed, I am depressed, I am ever so excited etc. So, exclude all such nouns and pronouns with reference to your mental image of yourself, your emotions, and feelings etc., from your answers. Finally, also exclude all such references, including all nouns and pronouns, which relates to the intellectual ideas that you may have about yourself, such as, I am a good person, I am a generous person, I am very polite person, and I am a team player, that is, all your qualities and moral and ethical personality attributes etc.

At the end of the above exercise, having exhausted all the possibilities, options and thoughts defining your body, mind, and intellect, thereafter, whatever remains is the correct answer and the real meaning of the '**Self**' within the context of Spirituality and Self-realization. A few of us may come up with words like Soul, Spirit, Atma, energy, power etc. Such answers, though, are correct answers, but unfortunately, our understanding about such words doesn't go beyond their word meaning or dictionary meaning. Do you really comprehend the meaning of these words? Do you feel that these words are really defining who you are? Do you really comprehend and identify yourself with and believe these words to be your real identity? Should you really believe that you are not the body, the mind, or the intellect but the Soul, Spirit, Atma, energy, power etc. Then in that case, your life must have been cleansed of all Negative Affectivity. For example, if someone insults you or accuses you of a crime in public, you do not get angry at all, if you suffer a loss, you accept it smilingly, and a horrible news of death or disease of a near and dear falls on your mind as water drops on the lotus leaf. You remain calm and collected and your emotions are not disturbed at all. You must, necessarily, be enjoying a life full of peace, love, and sustained happiness, completely insulated from the good and the bad, gain and loss, victory or defeat, insult or praise. All your struggles and toils in life must have ceased. Should such be the case, then you have good signs and symptoms that you have already realized the Self. I am afraid, in such a case, this book neither has anything more to offer you nor you require anymore. All your desires must have been purged and exhausted.

For all others, it's a common problem that most of us face. No one is to be particularly blamed for this ignorance. Getting to know oneself has never been part of any curriculum from nursery to PhD degree levels. Families have either given up on it or have no value for this subject. Preparing oneself for materialistic life, acquisition, preservation, and accumulation of sense objects to make one's life comfortable is the sole objective that propels and directs all our efforts throughout our lives. Spiritual Science, that can provide the knowledge on the subject of the Self, has been reduced to mindless idol worship and other ritualistic practices performed in a parrotlike mechanical fashion.

The word **Self** in Vedanta refers to **the Life Principle** that sustains life and is the very power or energy that enlivens the body, mind, and intellect. It is this very Self, which is responsible for the vitalisation of BMI and for these to function. When this Self ebbs out, it renders the body, mind, and the intellect inoperative and unfunctional. Such a state of lifeless BMI is called Death in common parlance. It is this very Self which is responsible for Generating, Operating and Destroying vitality in my BMI. Therefore, this Self is and can be referred to as the **GOD**. In Spiritual literature this Life Principle, the Self is referred to as the GOD, Brahman, Supreme Self, Atma, Paramatma etc., call it what you may.

However, due to non-apprehension of this Self, since it is beyond the comprehension of my senses, I have no way of knowing my reality as the Self. From my birth onwards, as I became consciously aware of this beautiful world around me, I began to identify myself with my body, mind, and intellect. I have no choice but to believe myself to be the body, the mind, and the intellect. That is the only introduction I have of myself. Hence, I know nothing about myself other than being a body, mind, and intellect. Therefore, all experiences that I gain through these three instruments, I experience them as my experiences and consequently, I must naturally suffer and enjoy the pains and joys earned through these instruments.

Self-realization is the science, method and the process prescribed by our Vedanta scriptures (1) to understand my constitution as a combination of the gross and the subtle elements of my personality; (2) differentiate between the Self, the subtle element of my personality and the Not-Self, the gross elements constituting by body mind and the intellect;

(3) give me tools, techniques and procedures to help me to transit away from my identification with the gross toward gaining and evolving my identification with the subtle dimension of my personality.

3. How to realize the Self?

The very first misconception and a general belief is that things like Self-realization or reaching any height in spiritual practice is designed for some special ones. Ordinary people like you and me are only there to admire those who have achieved it. We generally hold a view in our mind that all the wise people, in the history that we know of, were special people, who were born blessed with a destiny to shine. We generally don't think we are cut out for such **Penance, Hardships and Tapasya** that these blessed souls have undergone. Here I would like to encourage all young seekers by suggesting them to the contrary to such established notions. **I believe that Self-realization is simple and easy**. One doesn't need to be a Super-Human. Anyone, irrespective of their socio-economic background, age, gender, educational qualifications, prior scriptural knowledge, intellectual ability and/or the knowledge of the Sanskrit language, is capable of Self-realization. Being a Super-Human is not the cause or a prerequisite but the effect of Self-realization.

Self-realization is as simple or difficult as one believes it to be. However, I am neither suggesting that it is a piece of cake, nor at the same time, I believe it is pie in the Sky or a rocket science. Like any worthwhile achievement or success in life, **it requires sincerity, commitment, dedication for the relentless Self efforts applied consistently over a sustained period of time**. Is becoming a Medical Doctor or Space Scientist easy or difficult? Is becoming an Olympic Gold Medallist or Cricket Super Star easy or difficult? Well, the answer to these questions is both. For those who took a firm resolve in their mind and remained focused and pursued their goal and with single-point devotion, sincerity, commitment, dedication, and relentless Self efforts applied themselves consistently over a sustained period of time, they achieve the goals of their desire. For all such aspirants, becoming a Medical Doctor, a Space

Scientist, an Olympic Gold Medallist, or a Cricket Super Star, or any unimaginable target has always been realistic, achievable, and possible. For the rest of the wishful thinkers and day dreamers, it has always been an unrealistic, unachievable, and impossible prospect.

In the same way, for all those sincere seekers of truth who have a burning desire for liberation from their miserable life; and those who seek peace, love and lasting happiness, Self-realization is very much possible with single-point devotion, sincerity, commitment, dedication, and relentless Self efforts applied consistently over a sustained period of time. Therefore, it can be summed up that Self-realization per say is neither easy nor difficult, at the same time, the people who achieve it are not extraordinary. For those, who with full faith in their strength of conviction, put forth relentless Self-effort with single-point devotion, sincerity, commitment, dedication, applied consistently over a sustained period of time, Self-realization is a piece of cake and for wishful thinkers and day dreamers, it always remains a pie in the sky and a rocket science.

The Second misnomer regarding Self-realization is about the skill and abilities, required in Spiritual Practice for Self-realization, difficult to acquire. This misnomer, in the minds of the young people, is mainly formed with the fairy tale perception gained through our religious and puranic stories they read and listened to in their childhood. Such confusions are sustained as blind faith, since young people do not have anyone around to offer them clarification, logic, or real import of these stories. The stories give the impression that the protagonist undertook penance over hundreds of years and performed extra-terrestrial, or Superhuman acts to gain Self-realization or pleasing the God or a Deity, only thereafter, they get the God's blessings in the form of boons. The examples of such penances involved, for example, standing on one leg in the ice-cold water, or sitting in meditation posture and chanting God's name or Vedic verses in a dark and dingy cave in a far and isolated place on earth for years, or leaving family and social life and spending life in exile in a forest etc.

Having said that one should not mistake religious or puranic stories (Kathas) to be fairly tales, misleading or irrational, On the contrary, these are highly philosophical with deep Vedic and Upanishadic imports and the language used in these texts is highly subtle, suggestive, and indicative in nature. For example, leaving family, social life and spending life in exile in a forest indicates a requirement of giving up attachments with material desires (thoughts) and dwelling in contemplation and meditation over one's own spiritual nature in the jungle of thoughts. Standing on one leg in the ice-cold water indicates relentless Self-effort with single-point devotion, sincerity, commitment, dedication, applied consistently over a sustained period of time. It also indicates a mental strength and ability to smilingly withstand all the pains and suffering in the path of spiritual practice. Such mental strength and the ability are called **Titiksha (तितिक्षा)**, which is one of the six mental qualities (shath-sampati - षट्-सम्पति, Six-Properties), e.g. Sam, Dam, Uparati, Titiksha, Kshama and Samadhan), prescribed by Adi Shankaracharya as a prerequisite for a sincere seeker of Atma-Gyan.

Let us investigate a couple of Puranic stories to get the above points across. For example, we all are familiar with the story of **Bhagirath**, who earned the credit for bringing Ganga from Heaven to earth. Among the various interesting stories of Ganga, the most popular story is from Brahma-Rishi Vishwamitra's Ramayana Bal-Kand, where he narrates about Bhagirath and the descent of Ganga to Earth. A brief summary of the story is as follow:

> *"King Sagar—the ruler of Ayodhya and an ancestor of Lord Rama decided to perform the Ashwamedha (great horse sacrifice) to become more powerful. Indra, the king of Gods, became jealous and stole the horse for yagna. Indira tied the horse near Sage Kapila's ashram, where the sage was meditating in the deep forest. The king along with his 60000 sons began to search for the horse in the nether world and at last found it near Sage Kapila.*
>
> *Assuming that the sage had stolen the horse, the princes began to insult the sage and tried to free the horse. The princes continued to disturb the meditation of the*

sage and made him angry. The furious sage with the yogic fire of his eyes burnt all the princes into ashes. King Sagar was disturbed and asked his grandson, Anshuman, to search for the princes.

Anshuman's search ended in the front of the yagna horse and a heap of ash. He also saw the Sage Kapila near it. He bowed and inquired what happened to the princes. The sage narrated the whole incident and Anshuman broke down in grief. He pleaded for forgiveness and for the salvation of the princes. Sage Kapila was pleased and instructed Anshuman to bring the holy Ganga to earth as she can only help them to wash away the sin and attain salvation.

In order to attain salvation to his relatives, Anshuman started doing penance on the Himalaya, but it was in vain. His son Dilip also tried to please Lord Brahma and bring Ganga. However, he also failed in his mission. Bhagirath, the son of Dilip, took penance after his father. Bhagirath was so dedicated that Lord Brahma was pleased and granted him permission to bring Ganga to earth.

Goddess Ganga was asked to descend to earth, but she felt it as an insult and decided to sweep away everything that came her way. Bhagirath felt the fierce power in the flow of her current and understood that he needed to do something in order to stop the mighty river from destroying the world. In order to avoid this catastrophe, Bhagirath prayed to Shiva and requested him to hold Ganga in his matted hair (Jata).

At the request of Bhagirath, Shiva agreed to hold Ganga in his hair locks. At first, Ganga thought that no one would be able to withstand her power and descended to the Earth with all her power. Shiva decided to teach her a lesson and held her in his matted locks. Ganga tried to get free but failed to escape from the Great Shiva. After one year of rigorous penance of Bhagirath, Shiva was pleased and released Ganga. Ganga understood the greatness of Lord Shiva and asked for his forgiveness. Shiva is known as Gangadhara as He absorbed the flow of Ganga and saved the earth from flooding."

I have highlighted a few phrases and sentences to interpret and translate their philosophical import as contained in our scriptures.

"Bhagirath": Bhagirath presents a sincere seeker of Spiritual Knowledge, who has taken a firm resolve to do so.

"The Ashwamedha": **Ashwa** means a horse and **Medha** means the Intellect, that is, Buddhi in the word Ashwamedha. The horse indicates **a Resolve**. Put together the phrase Ashwamedha refers to a committed resolution towards a target or a goal of achievement.

"Ashwamedha Yagna": Ashwamedha Yagna, as per the common understanding, is an attempt by a king to challenge all other Kings to accept his sovereignty as a lord of all Kings and come under his subjugation. Philosophically, however, it refers to an endeavor (Spiritual Sadhana) by a sincere seeker of Brahma-Atma-Gyan, to gain control over his mind and achieve his sovereignty over his Body, Mind, and Intellect and become their Lord (Swami), through his relentless Self efforts applied consistently over a sustained period of time with sincerity, commitment, dedication. Ashwamedha Yagna, therefore, means endeavors to bring wild, uncontrolled, and directionless thoughts, which are like a wild horse, under one's control. Ashwamedha Yagna is like taming a wild horse and eventually riding on its back. Meaning becoming a competent and a Yogi.

"Indra, the king of Gods, became jealous and stole the horse for yagna": In this statement Indra refers to our Body, which runs amok and the risk of a constant threat through temptations for sense objects and causing distraction and stealing away one's resolve and making them weaker. Whenever one tries to take a vow or a resolve, the senses, the sense pleasures, and the sensual habits become a major hurdle in the way, and if one is not careful and resolute, these succeed in stealing the resolve. The individual consequently gives in to the sense pressures and ends up giving up on his resolve.

"To bring the holy Ganga to earth as she can only help them to wash away the sin and attain salvation": Ganga refers to the Brahman Gyan and Atma-Gyan, which is the only solution for the liberation from the miseries of life (sins). The knowledge of the Self is the only antidote for the common human disease called ignorance of the Self. Therefore, one, who seeks liberation from the suffering and the miseries of life, must attain the knowledge of the Self (Ganga).

"In order to avoid this catastrophe, Bhagirath prayed to Shiva and requested him to hold Ganga in his matted hair (Jata)": Ganga refers to the Brahma and Atma-Gyan, which is vast and comprehensive, beyond the comprehension of our senses. Such is the knowledge, which can easily overwhelm an average intellect, who has not prepared oneself sufficiently and acquired the necessary mental and intellectual temperament, abilities and skills required for the job. Such an ill prepared seeker can have a catastrophic impact of the highly subtle, suggestive, and indicative nature of the Vedic and Upanishadic knowledge, and he could be intellectually devastated and consequently dissuaded from his resolve. The sincere seeker of Brahma Gyan must, therefore, essentially pray to Lord Shiva. Praying to Lord Shiva essentially means to acquire all his iconographical attributes in order to become a Yogi, the one who has become the master of his senses, who is well poise, tranquil, and equanimous, only such an individual can be a qualified recipient, beholder, and the custodian of the knowledge. Once a seeker becomes the Yogi (Shiva) and acquires all the necessary mental and intellectual temperament, abilities, and skills, he becomes fit for the purpose.

"Ganga tried to get free but failed to escape from the Great Shiva": Having acquired all the iconographical attributes of Lord Shiva, the Yogi (the Seeker of Spiritual Knowledge) attains Shivhood (शिवत्व), the knowledge, that seemed difficult and incomprehensible, becomes easy and comprehensible and cannot escape the grasp of a well poise, tranquil, and equanimous intellect.

The philosophical import of the story, therefore, is that any worthwhile achievements or great successes require the dedication and devotion of Bhagirath. Self-realization for the salvation from the miseries of life is compared as harlequin a task as bringing Ganga down on the earth. The prescription from our Vedantic Subjective Scientists is to attain Brahma-Gyan, the divine knowledge of the Supreme Self. However, the prospect of attaining divine knowledge, which is not only so vast and comprehensive, but the subtle nature of the subject, in addition to its suggestive and indicative use of the language, can make an average intellect to be perplexed and bewildered. Most of such unqualified seekers, therefore, find no other option but to give up on it. This is compared with the massive force of flow of Ganga, which is coming down from the heights of Himalaya down to the planes. Therefore, one must become a Yogi (preparing one's mental temperament and texture) by acquiring and attaining all the attributes indicated by the symbolic iconography of Lord Shiva, so as to become capable of holding and containing, comprehending, and absorbing the subtlety and nuances in their bosom. Only, thereafter, with the relentless Self-effort with single-point devotion, sincerity, commitment, dedication, applied consistently, one is capable of Self-realization. Here the Ganga indicates the flow of unmanifest knowledge (heaven) at the thought level and making it manifest (Earth) in the form of words and their expressions. In short, what it implies is the revelation of divine knowledge gained through relentless efforts. That is why Bhagirath has become the synonym for all impossible prospects and such efforts are also referred to as Bhagirathi efforts.

In a similar story about Valmiki, it is said that when he sat down on the seat of contemplation for years, he was so consumed deep in his meditation that he did not realize that ants built a nest around his body and his entire body was covered under the anthill. It seems like an impossibility to a modern man. How could he not realize that an army of ants were crawling all over his body and how could he possibly remain unmoved and undisturbed? Again, it appears an impossible prospect, particularly when we compare it with our own experience where we can't even tolerate the sight of an insect, let alone them crowing over our body and biting us. Such an Upanishadic description, however, is trying to indicate and point to the height and depth of Valmiki's meditation and his single pointed devotion. While consumed in his meditation, he was not consciously aware of his physical discomforts at the body level, his emotions and feelings at the mental level, and any distractions at the intellectual level.

It's not that such a highly devotional, focused, and meditative state of mind was achieved by our great rishis and sages and other revered personalities only in the Puranic era and tales therein. There are numerous examples of such personalities in the world in the modern times too. Pick up any field such as science, sports, academics, literature, politics, or social work. You will find a galaxy of performances is glittered with numerous shining stars. Let us consider a few examples here.

Late president of India, **Dr APJ Abdul Kalam**, was born to a Tamil Muslim family in the pilgrimage center of Rameswaram on Pamban Island, it was the Madras Presidency then and now it is known as state of Tamil Nadu. His father Jainulabdeen Marakayar was a boat owner and Imam of a local mosque; his mother Ashiamma was a housewife. His father owned a ferry that took Hindu pilgrims back and forth between Rameswaram and the now uninhabited Dhanushkodi. Kalam was the youngest of four brothers and one sister in his family. Despite a humble beginning to his life in uncertainties and poverty, Dr. Abdul Kalam climbed to the heights of becoming an Indian aerospace scientist and statesman who served as the 11th president of India. He studied physics and aerospace engineering. Following his formal education, he spent the next four decades as a scientist and science administrator, mainly at the Defence Research and Development Organisation (DRDO) and Indian Space Research Organisation (ISRO) and was intimately involved in India's civilian space programme and military missile development efforts. He thus came to be known as the Missile Man of India for his work on the development of ballistic missile and launch vehicle technology. He also played a pivotal organizational, technical, and political role in India's Pokhran-II nuclear tests in 1998, the first since the original nuclear test by India in 1974.

Another such personality in India is **Scientist Nambi Narayanan.** He was born in the house of Tamil Hindu parents in Nagercoil, in the erstwhile Princely state of Travancore (present-day Kanyakumari District). He completed his schooling at Higher Secondary School, Nagercoil. He received a Bachelor of Technology in Mechanical Engineering from Thiagarajah College of Engineering, Madurai. Narayanan lost his father while pursuing his degree in Madurai, with his mother falling sick soon after.

Like Dr. APJ Abdul Kalam, **S. Nambi Narayanan** rose to the pinnacle of his career and became an Indian aerospace scientist who worked for the Indian Space Research Organisation (ISRO) and contributed significantly to the Indian space program by developing the Vikas rocket engine. He led the team which acquired technology from the French for the Vikas engine used in the first Polar Satellite Launch Vehicle (PSLV) that India launched. As a senior official at the ISRO, he was in charge of the cryogenics division. He was awarded the Padma Bhushan, India's third-highest civilian award, in March 2019.

In 1994, he was arrested on trumped up charges of espionage, being subjected to physical abuse while in the custody of the Kerala Police, which were later found to be baseless by the Central Bureau of Investigation (CBI) in April 1996. The film *Rocketry: The Nambi Effect*, based on his life, starring, and directed by R. Madhavan, was made and released in 2022.

Albert Einstein was born in Ulm, in the Kingdom of Wurttemberg in the German Empire, into a family of secular Ashkenazi Jews. His parents were Hermann Einstein, a salesman and engineer, and Pauline Koch. In 1880, the family moved to Munich, where Einstein's father and his uncle

Jakob founded Elektrotechnische Fabrik J. Einstein & Co., a company that manufactured electrical equipment based on direct current. Albert attended a catholic elementary school in Munich, from the age of five, for three years. At the age of eight, he was transferred to the Luitpold-Gymnasium, where he received advanced primary and secondary school education until he left the German Empire seven years later.

Albert Einstein reached to the heights of becoming a scientist of great imminence. He was a German-born theoretical physicist, widely acknowledged to be one of the greatest and most influential physicists of all time. Best known for developing the theory of relativity, he also made important contributions to the development of the theory of quantum mechanics. His mass–energy equivalence formula $E = mc^2$, which arises from relativity theory, has been dubbed 'the world's most famous equation.' His work is also known for its influence on the philosophy of science. He received the 1921 Nobel Prize in Physics 'for his services to theoretical physics, and especially for his discovery of the law of the photoelectric effect,' a pivotal step in the development of quantum theory. His intellectual achievements and originality resulted in 'Einstein' becoming synonymous with 'genius.' Einsteinium, one of the synthetic elements in the periodic table, was named in his honor.

Milkha Singh, also known as 'The Flying Sikh,' was an Indian track and field sprinter who was introduced to the sport while serving in the Indian Army. He is the only athlete to win gold at 400 meters at the Asian Games as well as the Commonwealth Games. He also won gold medals in the 1958 and 1962 Asian Games.

Major Dhyan Chand is another such example of superior accomplishments. As one of the greatest field hockey players in history, he was known for his extraordinary ball control and goal-scoring feats, in addition to earning three Olympic gold medals. For his extraordinary skills, he was known as 'The Wizard' or 'The Magician' of hockey for his superb ball control.

Edson Arantes do Nascimento, better known by his nickname **Pele,** was a Brazilian professional footballer who played as a forward. Widely regarded as one of the greatest players of all time, he was among the most successful and popular sports figures of the 20th century. In 1999, he was named 'Athlete of the Century' by the International Olympic Committee and was included in the Time list of the 100 most important people of the 20th century.

These are only a few examples of modern-day Rishis, who excelled in their chosen field of endeavor. However, what remains common in all these personalities, whether in the past or in the present day, is that despite being ordinary people, they all discovered the sleeping giant within and with their extraordinary efforts invoked and realized their true potentials. They dedicated and devoted themselves to a higher purpose in their respective fields of work. They wanted their best and excelled. The moment one sincerely commits, dedicates, and surrenders oneself to a higher purpose in life, all the divine powers lying dormant within get invoked and dynamised.

We admire and appreciate high performers and achievers when spotlight shines on them. However, if we spare a few moments to look at their lives and their journeys, we will find that they all went through the hell of physical, mental, and intellectual challenges and difficulties. But none succeeded in defeating their resolve. It is only possible when one has won over their mind. A meditative state of mind, where the mind becomes highly focused and pointed on a chosen thought or a similar stream of thoughts, while and despite all sensory distractions still goading you, is referred to as **going beyond the body, mind, and intellect.** Such an expression is very commonly used in various spiritual texts. This is one of the main purposes of meditation and also a skill and a competence that one must acquire for effective contemplation and meditation.

When we read or listen to religious stories, even though we might understand their philosophical import, we often underestimate our abilities and affirm to ourselves that I don't think I would be able to ignore my physical discomforts, my emotions and feelings and avoid distractions. Bhagirath must have been a superhuman, who could do what he did. But I don't think I am capable of doing even one percent of it. Such thoughts breed Self-doubt and erode our confidence and take us away from the possibilities of being able to venture into impossibilities. However, the fact remains that we, the humans, have been blessed and bestowed with all necessary skills and competences to live a successful and peaceful life. Not only do we have these skills and competences, we also have already invoked and employed these skills and abilities on several occasions in our lives. It's just that we are not aware that we have done so. I have already discussed this topic in detail in the section entitled '**The Path of Spirituality**' under myth 3. **So, we do not have to learn these afresh but learn to invoke these.** Let me repeat those passages here again, so that you, the reader can relate it with the above stories.

4. Skills and abilities required for Self-realization.

Spirituality is waking up to the idea that **you are a spirit with a body, not just a body with a spirit** and becoming consciously aware of who you really are, your real essence. It requires one to wake up from the ordinary, everyday consciousness, to a wider consciousness and work on **identifying and removing dysfunctional concepts** about the Self. Thereby ensuring a peaceful and misery free life.

Let us now revisit myth 3, discussed earlier in this book to understand and realize the scientific fact about our inner personality mechanics (अंतःकरण). The moment one sincerely commits, dedicates, and surrenders oneself to the higher purpose in life, all the divine powers lying dormant within get invoked and dynamized. Let us discuss again how our inner personality mechanics come into play when you sincerely commit yourself to a higher purpose. At the time, a couple of months prior to your final examination, you wanted to pass with a distinction. In order to achieve this objective of yours, let us review and peep into the subconscious mental processes and the sequence of invocations that our inner personality mechanics goes through.

The desire to pass the examination with a distinction must be sufficiently intense in your mind, for you to have any chance to get the highest possible marks. Such an intensified or burning desire, in Sanskrit, is called Mumukshutva (मुमुक्षुत्व), which is the very first qualification for a sincere seeker of spirituality.

When the burning desire intensifies in your mind, you automatically have a sense of discrimination in your mind. This power of discrimination (विवेक-शक्ति) of your mind between the good and the bad, beneficial and detrimental, Real and unreal, fleeting and permanent etc., is called Vivek-Buddhi (विवेक बुद्धि), which is the second qualification for a sincere seeker of spirituality.

This burning desire to perform well in your examination, leads you to prioritize and use your time effectively. You automatically begin focusing on those specific activities which you know are beneficial for your objective. While all physical, mental and intellectual distractions are still happening all around you, you remain oblivious and only focused on one and the only thing, that is, your studies, revision, and practice from morning to night every day without a break.

Your mind remains preoccupied with the only thoughts of studies and examination from morning to night. You willingly and effortlessly give-up all above mentioned tempting and tantalizing activities, which were so very dear to you. This ability to become dispassionate and ability to withdraw your attention, willingly and effortlessly, away from unhelpful activities and invest into what you consider good, is called **dispassion** in English and **Vairagya** (वैराग्य) in Sanskrit, which is an automatic result of a burning desire and discrimination and is achieved effortlessly.

The truth about our inner personality mechanics is that when you bring your mind to focus on a bigger, better and the higher value or a purpose in life, the lower or invaluable pursuits automatically either disappear or are side-lined. You automatically develop a dispassion about them. Vairagya, therefore, is considered the third qualification for a sincere seeker of spirituality.

Here I have demonstrated to you that you already have and used the skills of **Meditation, Concentration, Discrimination and Dispassion** in your life so many times. You have been invoking these skills, not just in educational fields, but in many fields of your interests. Be it sports or any of the extra-curricular activities that you sincerely committed yourself to, you were able to invoke these skills every time. It's just that you were not aware of these powers within you, and you didn't understand the mechanism of invoking these powers. Therefore, when you decide to take up the path of spirituality, you need not to learn anything new. All you have to do is **to commit yourself sincerely for Self-realization and invoke the burning desire in you**. The technique and the mechanism to invoke these powers, lying dormant within, will be effortlessly awakened.

14

Deepest Essence Of Vedanta

Before we embark on the discussion on Spiritual Practices (Sadhana), let us glance an eye on the trajectory religion and spirituality has taken in its conception, evolution, and development. How the philosophical thought has evolved, from time immemorial thousands of years ago, which laid the fundamental foundation of the present-day religious philosophy, thought and a spectrum of spiritual and religious practices up until what we witness today in our families, our communities, and the Hindu society at large. For a sincere practitioner of religion, it is important that he/she must know the fundamental purpose behind religion and all that it teaches.

We live in an era where rational explanations of science have made people question religion. When priests and padres of the time could not give clear answers, they dismissed all religion as fanciful hocus-pocus. It takes a rare teacher of vast intellectual erudition and deep inner experience to give a full, clear, and convincing explanation of what religion truly teaches. Pujya Gurudev Swami Chinmayananda, amongst many more, did exactly that through his lectures and jnana yagnas. His excellent commentaries on a large number of works of Adi Sankaracharya, including various Upanishads, Bhagavad Gita, Vivekchudamani, to name a few, does present a very scientific and logical explanation. Rejecting all blind faith and superstition, Swami Chinmayananda took a strictly scientific approach to spirituality, explaining every statement of scriptures in the light of logic and reason.

Through such analysis, he brought out the deepest essence of Vedanta in practical, easy-to-understand, contemporary language.

For a rational mind, who is keen to understand as to how the religion and spirituality was conceived, evolved, and developed by our revered Subjective Scientists to its present form, Swami Chinmayananda presents an excellent description of this evolutionary journey traveled by the Indian thought from stone age down to the present day in his book called 'Logic of Spirituality.' I am taking liberty to represent some of his thoughts here to help the readers gain a better perspective and an overview on conception, evolution, and development, thereby, gaining a better understanding of their religious practice today.

The physical world of plurality has always been at all times a mystery, a temptation, a conundrum, since the time of the caveman to the modern man of science and technology. Where did it all come from? What is the source of this universe? What is it that is happening all around me? These kinds of questions have always bothered the man from Adam and Eve onwards. Until today we have been questioning, investigating, and inquiring. Sometimes our inquiry has gone into mysticisms and religion, sometimes to superstition, sometimes to facts–but nowhere has there been complete satisfaction.

This problem, however, does not exist for animals, and therefore, philosophy or religion has never bothered them. It is only when you become an intelligent human being that you have hundreds of questions popping up in your mind and you start this investigation, since you are curious to understand the world outside. It is this questioning ability in the human intellect that has brought about all the so-called progress in the material world outside. All that we see around in the material world outside is a result of the human investigative anxiety to know, to understand the world. The Objective Scientists of the modern times are glorious people but are limited in their approach to this question. None of them are able to find out what is the fundamental reality, the Truth, the God. It is not their fault. They are trying to understand this concept with their intellect, which is, unfortunately, beyond the comprehension of human senses, mind, and intellect.

Origin of Inquiry

The question arises–Why Religion? Why Philosophy? The animals do not have it and they are living comfortably and dying away, and they live their life cycle very peacefully. Why should man have religion or philosophy? Why art, literature, and science? Animals don't have it, why do we have science? Animals don't have politics, economics and yet they survive. It is because the man is intelligent and therefore, he developed all these sciences. The human intellect asks questions; animals don't ask questions. To the animal, the world only has a utility value. A grazing animal smells a thing and if it is edible, it eats it or else it leaves it and goes away. Utility value is the only value that the animal can understand. Humans are not so. Animals do not have rational intellect to ask questions, but man has, therefore, he cannot stop asking questions. An animal will never ask any such questions as the inquisitive and investigative human mind does. A scientific mind, a well-developed intellect, a rational mind wants to know.

This is how various branches of sciences developed. They developed through inquisitiveness and a sense of wonderment, but in all of the branches of science, the scientist was fascinated only by a limited area of their investigation. For example, they wanted to know about the sun, moon, planets, and the star, so astronomy developed. In the same way various branches of science e.g. Botany, Zoology, Geology, Oceanography, Politics, Economics, Chemistry, Physics, Math etc., were developed by scientists. These are all specific areas of science and material world. Everywhere, we see the human intellect wanting to know, wanting to investigate and understand these very subject areas. It is this urge in man that developed all of the various sciences.

Ever since science has been developing, and in all the scientific research the fundamental question has always been–**What is the Cause of the** effect observed? Causation hunting is the only preoccupation of the human intellect. The rational intellect investigates things, searching for the cause of things. Whenever situations presented in the world caused discomfort for populations, scientists wanted to know the cause of the discomfort. For example, when Malaria became rampant and started to kill people, they wanted to know what the cause of the disease was. As soon as they were able to find the cause of the disease, they were able to develop the antidote for it and malaria as a pandemic was countered. Now for the last many decades, they have been trying to find out the cause of cancer. There is no doubt that the international efforts by the scientists will find out the cause of cancer and there will be a cure available soon.

Cause and Effect Relationship

This cause-and-effect relationship, which is called 'Karya-Karana Sambandha' (कार्य-कारण सम्बन्ध) in Sanskrit, was found by our Rishis of the Vedika period to be universal. In the past, present and the future, inquiring into the same cause-and-effect relations has been the preoccupation of all people all over the world. Therefore, our rishis said, "It is a universal thing, let us inquire into it." When they thus tried to understand the cause of the universe—**What is that ultimate reality from which the world has emerged?**—they failed completely and miserably.

In science there is no failure. Failures of the past become the stepping stone for future discoveries. The scientists avoid the mistakes of the past and make their discoveries based upon the failures of previous centuries. The great Rishis who were recorded in the Rig-Veda declared, **"We tried our best to understand the cause of this universe. We could not."** There is a Vedika Declaration: "यतो वाचो निवर्तन्ते अप्राप्य मनसा सहा" (yato vāco nivartante aprāpya manasā saha). This translates as, "He who knows the Bliss of Brahman from which all words return without reaching, It, together with the mind." This great truth appears to be beyond our abilities, our sense abilities, to observe or for our mental abilities to conceive of.

Scientific methods of investigation are generally direct in its investigation of the subject matter. However, at times when the subject cannot be approached directly, indirect methods of investigation are perfectly alright and accepted by modern science. When the great Masters of the Vedika period found that their faculties at this moment of their evolution were not capable of investigating into the cause of this entire cosmos, they said, "We will start an indirect investigation." So, they started a deep and exhaustive study of the cause-and-effect relations, through the study of the effects, that is, the observed material world. They reduced their entire data into three laws of causation.

The first law states, '**An effect can never be without a cause.**' The waves cannot be without the ocean. Ornaments cannot be made without gold. Pots can never be made without clay. An effect is not possible without a cause. All that exists in the world **must have a cause**, out of which it comes out or is made out of.

The second law states, '**Effects may be plural, appear different; they are nothing but the cause itself in different shapes and forms.**' The big waves, the medium waves, small waves, the ripple, the foam, the lather, the bubbles are all different forms of the ocean, the cause. The jug, the cup, the saucer, the plate, the flower vase are all different shapes and different names–for what? Clay in different forms! The bangles, the rings, the chain, and the earrings are all different names, different shapes, different uses, but all of them are gold in different forms.

The third law states, '**From the effect when the cause is removed, nothing remains.**' Can we think of the big waves, the medium waves, small waves, the ripple, the foam, the lather, the bubbles without the ocean? If the clay is removed out of a jug, the cup, the saucer, the plate, and the flower vase, what will remain? The bangles, the rings, the chain, and the earrings cannot be conceived of without the gold. The ocean, the clay, and the gold, therefore, in these examples are the respective causes of the effects produced by them. If the ocean is removed, there will be no wave, if the clay is removed there will be no pot and when gold is removed from the ornaments, nothing remains. Since the effect is nothing but the cause itself in different shapes and forms, when from the effect the cause is removed, nothing remains.

Hence, they deduced that the world that you and I see, hear, feel, and experience, cannot be without a cause, since an effect cannot be without a cause. It must have a cause. The cause of the world, religion calls it **'God,'** and philosophy calls it **'Reality' or the 'Truth.'**

However, there have been confusions regarding God. There is a God and God created the world but our doubt in the modern times is: Who is God? Where is God? Is he a man or a woman? Why did he create this world? How did he create it? When did he create it? The students in the Vedic period ask these questions to their Teacher. The teacher cried out, 'Shanti, Shanti, Shanti.' (Peace be, Peace be, Peace be). Why? Because unless the mind is peaceful, you cannot think rationally. An excited mind has no capacity to think logically.

The teacher said, "Let's apply the second law: Effects are nothing but the cause itself in different shapes and forms." Therefore, the assumption that God is above the clouds, that He, like a manufacturer, manufactures things and pushes them into the world is absurd, illogical. It's a falsehood, it's a superstition. The effect cannot be separate from the cause and therefore when the Lord, the God created the world, He must have created it from itself. The entire universe of names and forms, the mineral world, the plants, the animal and the human kingdom, everything that you are seeing here are all nothing but God in different forms.

Just as in a pottery shop, whatever size or shape or color the pots may be, all of them are permeated by clay. In the jewelry shop, everything there, whatever be the shape, and the use, are nothing but gold in different forms. Similarly, whatever that you are seeing, hearing, smelling, tasting, touching in this world of plurality, the entire objective world, is nothing but that '**Supreme Cause**' in different forms.

Now think very carefully. Let it sink into you. This cannot be demonstrated. It is a Subjective Science. Think for yourself. If thus the Lord permeates everything–just as clay pervades all pots, just as the ocean pervades all waves and gold pervades all ornaments–then He, the cause of the universe, is right here in the very world of plurality. He is a very democratic Lord, not a tyrant who is sitting there above the clouds, manufacturing everything, sending us here. He is with us. In fact, He is us. He pervades everything, including you and me! Maybe you are an atheist. Even an atheist who may say that he doesn't believe in God is able to express that because of the grace of God. The Lord, the God, is in everything–from a unicellular organism to the highest saint and prophet or genius in science or art or literature. Every one of us is enliven by his grace, by his presence. You may ask, If God is thus all-pervading and everywhere, pervading everything, where is He, what is He?

To answer such a question, let us apply the third law, '**When from the effect the cause is removed, nothing remains.**' What is it that is pervading all of us, plant, animal, and human? It cannot be the physical body. What is it that is common? The plant is **alive**, the animal is **alive**, man is **alive**. The spark of life is common in all, is it not? Now what is that which when removed, you and I will be rubbed out of this universe? What is it? It cannot be the nose, it cannot be the hand, it cannot be the leg. Any part of the body may be cut but we still survive. What is which, when 'minused' from you, you as an individual entity in the world are rubbed out, you are no more? **It is life.** Whoever you may be, a saint, or a great statesman, or an Einstein, it doesn't matter. You are there, you are functioning and performing, only because you are **alive**. Think!

Once life is gone, a dead Einstein has no more existence. The life that gives you existence, because of which you are what you are, which enlivens every activity of yours, is it not that life? This mysterious, miraculous, and mighty power in you and me makes us do what we are able to do, makes us function. The plants, the animals, the trees, the birds are functioning because they are alive. The dead bird will no longer chirp. The dead dog cannot bark. Anupam Srivastava will no longer write. Think!

Then who and what is this mighty power. **It is Life**! And this life in me is the life everywhere. The electricity in a bulb, which is now blinking at you, is the same electricity anywhere in the world. Chinese electricity is not different from Russian electricity or American electricity. Electricity is one everywhere. It expresses itself through all electrical equipment. Life is one. It expresses itself through the plant, kingdom, animal kingdom, the human kingdom. Everywhere it expresses itself.

Now, with this knowledge, look at the world through your window. Is it not the entire parade of happenings in the world of politics, economics, social life, and science? Are they not all the play of this mighty Lord? Why shouldn't we call it the Lord of the universe? Minus It, there is no universe. Minus life, this world itself has neither progress, nor science nor knowledge. Why? The planet itself would be called a dead planet. All that you are seeing, this scintillating life, that is seen all around, is all **His** play through the various kinds of equipment, no doubt. This one mighty presence, which is expressing itself through all living beings, at all times, our Subjective Scientists called it **the Reality, the Truth.**

We all know that we are alive. Is there anybody who has a doubt whether he or she is living or not? Everybody knows, whether a congenial idiot or a genius, everybody knows that he or she is alive. However, if we ask anyone, "What is life?" They don't know. They will only say, conditioned as we are by our circumstances, "Life is miserable, because my business is gone." Or "Life is wonderful, because there is some money in my bank, and I have a new wife or a husband." Such expressions are about what life has given us! Certainly not what Life is.

What is Life?–The Eternal Question

What is Life? Nobody seems to know this one life that is pervading everything, because of which everything is functioning. We know it is with us, but we don't know what it is. We want to search and discover it. Therefore, in Subjective Science, philosophy, they said, "Let us suppose this mighty presence in you called life is one life everywhere, it is Aum (ॐ)." Why Aum? - one may ask. One may call it with whatever name, but it is a name that has been taken and universally accepted. Same as in 2πr, one may question, why 'pi'? Well, in the world of mathematics, 2πr is the formula to calculate the circumference of a circle, where 'π' is an unknown common value to calculate the circumference of a circle. The value of the $\pi = 3.14$ is universally accepted. Similarly, **AUM (ॐ)** is a word, a sound symbol that represents the unknown common factor in all living beings. I know it is with me, but I am not able to grasp it and therefore it is called Aum.

Having applied the three laws, the Rishis concluded that all of us exist here now, only because **'life'** is in all of us. That one life, which is in the heart of all, is the Lord of the universe. Minus Him, there is no universe or world at all, no activities, no nothing. That mighty Reality, God, is essential in every one of us as the spark of life, the Consciousness. That consciousness–life–in us, cannot be seen. Each one will have to realize it only inside and not outside.

What is life? 'I don't know.' Because we know only the expression of life. But there is life in all of us–that we know. That life which we know is here, but about which we cannot say.

'I know what it is?' It is indicated in the science of philosophy by the symbol 'AUM.' In Algebra, when we don't know a thing we say, "Let it be x." In science, when we don't know a thing we say, "Let it be gamma or beta or theta." In philosophy, we say, "Let it be Aum." So, Aum is the secret, sacred presence. Because of it all of us are functioning. What it is, we don't know. To discover it, it is called the Science, the Technology, and the Method of Spirituality.

As it is declared at the end of each chapter of Gita, which is referred to as an Upanishad, the Brahma-Vidya, and the Yoga-Shastra: "Thus, in the Upanishads of the glorious Bhagavad Gita, in the Science of the Eternal, in the Scripture of Yoga, in the dialogue between Sri Krishana and Arjuna, the said discourse ends entitled..."

Since the time immemorial, this subject matter has been fascinating hundreds and thousands of inquisitive and scientific intellects. All are trying their best to read, grasp, and comprehend the Vedic literature to understand the mystery of Life and find ways to realize it. The main and the common challenge presented to most is the incomprehensible nature of the Self. Various scholars have tried to understand it from their individual perspectives, depending on their mental and intellectual bend of mind. Accordingly, they made prescriptions for the methods, process, skills, and abilities required to bring about necessary modifications in our inner equipment to become capable of realizing the Self. Let us therefore, in the next section, glance over the historical evolution of the knowledge, its application, and prescriptions, which are now established as various ritualistic practices and performances in our modern-day Hindu society. It would be useful also to note as to how far or detached our current religious practices have become from its original purpose. Having said that it must be said that the criticism is not of the original knowledge or the prescription, but **our understanding and our practices** thereof.

15

Vedic Philosophy And Approaches To Self-Realization

The works of a few main proponents of vedic philosophy and their respective approaches to the Truth in the historical context within which these approaches have evolved with time, has greatly influenced, and shaped our present-day spiritual knowledge, understanding and practices. The following account of how the vedic philosophy was approached by various thinkers and masters and their respective conclusions, provide the reader with a historical overview of the evolution of spiritual thought, knowledge, understanding and practices. Please read the following account with an open analytical evaluative mind, instead of a comparative perspective to draw your personal conclusions.

In my personal opinion, all perspectives on Indian spiritual philosophy presented below, have their respective historical and social context within which these were developed and grown, in addition to the proponents' bend of mind with which they have approached the subject matter to arrive at their respective conclusions. I would not like to judge one philosophical perspective better over the other. Each has its own unique selling points to suit the wide varieties of intellectual abilities and temperaments within the society.

Nondualism or Monism (Advaita Vedanta Philosophy- अद्वैत वेदांत दर्शन), whose main exponent was Sri Adi Sankaracharya in 8th Century. Most historians agree that Adi Shankaracharya lived in the 8th century

CE, or 1,200 years ago, 1,300 years after the Buddha. Adi Sankaracharya took birth at Kaladi in Kerala during 788 CE and he is believed to have disappeared in the year 820 CE at the young age of 32.

Adi Sankaracharya, based on his deep analytical study of the Vedic literature and personal experience thus gained, was of the belief that **Man is in essence God**. Those who insist that history is real, and mythology false, go against the very grain of Adi Shankaracharya's non-dualist maxim: **"Jagat Mithya, Brahma Satyam,"** which means the world, including measured scientific conclusions, that we experience is essentially illusory or rather, mind-dependent epistemological truths. The only mind-independent metaphysical truth is Brahma, variously translated as God, Soul, Consciousness, or the infinitely Expanded, Eternal, Unconditioned Mind.

In his commentary on the Brahma-sutra (1.3.33), Sankara observed, "One can say that there never was a universal ruler as there is none now," an acknowledgement of the fragmented nature of his society at his time, and refusing to accept the mythology of **Chakravarti**[18], or universal emperor, found in Buddhist, Jain, and Hindu lore.

Most historians agree that Adi Sankaracharya lived in a period, which was a major cusp in Indian history–between the collapse of the Gupta Empire 1,500 years ago, and the Muslim conquest of South Asia 1,000 years ago. Harshavardhan of Kannauj had died, the Rashtrakutas held sway on either side of the river Narmada, constantly at war with the Pratiharas of the North, Palas of the East, and Chalukyas of the South. Regional languages and scripts which are now so familiar had not yet emerged. South Indian temples did not have their characteristic gopuram gateways, the Ramayana had yet to be translated into Tamil,

---

[18] In Hinduism, a Chakravarti is a powerful ruler whose dominion extends to the entire earth. In both religions, the Chakravarti is supposed to uphold dharma, indeed being "he who turns the wheel (of dharma)."

Jayadeva had yet to write the Gita Govinda that introduced the world to Radha.

Sankara's philosophy is admittedly Vedic. Unlike Buddhists and Jains, he traced his knowledge to the Vedas and submitted to its impersonal authority, which made him a believer (Astika). In his commentaries (Bhasya) and monographs (Prakarana Granthas), he repeatedly sought a formless divine (Nirguna brahman) being the only reality, outside all binaries. This is evident in his commentary on Vedanta, the Brahma Sutra Bhasya, his Sanskrit Prakarana Granths Vivekchudamani and Nirvana Shatkam and his treatise Atma Bodha. Many consider this to be an acceptance of the Buddhist theme of the world being a series of disconnected transitory moments, hence amounting to nothingness (Shunya-vada), while giving it a Vedic twist, which is why Sankara was often accused of being a disguised Buddhist.

But Sankara's poetry (Stotras) also celebrates several tangible forms of the divine (Saguna Brahman) as they appear in the Puranas. He composed grand benedictions to Puranic Gods, for example, Shiva (Dakshinamurthi-Stotra), Vishnu (Govinda-Ashtak) and Shakti (Saundarya-Lahari). This makes him the first Vedic scholar, after Vyasa, to overtly link Vedic Hinduism to Puranic Hinduism, an idea further elaborated a few centuries later by other teachers of Vedanta, such as Ramanujacharya, Madhavacharya, and Vallabhacharya etc. Adi Sankaracharya even wrote on tantra, which made its presence explicitly felt around that time.

For all his talk of formlessness and nothingness, and the world being an illusion, Sankara went on to connect holy spots of India such as the 12 Jyotirlingas, 18 Shakti Peethas and four Vishnu-Dhaams to create pilgrim routes that defined India as a single land. In his legends, he traveled from Kerala to Kashmir, from Puri in present-day Odisha to Dwarka in Gujarat, from Sringeri in present-day Karnataka to Badari in Uttarakhand, from Kanchi in present-day Tamil Nadu to Kashi in

Uttar Pradesh, along the slopes of the Himalayas, the banks of the rivers Narmada and Ganga, and along the eastern and western coasts.

Sankara is not an ivory tower philosopher. He is a political sage, engaging with and responding to the historical context of his time. Through philosophy, poetry, and pilgrimage, he attempted to bind the subcontinent of India that was constantly referred to in Hindu, Buddhist, and Jain texts as well as in the Vedic ritual of Sankalp as Jambu Dvipa, the continent of the jambul tree, and Bharat-varsha, the land of the Bharata kings.

Adi Shankara, who traveled the breadth of the land, communicated through the one language that connected the intellectual elite of the land, that is Sanskrit. To appreciate the spirit of this time, we must understand the fundamental tension of Indian society between the world-affirming, ritual-bound householder and world-renouncing, ritual-rejecting hermit.

Scholars wonder if Sankara, the philosopher, who valorised knowledge, was also the Sankara who composed devotional poetry? Was the Sankara who established pilgrimages, the one who also spoke the futility of mindless ritual so beautifully expressed in Bhaja Govindam? Was he Vedic or Tantric? Was he Shaivite, Vaishnavite, or Shakta? Was he this or that, or both, or neither? Was he anti-Buddhist or a subversive pro-Buddhist? The diverse fragments of his life mirror the diverse fragmented worldviews shaped India in his time and continue to do so today.

This doctrine of reducing the world to mere illusion, popularly known as maya-vada, enabled Sankaracharya to do something remarkable, that is, to unite a land with diverse communities and diverse worldviews– from the Buddhists, the Mimansakas (old Vedic householders) and the Vedantins (the later Vedic hermits), to the Shaivas, the Vaishnavas, and the Shaktas. This is evident in his copious literary outpourings.

To understand Sankaracharya, we need to break free from the fixed Abrahamic binary of one true God and other false Gods, which even influences much of today's political and scientific discourse, and move into the Hindu, rather fluid, binary where the divine can be limited (Jivatma, the Limited Self) and limitless (Paramatma, the Supreme Self), and where the relationship of form and formless divine is much like the relationship between sound and meaning without which no word can exist.

Qualified Nondualism or Monism (Vasishta Advaita Philosophy - विशिष्ट अद्वैत दर्शन), whose main proponent was Sri Ramanuja, contended that **the devotee is part of the whole, not separate from Him**. Ramanujacharya, (1017 CE-1137 CE) was an Indian Hindu philosopher, Guru, and a social reformer. He is noted to be one of the most important exponents of the Sri Vaishnavism tradition within Hinduism. His philosophical foundations for devotionalism were influential to the Bhakti movement in India.

His Vishishtadvaita (qualified nondualism) philosophy has competed with the Dvaita (theistic dualism) philosophy of Madhavacharya, and Advaita (nondualism) philosophy of Adi Shankara, together the three most influential Vedantic philosophies of the 2nd millennium. Ramanujacharya presented the Vedic and theological importance of bhakti, or the devotion to a personal God (Vishnu in Ramanuja's case) to spiritual liberation. His theories assert that there exists a plurality and distinction between Atman and Brahman, while he also affirmed that there is unity of all souls, and that the individual soul has the potential to realize identity with the Brahman.

Dvaitadvaita (Dvaita-Advaita–द्वैताद्वैत दर्शन or Dualistic–Nondualism philosophy-द्वैतिक अद्वैतवाद), whose main exponent was Nimbarkacharya (1130 CE-1200 CE) known as Nimbarka, Nimbaditya or Niyamananda. He was a Hindu philosopher, theologian, and the chief proponent of the theology of Dvaitadvaita (Dvaita-Advaita) or dualistic–nondualistic philosophy. He played a major role in spreading the worship of the divine couple Radha and Krishna, and founded Nimbarka Sampradaya, one of four main traditions of Hindu sect Vaishnavism.

Nimbarkacharya is believed to have lived around the 11th and 12th centuries, but this dating has been questioned, suggesting that he lived somewhat earlier than Sankaracharya, in the 6th or 7th century CE. Born in Southern India in a Telugu Brahmin family, he spent most of his life in Mathura, Uttar Pradesh. He is sometimes identified with another philosopher named Bhaskara, but this is considered to be a misconception due to the differences between the spiritual views of the two saints.

The '**Nimbarka Sampradaya**,' also known as the '**Hamsa Sampradaya**,' and '**Sanakadi Sampradaya**' (सनकादि सम्प्रदाय), is one of the four Vaisnava Sampradayas. It was founded by Nimbarkacharya. It propounds the Vaishnava Bhedabheda theology of Dvaitadvaita (Dvaita-Advaita) or dualistic nondualism. Dvaitadvaita states that **humans are both different and non-different from Isvara (God or Supreme Being)**. Specifically, this Sampradaya is a part of Krishnaism—Krishna-centric traditions.

The Nimbarka Sampradaya is based on Nimbarkacharya's Bhedabheda philosophy and nonduality at the same time, or dualistic nondualism.

According to Nimbarkacharya, there are three categories of existence, namely: **Isvara** (God, Divine Being); **Cit** (Jiva, the individual soul); and **Acit** (lifeless matter). Cit and Acit are different from Isvara, in the sense that they have attributes (Guna) and capacities (Swabhava), which are different from those of Isvara. At the same time, cit and acit are not different from Isvara, because they cannot exist independently of him. Isvara is independent and exists by himself, while cit and acit exist in dependence upon him. Difference means a kind of existence which is separate but dependent, (परतंत्र सत्ता भाव - paratantra-satta-bhava); while non-difference means impossibility of separate existence (स्वतंत्र सत्ता भाव - svatantra-satta-bhava).

According to Nimbarka, the relation between Brahman, on the one hand, and the Cit and Acit on the other, is a relation of natural difference-non-difference (svabhavika-bhedabheda). Nimbarkacharya equally emphasizes both difference and non-difference, as against Ramanuja, who makes difference subordinate to non-difference, in as much as, for him **cit** and **acit** do not exist separately from Brahman but are its body or attributes.

Nimbarkacharya accepts parinam vad (परिणाम वाद), the idea that the world is a real transformation (परिणाम-parinama) of Brahman, to explain the cause of animate and inanimate world, which he says exist in a subtle form in the various capacities (shaktis), which belong to Brahman in its natural condition. Brahman is the material cause of the universe, in the sense that Brahman brings the subtle rudiments into the gross form, by manifesting these capacities.

For Nimbarkacharya, the highest object of worship is Krishna and his consort Radha, attended by thousands of Gopi's, or cowherdesses, of the celestial Vrindavan. Devotion, according to Nimbarkacharya, consists in prapatti (प्राप्ति), or Self-surrender.

Dualism (Dvaita Philosophy-द्वैत दर्शन), whose main exponent was Sri Madhavacharya in 13th century CE (1199-1278 CE or 1238–1317 CE), concluded that **the Lord and His devotee will ever remain as two distinct entities**. The relationship of the devotee to the Lord is one of complete surrender in love and reverence. The supreme goal of humankind is to reach his feet and remain there eternally, ever in His service.

Madhvacharya's teachings are built on the premise that there is a fundamental difference between Atman and the Brahman. These are two different unchanging realities, with the individual soul dependent on Brahman, but never identical. His school's theistic dualism teachings disagreed with the monist teachings of the other two most influential schools of Vedanta based on Advaita's nondualism and Vishishtadvaita's qualified nondualism. "Liberation," asserted Madhavacharya, "is achievable only through the grace of God." The Dvaita school founded by Madhavacharya influenced Vaishnavism, the Bhakti movement in medieval India, and has been one of the three influential Vedanta philosophies, along with Advaita Vedanta and Vishishtadvaita Vedanta. Madhvacharya's historical influence in Hinduism has been salutary, but not extensive.

Shuddha Advaita (Pure Nondualism Philosophy - शुद्ध अद्वैत दर्शन), whose main proponent was Vallabhacharya Mahaprabhu (1479 CE-1531 CE), also known as Vallabha, Mahaprabhu and Vishnuswami, or Vallabhacharya, is a Hindu Indian saint and philosopher who founded the Krishana-centered Pushtimarg sect of Vaishnavism on the Braj (Vraja) region of India, and the Vedanta philosophy of Shuddha Advaita (Pure Nondualism).

He is considered the Jagadguru acharya and Guru of the Pushti Marg bhakti tradition and Shuddhadvaita, which he founded after his own interpretation of the Vedanta philosophy.

Vallabha was born in a Telugu Tailang Brahmin family that had been residing in Varanasi, who escaped to Champaran of Chhattisgarh state while expecting a Muslim invasion in Varanasi, during the late 15th century. The name Vallabha means the beloved or lover and is a name of Vishnu and Krishna.

Vallabha studied the Vedas, Upanishads, Puranas, Shad Darshana, as a child, then traveled throughout the Indian subcontinent over 20 years. He became one of the important leaders of the devotional Bhakti movement. Vallabha's mother was Illamma who was the daughter of a family priest serving the rulers of the empire of Vijayanagar. The biographies written by his followers, just like those for other Bhakti leaders, claim that he won many philosophical scholarly debates against the followers of Adi Sankara, Ramanuja, Madhavacharya, and others, had visions and miracles.

He rejected asceticism and monastic life, suggested that through loving devotion to the deity Krishna, any householder could achieve salvation–an idea that became influential all over India, held by his 84 Baithakjis (बैठक जी - places of worship) in Uttar Pradesh, Rajasthan, Gujarat, Maharashtra, Tamil Nadu, Andhra Pradesh, Karnataka, Kerala, Uttaranchal, Madhya Pradesh, Orissa, Goa, Sindh, and various other parts of Indian subcontinent. He is associated with the Vishnuswami Sampradaya and is the prominent Jagadguru Acharya of Rudra Sampradaya out of the four traditional Vaishnava Sampradayas.

He authored many texts including but not limited to, 'The Anubhashya,' colloquially also called 'Brahmasutra Anubhashya' (his commentary on Brahma Sutra), *'Shodasa,'* or *'Sixteen 'stotras' (tracts) and several commentaries on the Bhagavata Purana.'*

Vallabha's writings and kirtan compositions focus on baby Krishna and his childhood pranks with Yashoda (unconditional motherly love), as well as a youthful Krishna's protection of the good (divine grace) and his victory over demons and evils, all with allegory and symbolism.

His legacy is best preserved with the acharyas of his Pushtimarg Vallabh Sampradaya, also in the Braj region, and particularly at Nathdwara and Dwarkadhish Temple in Mewar region of India–are important Krishna pilgrimage centers. He is regarded as an incarnation of Agni (Vaishvanara).

Achintya-Bheda-Abheda (अचिन्त्यभेदाभेद) is a school of Vedanta representing the philosophy of incarnation one-ness and difference. In Sanskrit achintya means 'inconceivable,' Bheda translates as 'difference,' and Abheda translates as 'non-difference.'

The Gaudiya Vaishnava religious tradition employs the term in relation to the relationship of creation and creator (Krishna, Swayam Bhagavan), between God and his energies. It is believed that this philosophy was taught by the movement's theological founder Chaitanya Mahaprabhu (1486–1534) and differentiates the Gaudiya tradition from the other Vaishnava Sampradayas. It can be understood as an integration of the strict dualist (dvaita) theology of Madhavacharya and the qualified monism (Vishishtadvaita) of Ramanuja.

The theological tenet of Achintya-Bheda-Abheda tattva reconciles the mystery that God is simultaneously 'one with and different from His creation.' In this sense, Vaishnava theology is panentheistic as in no way does it deny the separate existence of God (Vishnu) in His own personal form. However, at the same time, creation (or what is termed in Vaishnava theology as the 'cosmic manifestation') is never separated from God. He always exercises supreme control over his creation. Sometimes directly, but most of the time indirectly through his different potencies or energies (**Prakriti**). Examples are given of a spider and its web; earth and plants that come forth and hair on the body of a human being.

"One who knows God knows that the impersonal conception and personal conception are simultaneously present in everything and that there is no contradiction. Therefore, Lord Chaitanya established His sublime doctrine: Achintya-Bheda-Abheda-tattva, that is, simultaneous oneness and difference." (A. C. Bhaktivedanta Swami Prabhupada). The analogy is often used as an explanation in this context in the relationship between the sun and the sunshine. For example, both the sun and sunshine are part of the same reality, but there is a great difference between having a beam of sunshine in your room and being in close proximity to the sun itself. Qualitatively the sun and the sunshine are not different, but as quantities they are very different. This analogy is applied to the living beings and God - the Jiva being of a similar quality to the Supreme being, but not sharing the qualities to an infinite extent, as would the Personality of Godhead himself. Thus, there is a difference between the souls and the Supreme Lord.

Historically, within Hinduism, there are two conflicting philosophies regarding the relationship between living beings and God. Advaita schools assert the monistic view that the individual soul and God are one and the same, whereas Dvaita schools give the dualistic argument that the individual soul and God are eternally separate. The philosophy of Achintya-Bheda-Abheda includes elements of both viewpoints. The living soul is intrinsically linked with the Supreme Lord, and yet at the same time is not the same as God - the exact nature of this relationship being inconceivable to the human mind. The Soul is considered to be part and parcel of the Supreme Lord. Same in quality but not in quantity. God having all opulence in fullness, the spirit soul however, having only a partial expression of His divine opulence. God in this context is compared to a fire and the souls as sparks coming off of the flame.

16

Spiritual Practice (साधना) For Self-Realization

Having read about Spirituality, the Self, the God, the Path of Spirituality, and Self-realization so far in this book, you must have surely had a thought in your mind that all these description about spirituality, religion and the rituals therein are diametrically opposite to what you have seen, known, and experienced about the Sanatan Dharma. The display of Hindu religion that we witness all around us is all about Puja of various Deities, Paath, Bhajan, Kirtan, Pilgrimages, ritualistic reading of books of scriptures (Ramcharitmanas, Chalisas etc.), Fasting, celebration of religious festivals and important days during the year. There is a popular understanding amongst Hindus, if not an established belief, that if one has been performing or participating in these activities to whatever degree, your responsibility of being a religious person is satisfactorily completed. One feels happy and justified that they have done their bit of religiosity.

Unfortunately, various religious activities that one performs during the course of their life, seems to have become an end in themselves. Ritualistic performances undertaken mindlessly in a mechanical manner for the sake of it, seems to be the way the Hindu religion has been reduced down to. "I have no clue whatsoever what I am doing, nor do I have any clarity as to why I am doing it. I never stop to think if I am getting any material or spiritual benefits out of it, nor do I know what I was supposed to get out of it in the first place." So, we are on a search expedition, which is going on very devotedly, systematically, and continuously ever since my childhood and it carries on throughout my life. I had never known the object of my search at the beginning of the search and even now, I do not have any clue about what I have been searching. But the search, nonetheless, continues. This seems to be the case with the people who believe themselves to be religious Hindus.

Whether you are an atheist or a religious person, who regularly performs most of the above ritualistic practices, there is not much difference between the two, so far as experiencing life or the core objective of religious practice is concerned. Both continue to suffer the impact of Negative Affectivity irrespectively. The atheist person generally believes themselves to be logical and scientist in temperament, hence they cannot really be expected to undertake religious ritualistic practices or partake in such activities, since they believe that there is no God and/or these seem illogical and unscientific to them. Having said that, I am not suggesting that the above mentioned religious activities are useless and/or ineffective, illogical, or unscientific at all. Can my atheist friends explain what God is, which they do not believe in. I think when someone claims to be an atheist, they are suggesting that they do not believe in idol worship or undertake above mentioned religious activities etc. Since they do not believe in God, it is but natural for them not to get involved in anything which is remotely religious, let alone engaging in ritualistic Puja, Paath etc. At the same time, it is not possible for one to remain atheist if one knows God. So, my question to my dear atheist friends is very simple. How do you manage to **'not believe'** in something, which you do not know about. My logical and scientific mind tells me that to believe in something or not believe in something, I must know it reasonably well if not thoroughly.

We will now pay some attention at the Spiritual Practices with particular reference to some of the known practices in the common parlance e.g., Puja of various Deities, Paath, Bhajan, Kirtan, Pilgrimages, Ritualistic reading of books of scriptures (e.g. Ramcharitmanas, Gita, Chalisas etc.), Fasting, Celebration of religious festivals and important days during the year. Are these stand-alone religious prescriptions or have anything to do with Vedic literature such as Vedas, Puranas, and Upanishads? Let us now investigate the origin and the logic of rituals and their relevance within the wider context of Vedic literature.

I ask you to recall from previous sections of this book that our Rishis have classified the texture of our thoughts (moods) into three distinct categories and called these, the 'Gunas,' e.g., Sattvic, Rajasic and Tamasic. **Sattvic mood** is where an individual is not at all motivated by selfish desires or seeking sense pleasures. The people who have acquired such a mood, mostly undertake desireless activities. All their activities (at body, mind, and intellect levels) in the world outside are dedicated purely to the activities themselves as they seek joy from the work they do. In the **Rajasic mood,** having reached a certain level of Selfish satisfaction, the individual undertakes activities (at body, mind, and intellect levels) in the world outside for seeking personal glorification and acknowledgement in the society through undertaking charitable activities, apparently for the good of others, but primarily for social recognition, pride, and/or personal glorification. These people are working for the higher goal and values and working tirelessly to succeed in their endeavors. In the **Tamasic mood**, the individual has a total lack of pure consciousness and has full blown egoistic desires. All his activities (at body, mind, and intellect levels) in the world outside are performed with pure Selfish motives for the fulfillment of their sensuous desires, purely for the satisfaction of his and his family's needs alone.

Depending on our particular mix of Gunas, we see the world–as well as our relationship to the Supreme Reality–differently. To an ordinary person, his body is himself. His identification with the body is deep and strong. He lives for the body, strives for the body, and knows no other mission in life than seeking sensuous enjoyments. For one who exists in such a state, the only relationship to the supreme Reality can be one of **separateness** (Duality).

To another class of people–who have evolved to recognise that they are not only their bodies but also beings endowed with a mind and intellect–to such people, the human being is not just a perishable worm, but a sacred creature who possesses almost godly powers evident in the manifestations of the mind and intellect. Such people study the achievements of science and poetry. They recognise the great thinkers and discoverers. They consider the victory that man has so far gained over mighty nature. They see man as a thinking creature who has glory and might not be much inferior to God's. For people with this degree of development and intellectual evolution, the relationship to Reality is that of being **a part of the whole** (Qualified Nondualism).

For these two categories of people, our great Rishis of Sanatan tradition have provided two separate approaches to the Truth. Qualified Non Dualism/Monism (Vasishta Advaita Philosophy - विशिष्ट अद्वैत दर्शन) and Dualism (Dvaita Philosophy - द्वैत दर्शन). The former contended that the devotee is part of the whole, not separate from Him and the later concluded that Lord and His devotee will ever remain as two distinct entities. The third approach, that is the Non Dualism or Monism (Advaita Vedanta Philosophy- अद्वैत वेदांत दर्शन), of Sri Adi Sankaracharya which believes that **Man is in essence God**.

To a student of Dualism or Qualified Monism, the declaration of Sri Adi Sankaracharya may appear fanatical, for the former views truth in reference to his body while the latter views it with reference to his psychological personality. The perfect student of Vedanta, however, discovers through discrimination that neither his body nor his mind-intellect equipment is really himself. He feels that some power subtler than the mind and intellect plays hide-and-seek within him and forms a dynamic life center deep within the matter envelopments(BMI). The sincere student of Vedanta, through Guru's grace, gets the endorsement of his conclusions. He gains arguments and convictions, which leads him to the seat of life, the Self, that lies within the seeker himself. When the disciple comes to understand the significance of the scriptures' words and experiences, first hand, that he himself is that which he has been seeking, he gains perfect knowledge. **He is Self-realized**. Such an experience of the disciples and the seeker of Reality is expressed by our Rishis in the Vedic declaration of **"Aham Brahma Asmi,"** that is, **"I am Brahman."**

Our relationship with Reality can thus be explained in three different ways, depending on our state of mind. Even the greatest sages had moments when they were conscious of the sorrows of physical pain and inclement weather. At such moments, even they may prostrate at the Lord's feet and mentally seek his mercy. At other moments, they may be conscious of some inner mental agitations or irresistible poetic outbursts and may recognise within themselves a power that is almost a part of the Lord Himself. And then, in those rare moments when they had completely retired from the outer coverings of matter to the subtlest of the subtle within, they saw that **"I am That."** At that point, the individual and the supreme Reality constitute one perfect whole.

These schools of thought are not so much contradicting or competing theories, but as explanations of necessary stages, we must pass through in our pilgrimage to the peak of perfection. Only the intellectual pundits quarrel and seek to establish one or the other declaration as superior. The moment we step on the path of spiritual practice, we'll realize that these three philosophies, in fact, are wayside essential stopovers for our pilgrimage in linear order of our physical, mental, and intellectual evolution. These indicate a necessary evolutionary progress each individual goes through in their spiritual journey. We can rest at each and proceed ahead. All individuals are body conscious at first and believe their personality with reference to the body alone. With growing knowledge and experience, they encounter the pivotal role of mind and intellect in all their experiences and eventually realize the need to go beyond their body, mind, and intellect, in order to realize their Real personality. Every pilgrim, therefore, depending on his/her evolutionary stage in life, must first visit Sri Madhvacharya, take his blessings, and proceed to worship Sri Ramanuja; then alone can one reach the portals of Vedanta, the abode of Sri Adi Shankaracharya, where he can find the release from thraldom of Maya and ultimate liberation from the miseries of life.

Spiritual and Religious Practices (साधना)

Most belief systems and ritualistic practices within the Hindu fold, we observe today, are rooted into and/or are influenced by one of the approaches discussed above or are a combination of them. The sole purpose of spiritual and religious knowledge and practice, according to our Subjective Scientists, is to realize one's real potential, and the true nature, gain mastery over one's body, mind, and the intellect, so as to live an effective, purposeful, and successful life full of perpetual and everlasting peace, happiness, and contentment.

What religious and ritualistic practice one follows in life, however, is seldom based on education, knowledge and/or informed choice. In most situations, it is either the family tradition, which one must carry forward or in any case it is a blind faith, and/or the fear of the unknown, which are unfortunately the fundamental reasons supporting the prevalence of Hindu ritualistic practices today. Does it serve any worthwhile purpose in our day-to-day life? Everyone has their own personal justifications to support their argument in response to this question, but rarely anyone can give an answer which is in line with the Vedic or Upanishadic understanding.

Most young people in Hindu families, whether in India or living abroad, often find themselves confused, confounded, bewildered, about their religion. Their knowledge and understanding about Hinduism and its practices seem very cursory, shallow, and superficial. They often find themselves on a flimsy ground to hold a sensible discussion, let alone holding a logical debate. They are not to be blamed. Unfortunately, they do not have any credible resources available to them, which they can rely upon for a consistent, logical and/or scientific explanation to a wide range of religious practices, they witness within and without the family. They are expected to take part in these activities, since they are born in a Hindu family. At the same time, most Hindu parents find themselves ill equipped with answers and logical explanations to the religious practices that they themselves perform and which they expect their young ones to participate in. This is just a pen-picture of the current state of affairs of Hindu society today.

One must wonder as to how a rich society, which was nurtured by highly erudite saints, seers, and sages, who led an incredible Gurukul System of education for thousands of years, well balance in both secular and sacred education, which mastered the art of man-making and was leading in scientific advancements, saw a pathetic decline to its present state in past two thousand years. Let us glance over a few major historical upheavals, which systematically caused the erosion of the Gurukul System of education, thereby weakening the scaffolding of Hindu society. Once we appreciate the calamitous journey traveled by the Hindu society over the last two thousand years, we would be in a better position to contextualize the current pathetic state of affairs of Hinduism, its knowledge, understanding and practices in the modern-day Hindu society.

India has been subjected to a systematic erosion of Indian Vedic, philosophical and cultural education, ever since the advent of Gautam Buddha on the scene. In the 6th century B.C., the world saw Siddhartha becoming Buddha. He, at first, did not like to preach his new doctrine to people because he thought that the people would not understand or accept it. But he changed his mind and once he did, there was no stopping him. There was no persecution but an air of persecution, carefully created by Gautam Buddha to carry out his missionary ambitions to convert Hindu population that was adhering to the Vedic culture of education in Sanskrit into a Buddhist mob who knew Pali, a language of mediocre minds. The stage was set, Hinduism and its eminent system of education was set on a course of its demise and the pre-final nail in its coffin was the Islamic invasion.

The influence of Islamic invasion on Indian society, and the old Indian education system was much stronger. There were many different Muslim rulers in different parts of India. The first spreaders of Islam in India were traders or preachers who arrived in India from Bukhara, Turkey, Iran, Yemen, and Saudi Arabia. The process of converting Indians to Islam began in the 8th Century when the Arabs began invading North India and present-day Pakistan. Most of these invaders were Islamic fanatics. During their term, the non-Muslims suffered a lot. Many worshiping sites of different religions were destroyed and transformed into mosques. Most of the Indian Muslims trace their origin from the lower strata of the Hindu societies because they were the most brutally exploited and had to convert to avoid the sufferings of paying heavy taxes. The Jamaat (The group of Sufia-E-Karam) took keen interest to preach the teachings of Islam.

The sharp contrast between the spread of Buddhism and the spread of Islam was that Buddhism being an offshoot from Hinduism, never tried to eradicate the teachings of Hinduism whereas Islam, an independently developed foreign religion, was keen on tearing the fabric of Hinduism and trying to mock the profound teachings of the Vedas. The result of years of invasion, annexation and offense against the Hindus led to the deterioration of the education system of ancient India. The Gurukul system was highly decentralized. There was no center of learning in each Nagaras (old cities) to which protection could be provided. Few places, where it was so, were destroyed by the Muslims.

Historically, India had a strong tradition of education, with institutions such as Nalanda, Takshashila, and Vikramashila, among others, dating back to ancient times. The parts of Nalanda were destroyed by fire between 1197 and 1206 A.D. since heaps of ashes and charcoal were found at the excavation sites. Nalanda suffered gravely during the conquest of Bihar Nagaras by the Muslim general Muhammad Bakhtiyar Khilji, a sellsword who rose from being a slave to being a general who put to an end the epitome of knowledge ever created.

However, during the colonial period, the British introduced a new education system that was geared towards producing servants, clerks, and administrators to serve the British Empire. This new system prioritized English education and western knowledge over traditional Indian knowledge systems. While this led to the establishment of new schools and colleges, it also resulted in the decline of traditional educational institutions. This was the final nail in the coffin of the demise of Hinduism and its eminent system of education.

Furthermore, after India gained independence in 1947, efforts were made to expand access to education across the country. This led to the establishment of new institutions, including universities, colleges, and technical schools, and the growth of existing institutions. Unfortunately, Hindu society wasn't going to benefit from Independence as there was a silent and covert invasion of the left communist ideology, which had a very serious and detrimental influence on the modern education system in India. Slowly and systematically, the sacred education was completely removed from the syllabus. However, many old educational institutions were unable to keep up with the changing times and were not able to adapt to new trends and technologies. This, coupled with a lack of funding and support, has led to the decline of many old educational institutions in India.

In addition to the removal of sacred education from the curriculum, there were systematic covert attempts being made in India to decouple new Independent India from its thousands of years of cultural heritage. Until the second decade of the 21st century, the Indian administration seemed under some invisible pressure to prove and declare itself the most secular nation in the world. In its attempt to do so, the administration was heavily inclined to please the Muslim population at the expense of Hindu rights. Deliberate attempts were made, since its independence, to undermine and denigrate Hindu cultural and religious practices.

Hindus lost control of their temples. Hindus could not get their children educated in religious texts in schools, these are just a few observations to name. Hindus of India did not find a socio-cultural environment within the country, wherein their religion could thrive with pride.

In conclusion, the decline of old educational institutions in India is a complex issue that cannot be attributed to a single factor. Rather, it is the result of a combination of historical, social, economic, and political factors that have impacted, both the decline of the sacred Indian Vedic and Philosophical education system and the development of the new secular and western education in India over time. This titanic shift in the education policy in the independent India also shifted the core purpose of man making and nation building which was deeply rooted in the Indian Vedic thought of **'Vasudev Kutumbakam'** and stooped down to its lowest rank of materialistic western value based, individualist society, where money making by hook or by crook to serve 'me, mine, and myself' and looking after number one has now been established as the only philosophy of life. Raising the standards of living (materialism) became the sole purpose of education and raising the standard life (spiritualism) is not a concern, whatsoever, of anyone, be it parents, teachers, families, society, or the nation.

So, if our young people and their families are bereft of the knowledge about their own culture, religion, and ritualistic practices, they can't really be blamed. However, when they face other cultures and compare themselves with them, all they have is a sense of shame and low Self-esteem. It is no more wonderous to come across many, perhaps in hundreds of thousands, who do not like associating themselves with Hinduism. Yet there are millions, who take pride in disrespecting and devaluing their own culture and religion and make fun of symbols of religious significance.

They know they are Hindu, but they do not know why they are Hindus or what makes them Hindus. They celebrate Diwali, for example, but they have no clue about it, except that Lord Ram came back and it's a celebration of victory of good over evil. I would not be surprised if you can find anyone who knows anything different from these two most common responses, both in India and abroad. Today's school students do not even know who the author of the epic Ramayana was. They would, however, take a lot of pride in their knowledge of Shakespeare and have a definite knowledge of the author of Harry Potter. Parents prefer their children to speak in English and recite Humpty-Dumpty sat on a wall. Parents take pride and a sense of being modern when they talk to their 3–4-year-olds in English in public places. There are schools in India who levy fines on students if they speak in their mother tongue over English. Using your mother tongue is an indication of belonging to a lower social strata. You may be a congenital idiot of the finest degree, but if you are blessed with English language, you will enjoy good respect in Indian society.

Sanskrit, anyway, is worse than a foreign language in India. No one wants it and only a few know it. It has no utility or purpose that it can serve in modern Indian society. Since independence we have made sure that McCauley[19] and his sinister policy was kept alive. His objective was to create English speaking buffoons to work as servants for the East India Company and he was extremely successful. He wanted to destroy our language in order to not only drive the Indian society away but to eventually uproot them from its rich cultural heritage. The lack of Sanskrit is one of the main reasons as to why Hindus in general and Hindu young people, in particular, are bereft of their own cultural knowledge and heritage.

---

[19] *In India, Thomas Babington Macaulay is fully credited with the official introduction of English education, though the necessary order on the subject was issued by Bentinck, the Governor-General of India, on March 7, 1835. According to Macaulay, the sole purpose of the introduction of English education in India would not be merely an indoctrination of Indians through textbooks and curricula for subordinate positions in the establishments of the East India Company but to achieve cultural transmission among the educated Indians.*

Spiritual practices, which manifest themselves in various ritualistic performances, are fundamentally designed to help every Hindu and particularly the seeker of spiritual knowledge to create and provide one's body, mind, and intellect a conducive physical and mental environment for higher spiritual practices. It is a vedic declaration that "The mind is the cause of all problems experienced, and the mind is the tool, technique and the solution for all problems experienced." Within this context, it can be concluded that all spiritual practices are, fundamentally and essentially, designed, prescribed, and recommended to train the wild and wandering nature of the mind and bring it under sway of one's intellect to purify mind and maintain a sustained poise and tranquility.

Toward these objectives, there are a range of ritualistic activities which are recommended to Hindu to observe and practice. These practices can be divided in two broad categories, namely, **Bahiranga Sadhana (बहिरंग साधना)**, primary or external spiritual practices, which essentially are preparatory techniques to tame the wandering mind and bring it under one's control and gain an ability to focus one's mind on a chosen thing or a thought. Such a state of mind is called the **meditative state of mind** and it is an essential prerequisite for the advance or internal spiritual practices, which are known as the **Antaranga-Sadhana (अंतरंग-साधना)**. Antaranga-Sadhana, essentially, are the practices wherein the meditative mind is engaged in contemplation on the higher Self.

Bahiranga Sadhana (बहिरंग साधना)

What is Bahiranga Sadhana?

Spiritual Discipline for purification of the Mind is called Bahiranga Sadhana. For example, Yagna (यज्ञ), Charity (दान), Service (सेवा), Chanting (जप), Penance (तप), Vow (व्रत), Pilgrimage (तीर्थ), Contemplation (विचार एवं ध्यान) etc., all these spiritual practices fall under this category of primary external practices. The main purpose of these practices is preparation and purification of the mind of the spiritual seeker, ready for the advanced spiritual practices.

Yagna means to worship God (ब्रह्म उपासना). If we fulfill our duties considering them as worship, that itself is yagna for the welfare of an individual or society. The worship of God performed through fire is called Yagna. It is also called Havana or Homa. Yagna performed as a daily routine is called **'Samidha-Dana'** or **'Agnihotra.'** Actually, Fire Yagna is a symbolic worship indicating the need to sacrifice one's Ego in the fire of life (God-Realization) and thus destroying ignorance is the ultimate aim to be realized by the spiritual seeker.

That means, work itself is worship or Yagna. So, then why does one worship God in some particular form (साकार उपासना)? Considering the Idol of one's chosen Deity to be the God Itself and adoring it as such is worship. Just as the cloth of a flag, its color and design are a symbol of a nation, country's ideals. The traffic signs on the roads are the symbols, indicating distance and the direction to follow in order for us to reach our destination safely and on time. In the same way, an Idol is a symbol of a particular idea of God, which is superimposed on an image or an object or a stone. That is why 'Idol Worship' is also known as a 'Symbolic Worship' (सांकेतिक उपासना या प्रतीक उपासना).

Symbolic Worship is a primary stage of spiritual practice, which is a prerequisite for children, young people, and new seekers of knowledge. Bahiranga Sadhana or primary spiritual practices help in creating an external environment conducive for our mind to have a continuous and regular supply of Sattvic stimuli for it to be ready and prepared for the inner, higher, and advanced spiritual practices. The main objective of Bahiranga Sadhana or primary spiritual practice, therefore, is undoubtedly preparing and purifying our mind. Hence the Bahiranga Sadhanas or primary spiritual practices must be performed with full clarity, knowledge and understanding of their respective purpose and goals in mind.

In Hinduism, **Yagna** is a ritual of offerings accompanied by chanting of Vedic mantras also referred to as 'worship, prayer, praise, offering, oblation, and sacrifice' derived from the practice in Vedic times. Yagna is an ancient ritual of offering and sublimating the herbal preparations (हवन सामग्री - Havana Samagri) in the fire. There are many concepts that are based on and evolved from the concept of Yagna. The word Yagna comes from the root- **'Yaj'** which means to worship. Yagna is a broad concept which is hard to translate into English. The closest single English word for Yagna is 'Sacrifice.' There are multiple synonyms of the word Yagna that convey different aspects of this broad concept.

The term 'Yagna' borrowed from our scriptures, is employed in Bhagavad Gita by Lord Krishna to yield a more elaborate sense implying a wider and a more universal application. According to the Gita, the Vedic Yagna has become a Self-dedicated activity performed in a spirit of service to the many. All actions, performed without Ego, and not motivated by one's egocentric desires, fall under the category of 'Yagna.' When a sage[20] performs action in a spirit of Yagna, they dissolve away without leaving any impression upon his mind, just as the rainbow that disappears when the thin shower falling against the sunlight ends.

If this be so, the question arises, "For what reason then do all actions which they perform, entirely dissolve, without producing their natural impression on their mind?" This inquiry of the reader is dealt with in the following verse from chapter 4 of Bhagavad Gita.

ब्रह्मार्पणं ब्रह्म हविर्ब्रह्माग्नौ ब्रह्मणा हुतम् ।

ब्रह्मैव तेन गन्तव्यं ब्रह्मकर्मसमाधिना ॥

-भगवद् गीता ४.२४

---

[20] *Sage is considered a profoundly wise person; a person known and venerated for the possession of wisdom, judgment, and experience.*

"Brahman is the oblation; Brahman is the clarified butter, etc., constituting the offerings; by Brahman is the oblation poured into the fire of Brahman; Brahman verily shall be reached by him who always sees Brahman in all actions."

The Infinite Reality is indicated by the Vedic term 'Brahman,' which is the same **Truth** that functions through the body but is called 'Atman.' But though the Eternal Truth has been thus indicated by two different terms, Vedanta declares that **"The Atman is Brahman."** The metaphor is borrowed from the very well-known divine ritualism of the Vedas, the Yagna. In every Yagna there are four essential factors, (1) the Deity invoked to whom the oblations are offered, (2) the fire in which the offerings are poured, (3) the material things that constitute the offerings and (4) the individual who is performing the Yagna.

The fire Yagna, therefore, is a symbolic spiritual act, which indicates towards the mental attitude and the experience of the Perfect-Sage when he performs the Yagna. To him Truth alone exists and not the delusory plurality which his erstwhile ignorance had conjured up for him in his mind. Therefore, to him, all Yagna arise from Brahman; in which Brahman, the Truth, is the performer; offering Brahman, the material to the sacred fire, which is also nothing other than Brahman; invoking but Brahman. If an individual can thus see the substratum, or the essential nature, in and through, all names and forms, actions and behaviors, to him, irrespective of all, external and internal, conditions and circumstances, all beings and things are but a remembrance of the Infinite Blissful Truth. If actions are performed by a Saint, invoking no deity other than Brahman, all his actions dissolve away because he is invoking the One Truth through all his actions.

The significance of the above verse, which is said before food is amply Self-evident. To live we must eat. Food is necessary for existence. Whatever be the type of food, when one is hungry one will enjoy one's meals. The suggestion is that even at this moment of natural enjoyment while eating, we are not to forget the great Truth that it is Brahman eating Brahman, and that is Brahman, invoking nothing but the grace of Brahman. To keep this idea constantly in the mind is to get perfectly detached from the enjoyment and raise us to a greater and endless beatitude, which is the reward of Super-manhood. Even the simplest activity, such as eating food must be considered and completed in a Yagna spirit. The entire digestive process is a very complex system and process, but if we think carefully, God has graciously taken on responsibility of the entire system and process of decomposing the food by mixing various enzymes and juices into it, extracting, and distributing nutrition and take the essence of the food, that is, the nutrition to each and every cell of the body and discard the waste. We are only required to chew our food in our mouth but we do not even do that properly. That's why our Rishis have recommended that in order for our body, mind, and intellect, necessary instrument required is in the meditation upon the Self, to be nourished and healthy, eating/chewing food should be considered a Yagna and must, therefore, be performed in the Yagna spirit. It is therefore recommended by our spiritual masters that the food must be considered as God's Prasad and must be accepted and consumed with love and reverence.

The sublime meaning of the word Yagna has a three-fold meaning of (1) Worship of Deities (देव पूजन- Devapujana), (2) Unity (संगति करण- Sangatikarana) and (3) Charity (दान- Dana). An essential element is the ritual fire–the Divine Agni–into which oblations are poured, as everything that is offered into the fire is believed to reach God.

For instance, it is also called 'karma,' meaning action or the act of sacrifice/offering/worshiping. In the general sense it can be understood as any action done with the sense of sacrifice, like praying, remembering, meditating. In the specific sense it is the act of offering oblations to propitiate a Devata.

The primary constituents of a Yagna are the:

- inspiration or sacred urge of the doer (भावना - Bhavana)

- learning (स्वाध्याय - Svadhyaya)

- rites involved (कर्म - Karma)

- offerings (त्याग - Tyaga-Renunciation)

- devata (देवता - Propitious and/or illumining potentiality)

- the results (फल - Phala-the result, the outcome)

The spiritual import of Yagna, therefore, essentially is a selfless action, in a mood of surrender and dedication, performed by an inspired seeker of knowledge to gain insight in his own propitious potentialities. Since we know that the style of writing in the Vedic and Upanishadic literature uses symbolic and indicative language to point to the subtle and sublime meanings of its teachings. The practice of pouring oblation in the fire by five priests indicates a spiritual practice where a sincere seeker is advised to pour all his Ego, egocentric desires, and the sense of doership by the five sense organs and the organs of action into the fire of life. This is indicative of a stage of intellectual evolution where a spiritual seeker comes to realize that he is not the BMI, but the supreme Reality and all actions performed by his body, mind and intellect are, in fact, enlivened by the Reality, therefore, all actions thus performed, must be necessarily credited to the Reality itself.

Performance of regular Yagna, therefore, is a spiritual prescription for a sincere seeker to be reminded of, every now and then, in his evolutionary journey. All actions performed in a Yagna spirit, where the mental energy is not wasted in the worry of future results of the actions, rather conserved and invested into the task in hand, has much higher possibilities of **'Dexterity in Action,'** that is, becoming competent in action or work. Gaining such a skill in action is referred to as **'Yoga'** by Lord Krishna in Bhagavad Gita.

बुद्धियुक्तो जहातीह उभे सुकृतदुष्कृते ।
तस्माद्योगाय युज्यस्व योग: कर्मसु कौशलम् ॥

-भगवद् गीता २.५०

"One who has an evenness of temper accomplished by his perfect withdrawal from the realm of sentiments and emotions, and who is established in his resolute intellect, gets himself transported from the arena of both the good and the bad, merit and demerit."

A Yogi is one who is always trying, through all the means that are in him, to raise himself from his state of physical, mental, and intellectual imperfections to a more perfect state of existence. The word **'Deva'** (देव) comes from a root, meaning 'illumination.' Subjectively viewed, the greatest 'Devas' are the five sense organs. Eyes illuminating forms and colors; ears illuminating sounds, the nose illuminating smells, and the tongue and skin illuminating taste and touch respectively. Seekers and perfect Masters (Yogis) too, when they move in the world, no doubt, perceive sense-objects through sense stimuli. But in their understanding and experience, perception is but "a world of sense-objects continuously offering themselves into the fire of his perception in order to invoke the Devas (sense-perceptions)." Such seekers and masters walk out into life, and when they come across the sense world, they only recognise and experience that the world-of-objects is paying a devoted tribute to the powers of sense perception!

When this mental attitude is entertained constantly by a seeker, he comes to feel completely detached from the sense experiences and, irrespective of the quality of experience, he is able to maintain a constant sense of inward equanimity. Such an action is called a **Deva-Yagna** (देव-यज्ञ). As contrasted with this method, there are others who perform **Brahma-Yagna** (ब्रह्म-यज्ञ), says Krishna, wherein they come "to offer the Self as a Sacrifice by the Self in the fire of the Self." This statement becomes perfectly clear when subjectively analyzed and understood. As long as we exist in the body manifestation, we have to come across the world of sense-objects. The outer world can yield to us its joys and sorrows not by itself but only as a result of our healthy or unhealthy attitude towards it. The objects in themselves are impotent to give us either joy or sorrow.

The Yagna metaphor is taken from the most familiar ritualism known at the time of Arjuna. Oblations were offered, in Vedic ritualism, into the sacred fire in order to invoke the blessings of the deity. These examples show that when we offer material into a sacred fire, not only the oblations get burnt up and consumed by the fire, but also, as a result, a great blessing accrues. In the same way, some masters live on in life, constantly offering their senses into the fire of self-control, so that the senses of their own accord get burnt up, contributing a greater freedom and joy in the inner life of a man. It is also a fact very well experienced by us all, that the more we try to satisfy the sense-organs the more riotous they become and loot away our inner joy. By self-control alone can the sense organs be fully controlled and mastered. This is yet another method shown to the seekers by which they can come to experience and live a more intense life of deeper meditation.

As restraining of the senses is suggested as a method above, to make the mind non-perceptive to the perceptions of the senses (Indriyas) is a method by which one can gain a better poise in life for purposes of meditation. Such an individual who has controlled the mind completely and has withdrawn it totally from sense-centers is indicated as a Yagna. The former method is a technique of controlling the stimuli at the very gateway of the senses, the latter is a different technique of controlling the same from the inner, and therefore, more subtle level of perception, called the mind. Adi Sankaracharya presents these two techniques by the name of **"Sama & Dama"** (सम एवं दम) as part of six essential mental qualities (षड्-सम्पति) for a sincere seeker to acquire.

All the activities of the sense-organs (Jnana-Indriyas), and the organs of action (Prana-Indriyas) are offered into the knowledge-kindled fire of the right understanding–Control of the Ego by the better understanding of the Divine Reality is called, by Lord Krishna, as the **'Yoga of Self-restraint'** (Atma-Samyama-Yoga, आत्मसंयम योग). A few more types of Yagna have been enumerated in the Gita, in addition to the ones already mentioned above.

Dravya Yagna (द्रव्य-यज्ञ, Offering of Wealth)

Sacrifice of Wealth is to be understood in its largest connotation. Charity and distribution of honestly acquired wealth (Charity- दान), in a sincere spirit of devotion to and in the service of the community, or of the individual who is the recipient of the benevolence, is called **Dravya Yagna**. This includes more than a mere offering of money or food. The term Dravya includes everything that we possess, not only in the world outside, but also in our world of emotions and ideas. To pursue this life of charity, servicing the world as best as we can, with all that we possess physically, mentally, and intellectually is the noble sacrifice called **'Wealth Sacrifice.'**

In order to perform this, it is not necessary that the devotee should be materially rich. Even if we are poor and physically debilitated, from our bed of pain and poverty, we can still be charitable, because our inner treasure of love, kindness, sympathy, and affection, do not at all depend either upon our material circumstances nor on our physical condition. Sometimes a word of sincere sympathy, a look of love, a smile of true affection, or a word registering true friendship, can give to the receiver more than a heartless cheque, even if it be for a very fat sum. Service rendered to a deprived person or a being with love and respect, considering him to be Lord Narayana, is called Charity (दान), the Dravya Yagna. Sharing one's time, service, knowledge, and skills, that too is Charity. That too, should not be for a reward or recognition. The mind gets purified only when it is rendered selflessly.

Tapo-Yagna (तपो-यज्ञ)

Some live, offering unto their Lord, a life of austerity. There is no religion in the world which does not prescribe, by some method or the other, a period of austere living. These austerities (Vrata–व्रत) are invariably undertaken in the name of the Lord. It is very well known that the Lord of Compassion, who feeds and sustains even the lowest of the low, can gain no special joy because of a devotee's Self-denial. But it is generally done in the spirit of dedication, so that the seeker might achieve some self-control and gain mastery over the temptation of the sense objects and to withstand the sense pressures. This activity, in some extreme cases very painful indeed, is undertaken in order that the devotee may learn to control himself in his life.

Svadhyaya Yagna (स्वाध्याय-यज्ञ)

The daily deep study of the scriptures is called **Svadhyaya**. Without a complete study of the scriptures we will not be able to know the logic of what we are doing in the name of spiritual practice, and without this knowledge our practices cannot gain the edge and the depth that are essential for sure progress. Thus, in all religions, the daily study of the scriptures is insisted upon, as an essential training during the seeker's early days. Even after Self-realization, we find that the sages spend all their spare time reading and contemplating upon the inexhaustible wealth of details and suggestion in the scriptures.

In its subjective implication, Svadhyaya means 'study of the Self including the art of introspection pursued for understanding our own inner weaknesses.' If, in the case of a seeker, it is a technique of estimating his own spiritual progress, in the case of a Seer, it will be for reveling in his own Self.

Jnana Yagna (ज्ञान-यज्ञ)

The sacrifice-of-knowledge–this word has, very often, been used in the Gita and it constitutes one of the many original terms coined out by Ved Vyasa to beautify the Lord's declarations. The sacrifice-of-knowledge is the term given to that activity in man by which he renounces all his ignorance into the fire-of-knowledge kindled by Him and in Him. This is constituted of two aspects: (1) negation of the false, and (2) assertion of the Real Nature of the Self. These two activities are effectively undertaken during the seeker's meditation.

All these methods of Self-unfoldment - sacrifice of wealth, austerity, Yoga, study, and knowledge—can be practiced with profit only by those who are men of rigid determination and who can find in themselves an inexhaustible enthusiasm to apply themselves consistently to reach this great goal. It is not sufficient that we know these paths, or that we decide to gain these developments. Progress in spirituality can come only to one who is sincere and consistent in his practices.

Pranayama Yagna (प्राणायाम-यज्ञ)

This has been discussed for its usefulness as a Yagna in following verse of Gita to be undertaken by a sincere seeker, which helps him to gain a capacity to withdraw all his perceptions and is indeed considered a great help to a meditator.

अपाने जुह्वति प्राणं प्राणेऽपानं तथापरे ।
प्राणापानगती रूद्ध्वा प्राणायामपरायणा: ॥

-भगवद् गीता ४.२९

In this verse, the technique of breath-control (Pranayama) regularly practiced by some seekers is described, in order to keep themselves under perfect self-control, when they move amidst the sense-objects in the work-a-day world.

As a sacrifice, some offer the Outgoing Breath into the Incoming Breath and others offer the Incoming into the Outgoing. The latter, in the technique of **Pranayama**, is called '**Purak** (पूरक, Inhalation),' meaning the process of filling in; while the former is the process of blowing out, technically called '**Rechak** (रेचक, Exhalation).' These two processes are alternated with an interval, wherein the breath is held for some time, within and without, which is called '**Kumbhak**' (कुंभक). The process of **Purak-Kumbhak-Rechak-Kumbhak,** when practiced in a prescribed ratio, becomes the technique of breath-control. This technique is again explained here as Yagna by which the practitioner, in the long run, learns to offer all the subsidiary Pranas into the main Prana.

Prana (प्राण): Prana is not the breath; this is a general misunderstanding. Through breath-control, we come to gain a perfect mastery over the activities of the Pranas in us. When very closely observed, we find that the term 'Prana' used in the Hindu Scriptures indicates the various manifested activities of life in a living body. They generally enumerated five different kinds of Pranas, which, when understood correctly, are found to be nothing but the five different physiological functions in every living body. They are: (1) the capacity in a living-creature to improve himself in his mental outlook and intellectual life (प्राण, **Prana**), *(not to be confused with the undivided main prana)*, operates at the head and the chest region, and governs intake, inspiration, propulsion, forward momentum. (2) the function of the perception (उदान, **Udaan**), operates at the throat region and governs growth, speech, expression, ascension, upward movement, (3) the circulatory system, which distributes the food to all parts of the body (व्यान, **Vyana**), operates at all body level and governs circulation on all levels, expansiveness, pervasiveness (4) the function of digestion and assimilation (समान, **Samaan**), operates at the navel region of the body and governs assimilation, discernment, inner absorption, consolidation, and lastly (5) the function of excretion (अपान, **Apana**), operates at the pelvis region and governs elimination, downward and outward movement.

These activities of life within, which an ordinary man is quite unconscious, are brought under the perfect control of the individual through the process of Pranayama, so that a seeker can, by this path, come to gain a complete capacity to withdraw all his perceptions. This is indeed a great help to a meditator.

Chanting (जप): This Chanting (जप, जाप) means constantly repeating one mantra (or an idea or a thought) remembering God's name is called '**Naam-Smarana (नाम-स्मरण).**' Worship in the form of chanting and Naam-Smarana is prevalent in almost all religions. Chanting is both a technique of turning the attention of our mind inward, which normally wonders about and keeps running out and revels with sense objects, and also to provide our mind a focal point to concentrate on and remain detached from the external world. As a technique, Chanting, if practiced daily, regularly and over a long period of time, can bring enormous profits to the seeker, in helping him to gain control over his wandering mind and gain an ability to remain focused on, dedicated, and committed to one thought, one idea amongst the din and roar of distractions and disturbances created by the sense organs.

Penance (तप, तपस्या, तपश्चर्या): Striving hard, physically, and/or mentally, to achieve a great goal is penance. It means concentration of the mind and senses.

मनसा च इन्द्रियाणां एकाग्रयम परमं तपः ।

Mansa ca indriyanaam aikagrayam paramam tapah.

Mahabharata 12.242.4

Adi Sankaracharya has discussed this mental ability as a prerequisite for a seeker of the Truth and referred to this spiritual stamina for forbearance or silent endurance as Titiksha (तितिक्षा, Forbearance). Titiksha as an essential mental quality has been further elaborated later in Antaranga Sadhana section later in this chapter.

A Pilgrimage (तीर्थ): Visiting a sacred place, worshiping God, bating, doing charity, and spending time with good people is called pilgrimage, which has been an important part of the Hindu ritual and spiritual practices since Vedic times. In many respects they contributed to the growth of Indian civilization and the emergence of numerous sacred cities and urban centers. In the process, they contributed to the preservation of Hinduism, elevating the character and consciousness of its people, uniting them into one nation despite their regional and cultural diversity, and creating feelings of belongingness and brotherhood.

Pilgrimages are beneficial both mentally and spiritually. They are an important part of Hindu ritual and devotional worship. Devotees go on pilgrimages to fulfill their vows or perform their obligatory duties such as marriage, initiation, or tonsure (Mundan) ceremony. Some pilgrimages are undertaken to atone for past sins or express gratitude. People also go on pilgrimages to holy sites to mix the ashes of their deceased relatives to help them obtain a good birth in the next life or ensure their safe journey to the next world.

Tirtha means a passage, a roadway, a fjord, a staircase, or a descent into a river. Customarily and traditionally these attributes are associated with pilgrim places which happen to be upon the banks or near rivers and water bodies or on the top of a hill or a mountain.

In a wider spiritual context, pilgrimages serve as a reminder of our essential nature and our highest purpose upon earth. These symbolize the life of mortal beings as pilgrims who are caught in the web of life. We all are on a spiritual journey in search of liberation. Our final destination is the immortal heaven, upon reaching which no one returns. In Hinduism, pilgrimages remind us of this singular truth. We may undertake them for a number of purposes, but as the scriptures say the best ones are those which are undertaken to express love and devotion to God rather than for selfish motives.

Thus, pilgrimages serve an important purpose in our lives, by helping us practice Dharma and keep our Gods happy and nourished through offerings and sacrifices. By that, they contribute to the preservation and continuation of our Dharma. Because of their beneficial effect, we should not look down upon them as mere acts of superstition. India is considered a sacred land because it is home to numerous Deities, saints, and seers. They are spread all over the country. Each year, millions of people go on pilgrimages to visit them and seek their blessings. In the process, everyone is benefited.

However, one should not expect too much from pilgrimages or solely rely upon them for their spiritual well being. Although they have a symbolic parallel with the spiritual journey of individual souls upon earth, they form a part of the Hindu ritual worship. Hence, it is still a part of the lower knowledge, which is helpful to gain a good birth in the next life, but not very helpful to achieve liberation or escape from suffering in the mortal world. For that you have to practice virtues, detachment, renunciation, sameness, etc. You have to cultivate purity and become pure to achieve oneness with the Supreme Self.

Vow (व्रत) or Fasting (उपवास)

Why do people observe Vow or fasting? Are Vowing and Fasting two different things?

Vow means solemn promise (संकल्प), for example, vow of silence. It helps to keep the obstinate and impudent mind disciplined. Only with the help of vows, does the fickle mind acquire spiritual depths. You would have noticed that our mind is so conditioned to follow and fulfill the demands of our sense appetites and makes us a slave of our senses. In order to regain our control and mastery over our senses, our Subjective Scientists have recommended the practice of Vow.

Fasting (उपवास) is a form of vow, which is very commonly witnessed as a religious and/or a health-related practice in our present-day Hindu society. Giving up, restraining, or restricting intake of food or drink for a fixed period on specific important days in the year as a means of contemplating upon God is considered a real fasting. This is, however, a general understanding of fasting. When we say restricting or giving up food, in Vedanta, it refers to giving up or restricting the intake of sense objects (stimuli) for all sense organs, not just the sense of taste, that is, the mouth. This is, however, a concept of real fasting for spiritual purposes. **Kinaesthetic Restraining** of all senses from running after sense temptations and restraining of the mind from running out to court and revel amongst the sense objects is a necessary condition of fasting. The idea of food fasting (उपवास), therefore, essentially must not only be to refrain from consumption of food alone but also to not even think about food at all on the day of fasting. The seekers of spirituality, therefore, commence their practice of restraint with food-fasting, which is a technique to overcome taste temptations. The seeker of spirituality increasingly evolves into restraining other sense organs as he progresses in his path of spirituality. Sitting in quietude with eyes closed is a 'visual fasting,' to restrain visual stimuli entering in, **'Mauna Vrat'** (मौन व्रत) is an **auditory fasting**, wherein the seeker takes a vow not to speak for a day or a duration. Developing forbearance to withstand climatic conditions, such as hot and cold weather conditions felt on his skin while sitting in for meditation, contemplation or undertaking any Yagna, is a **sensory fasting**, similarly includes withstanding the smell and not letting your mind get distracted by the good or bad smells, is an **'Olfactory fasting'** to restrain against smell.

Upasana (उपासना) and Upvas (उपवास): The term Upasana is made up of two syllables. 'Upa' means near (समीप) and 'Aasan' (आसन) or 'Vasa' (वास) means to sit. Sitting near lofty or God is called 'Upasana' (उपासना) or 'Upvas' (उपवास). Sitting near God doesn't mean to literally, but to notionally sit. Philosophically, it means a process of meditation and contemplation over the attributes of the chosen Deity with an objective to know, acquire, and eventually absorb these into one's bosom, thereby, spiritually evolving, and rising to the height of or close to the Deity. Upasana is a process where the worshiper becomes the 'worshiped.'

Upasana literally means 'worship' and 'sitting near, attend to.' It refers to the worship of, or meditation on and contemplation over the formless, the Absolute Truth, the Self, the Atman, the Life Principle, distinguishing meditative reverence for an internalized and intellectual concept from earlier forms of physical worship, actual sacrifices, and offerings to Vedic deities.

In one contemporary context, Upasana means methods of worship (भक्ति Bhakti), usually of meditative kind. Upasana is also sometimes referred to as Puja. However, a formal Puja is just one type of worship in Indian philosophy. The concept of Upasana developed a large tradition in Vedanta era and that Upasana in Vedic text initially developed as a form of **'substitute sacrifice,'** where symbolic meditation of the Aranyakas practice, instead of actual sacrifice ritual, offered a means to gain the same merit without the sacrifice. Over time, this idea shifted from meditating about the ritual, to internalization and meditation of the ideas and concepts associated. This may have marked a key evolution in Vedic era, one from ritual sacrifices to one contemplating over spiritual ideas.

It flowered into the meaning of an intense kind of systematic meditation and identification. Adi Sankaracharya described Upasana as a kind of meditation about someone or something, consisting of continuous succession of comparable basic concepts, without interspersing it with dissimilar concepts, that proceeds according to the scriptures and on idea enjoined in the scriptures. It is a state of concentration where whatever is meditated upon is completely identified with, absorbed within Self, and unified with as one identifies Self-consciousness with one's body. The two become one, "you are that." The 'someone' or 'something' in Upasana can be a symbolic Deity or an abstract concept, states Adi Sankaracharya. Upasana entails more than mere concentration or sitting in dhyana; it is being one with God, which manifests as 'be a God,' and by being a God, he attains the God, living this identity with God in daily life. Therefore, Upasana can be defined as daily, regular, and continuous contemplation over the attributes of the deity or the ideal with an objective of becoming one with the deity.

Contemplation (विचार एवं ध्यान): Likes, dislikes, desires, anger, agitation, ambition, envy etc., prevent a person from progressing on the spiritual path. Contemplation helps an individual (1) to annihilate all these vices from his bosom, thereby, removing the cause of Negative Affectivity, and (2) to Svadhyaya, literally meaning 'the study of the Self.'

Svadhyaya (स्वाध्याय) is a Sanskrit term which means Self-study and especially the recitation of the Vedas and other sacred texts. It is also a broader concept with several meanings. In various schools of Hinduism, Svadhyaya is a Niyama (virtuous observance) connoting introspection and **'study of Self.'** Svadhyaya is a compound Sanskrit word composed of Sva (स्व) + Adhyaya (अध्याय). Adhyaya means 'a lesson, lecture, chapter, and/or reading,' and Sva means 'own, one's own Self,' referring to Jiva within the body, mind, and intellect. Svadhyaya is also a compound Sanskrit word composed of Sva (स्वा) + Dhyaya (ध्याय). Dhyaya means 'meditating on.' The root of Adhyaya and Dhyaya is 'Dhyai' (ध्यै) which means 'meditate, contemplate, think of.' The term Svadhyaya, therefore, also connotes 'contemplation, meditation, reflection on oneself,' or simply 'the study of Self.'

The term Svadhyaya has other meanings. In the Sruti, it refers to the historical practice of Self-reciting Vedas to ensure it is memorized and faithfully transmitted, without writing, by the word of mouth, to the next generation. In various schools of Hinduism, particularly Yoga, Svadhyaya is also a niyama, a virtuous behavior. As a virtue, it means 'the study of Self,' 'Self-reflection,' 'introspection,' and 'observation of the Self.' Svadhyaya is translated in a number of ways. Some translate it as the 'study of the scriptures and Darshanas (Philosophies).' Some translators simply use the word 'study' without qualifying the type of study. Dhyaya, when used in the context of the Self-study in ancient and medieval Indian texts, is synonymous with Abhyasa, Adhi and Viks; while Adhyaya, when used in context of reciting and reading in Indian texts, is synonymous with Anukti, Nipatha and Patha.

Taittiriya Upanishad's hymn 1.9.1 emphasizes the central importance of Svadhyaya in one's pursuit of Reality (Ṛta), Truth (Satya), Self-restraint (Dama or broadly Brahmacharya), Non-injury (Ahimsa), Perseverance (Tapas), Tranquility and Inner Peace (Sama), Relationships with others, family, guests (Praja, Prajana, Manush, Atithi) and all Rituals (Agnaya, Agnihotram).

Taittiriya Upanishad, however, adds in verse 1.9.1, that along with the virtue of Svadhyaya process of learning, one must teach and share (प्रवचन-Pravacana) what one learns. This is expressed by the phrase "स्वाध्याय प्रवचन च- Svadhyaya Pravachan cha" translated as 'and learning and teaching.'

In verse 1.11.1, the final chapter on the education of a student, the Taittiriya Upanishad reminds,

सत्यंवद । धर्मंचर । स्वाध्यायान्माप्रमदः ।

"Speak the Truth, follow the Dharma, for Svadhyaya never cease."

One of the earliest mention of Svadhyaya is found in Taittiriya Aranyaka 2.15: "svadhyayo-adhyetavyah" ("Svadhyaya must be practiced"). Satapatha Brahmana also repeats it. Chandogya Upanishad verse 4.16.1-2 recommends both silent (manas) and vocal (vachika) types of Svadhyaya. The range of ritualistic practices and disciplined methods, discussed above, of getting the mind-and-intellect equipment, which is full of Vasanas, adjusted for greater and more effective Self-application in meditation, are called 'Bahiranga Sadhana.'

यज्ञदानतपः कर्म न त्याज्यं कार्यमेव तत् ।
यज्ञो दानं तपश्चैव पावनानि मनीषिणाम् ॥

"Yagna, charity, and vows should not be given up. In fact, they should be done constantly. Yagna, charity, and vows purify the minds of even intellectuals."

भगवद् गीता-१८.७

All the Yagnas or the techniques discussed under the heading of Bahiranga Sadhanas above, are suggested and recommended by our great masters and Rishis that one who knows the art of living these techniques, when practices them in a spirit of Self-dedication and selfless enthusiasm, can fully come to profit by them. These methods and techniques do not promise that they will, of themselves, guide us or lead us to the Supreme. It is, however, promised that all those who practice all, or a few, or even one of them for a sufficiently long period, can become purified of their sins.

'Sins,' as defined and explained in the Gita, is **a wrong pattern of thought-channels** that is etched in a mind by devolutionary thoughts, entertained by a deluded Ego in its extreme misunderstanding and its consequent attachments with the body, and sense-objects. It is these sinful vasanas that make the Ego act like an animal and force it to commit low and vicious criminalities. The above-mentioned practices, discussed under the bracket of Bahiranga Sadhanas, not only wipe clean the existing wrong vasanas but cut out in their place new channels of thoughts more constructive and evolutionary in their very nature.

Thus, it must be carefully noted that all religious and/or spiritual practices, physical, mental, or intellectual, that is, Yagna (यज्ञ), Charity (दान), Service (सेवा), Chanting (जप), Penance (तप), Vow (व्रत), Pilgrimage (तीर्थ), Svadhyaya (स्वाध्याय), and Contemplation (विचार एवं ध्यान) etc., are generally known as divine and religious. These are, though, at their best, without exception, only techniques by which the mind-and-intellect equipment gets adjusted for greater and more effective Self-application in meditation (Antaranga Sadhana). Meditation is the 'Path' in which the Ego learns to withdraw its false evaluations of itself in particular, and of life in general, and comes to the final experience of its own divine nature. We often find sincere seekers getting so extremely attached to their own 'Path' of practice that they constantly argue about it among themselves. Therefore, Lord Krishna, through his advice to Arjuna in fourth chapter on Gyan Karma Sannyasa Yoga (ज्ञानकर्मसंन्यास योग), instructs us all that all 'Paths' however, noble, and great they may be, are all but means, and not an end in themselves.

'Antaranga-Sadhana- अंतरंग-साधना'

The mind alone is the cause of all bondages and is the only tool available for liberation. The mind's dwelling in sensual pleasures is the cause of bandage and as soon as the mind moves away from pleasures it becomes the cause of liberation. So, a spiritual aspirant must detach his mind from sensual pleasures. The one who has mastered preparatory spiritual practices (Bahiranga Sadhana- बहिरंग-साधना), progresses swiftly even in advance spiritual practices (Antaranga Sadhana- अंतरंग-साधना). Due to Yagna, Charity, Service, Chanting, Penance, Vow, Pilgrimage, Contemplation etc., his mind has already become focused. Such aspirants acquire Self-knowledge, by listening (श्रवण), reflecting (मनन) and contemplation (विचार, ध्यान, एवं निद्विध्यास). Listening, reflecting, and contemplating are the stages of advanced spiritual practices.

Sravana does not mean just hearing. It means attentively and faithfully listening to Vedanta from an experienced and Self-realized teacher and ascertaining its import, which is possible only by consciously paying attention. That's why a seeker should listen to Vedanta from his Guru attentively and carefully. The next stage is that of Reflecting. It means logical analysis and verification of the Guru's teachings, through regular and constant Reflecting over, an aspirant transforms the knowledge acquired from the Guru into his direct personal experience and wisdom.

Advaita Vedanta philosophy accepts that Jiva and Brahman are one, yet the 'Not-Self' (material sensuous things and beings) continues to exist at the causal body level. In order to get rid of this Vasana for the Not-Self, the thought that **'I am Brahman- अहं ब्रह्मास्मि,'** should be contemplated upon regularly and consistently, so that the mind gets more focused on this thought and consequently, the other thoughts of difference stop arising.

In order to get rid of the Vasana for the 'Not-Self,' contemplation is required. The process of making the experience of **'I am Brahman- अहं ब्रह्मास्मि'** firm in one's bosom is called Niddhidhyas or Dhyana. Constantly and regularly reflecting and contemplating over the thought **'I am Brahman- अहं ब्रह्मास्मि,'** there comes a stage when even that thought ends. The seeker becomes one with the Brahman. The Jiva merges into Brahman. This is the state of pure consciousness or Supreme Reality.

One becomes Liberated while alive. Such a liberated person is called **Jivanmukta**.

The one that finds out the secret of 'Antaranga-Sadhana' becomes one with the auspicious (शुभ एवं शिव) and infinite one. It is rightly said that a Self-realized one is Brahman itself.

श्रुतेः शतगुणं विद्धान्मननं मननादपि ।
निदिध्यासं लक्षगुणमनन्तं निर्विकल्पकम् ॥

In Vivekachudamani, Sankaracharya said,

> "Reflecting should be considered 100 times superior to listening; contemplation or meditation should be considered 1000 times superior to reflecting. But the sacredness of 'Samadhi' (Abidance in the Self) is infinite."

-विवेकचूडामणि-३६५

Self-realization is an evolutionary process of transition from one state of ego-centric consciousness to another state of pure, uncontaminated consciousness. It is a transition from a limited sense of one's being to a realization of one's limitless personality. It is a transition from a sense of incompleteness to the realization of completeness. It is a process of transition of Nar (Manhood) into Narayana (Godhood). It is all about reaching the pinnacle of one's supreme personality and of peace, fulfillment and tranquility. Such a transition is called **Self-realization**. A process of constantly working on cleansing away from our real nature, the accumulated conditioning that hides its pristine beauty.

Self-realization is an evolutionary process and could never be an event, very similar to academic evolution. A very similar process discussed and expounded upon through an analogy of how an author, an expert linguist, in the beginning of this book, commences his journey with familiarization of alphabets, moving on incrementally from one stage to another, learning various facets of the language and its grammar, learning to read, understand and write, gains his competency in expressing his thoughts in and through words and further with practice becomes a prolific author with an excellent style in expressing subtlest of thoughts through his word pictures.

In the same way, to reach to the pinnacle of peace, fulfillment and tranquility, called Self-realization, one must work on cleaning away from our real nature, the accumulated conditionings that hide its pristine beauty. That process of cleansing is called spiritual practice or sadhana in Sanskrit. A sincere seeker of spirituality, desirous of Self-realization, must commence his journey to learn, reflect and practice with a daily, regular, and forever (चिरं, नित्यं, निरंतरम्) Self-effort with sincerity, supported by burning desire for liberation, unwavering commitment, and infallible dedication.

Spiritual seekers often suffer chronically from lack of progress on the path. The cure for such seekers is easy to prescribe, but perhaps more difficult to practice. What they need is a sharpened tempo in their spiritual seeking, which refers to a quickening of perception, an alertness of the soul, and a warmer ardency in their embrace of the goal. These qualities cannot be developed by themselves, one at a time; but seekers will find themselves absorbing them when their minds gain a deeper harmony, which comes as a result of following two processes:

1. **Discrimination (विवेक- Viveka):** The positive process of gaining a clear picture of the all-satisfying goal and the straight path to it.

2. **Detachment, dispassion (वैराग्य- Vairagya):** The negative process of detaching from all dissipating urges.

Once these two qualities are carefully cultivated and fully developed—discriminating appreciation of the Real and detachment from the false—the rest of the pilgrimage becomes pleasant and sure. Though, for some it may feel that it is in no way easy, however, for a sincere seeker of spirituality, who is desirous of Self-realization, with a daily, regular, and forever (चिरं, नित्यं, निरंतरम्) Self-effort with sincerity, supported by burning desire for liberation, unwavering commitment, and infallible dedication, the pilgrimage is not only possible but simple and easy.

Discrimination (विवेक-Viveka)

A mind that rushes out into the world of objects is full of desires and agitations. Such a state of mind is not conducive to quiet contemplation upon the Truth. Withdrawal of the mind from preoccupation with the world quiets the agitations in it and prepares the ground for contemplation. In such a calmed mental atmosphere, the intellect begins to distinguish between the ephemeral objects of the world and the eternal Principle of life. In other words, we learn to discriminate between (1) the Real and the unreal, (2) the Changeless and the changing, and (3) the Imperishable and the perishable.

We all have experiences with discrimination in our daily lives. We discriminate between good coffee and bad coffee. We can distinguish a loyal friend from a fickle one. We know how to be very discriminating in choosing our next car, house, or the latest model of laptop or a mobile phone. Now let's try to apply discrimination to the spiritual field. We know that time is a product of the mind; it has no separate existence from the mind. We also know Brahman, the supreme Reality, transcends the mind; therefore, Brahman cannot be bound by time. Even though we may not yet experience the nature of Brahman directly, we can have the intellectual conviction of its timeless, unchangeable nature. Once that conviction becomes strong in us, we inherit the consequent ability to reject all that is impermanent.

In this way, we learn to discriminate between the Permanent and the impermanent, the Changeless and the changing, the unconditional Self and our various conditionings. As Adi Sankaracharya say:

निषिध्य निखिलोपाधिन्नेति नेतीति वाक्यतः ।

विद्धादैक्यं महावाक्यैर्जीवात्मपरमात्मनोः ॥

> "By a process of negation of the conditionings (Upadhis) through the help of the scriptural statement "Not this, not this" (neti, neti), the oneness of the individual soul and the supreme Soul, as indicated by the great Mahavakyas, is realized."
>
> -Atma Bodh, verse 30

We, as seekers of Truth, analyze our various conditionings—the body and the sense objects, the senses, the mind and its feelings, the intellect, and its thoughts. With our power of discrimination, we reject every one of them as the not-Self. We even reject time, space, and causality as perceptions of the mind and intellect. In this process of negation (Not this, not this - neti, neti), we realize that we are none of these not-Self vestures, but the pure, supreme Self Itself.

Detachment (वैराग्य-Vairagya)

Once the mind knows discrimination between the Real and the unreal, detachment follows of its own. Even our daily experiences prove that detachment flows naturally from understanding:

"In your dream, you get married to a lovely person, and you love her dearly. Once you are awakened, you cannot maintain your attachment to that dream-love, for the moment you're awake you realize the falsehood of the dream, so your mind quite effortlessly rolls away from dream attachment."

Before our mind can be fit for higher contemplation and finally for the realization of the divine Self, we have to develop our sense of detachment from the fascinations of the world, and we have to cultivate such detachments at the mental level. We cannot achieve true detachment by merely physical retirement from the world, but rather, by maintaining a proper mental relationship to it. We have to renounce our infatuations with the extroverted life and explore the possibility of rediscovering the pure Self deep within.

The word detachment has often been misunderstood. For many it holds an uncanny fear, for it seems to point more to a condition of living death than to a state of a better and fuller life. Others have found it as an excuse to escape their obligatory duties and abandon life overall. Every human being has a purpose in life and should use the world to fulfill it. In fact, Hindu way of life prescribes that we have a life of Dharma, that is, we fulfill the duties that our nature imposes on us. The world provides a field for exhausting our inherent tendencies, our Vasanas. But while on the path of evolution we often fall prey to the bewitching objects of the world and our infatuation with our loved ones. These worldly attractions distract us from our goal. The advice of the scriptures, therefore, is: While remaining in the world, earn to maintain the right relationship to it. We can practice detachment from the world by questioning ourselves thus:

- Who is my wife? Husband? Mother? Father?

- Who was my father before I was born? Who was my husband before I married him? How have I developed an attachment to him?

- Where was my daughter before I gave birth to her?

- Where was I before I appeared in this world?

Reflecting on such questions over and over again, we develop detachment from the usual fascinations of the external world. In time, we will come to the final question:

- Who am I?

Once we start asking such self-introspective questions, we kindle in ourselves the desire to seek the pure Self, which lies beyond all bonds we may feel with objects and beyond any attachments we may cherish to other human beings. Even as we release from false relationships to the world, we must establish ourselves in the higher aspects of life. We need to substitute attachment to the higher for detachment from the lower. For this purpose, the scriptures advise us to cultivate healthy contacts at all levels of the personality by:

- Associating with good people.

- Maintaining noble emotions.

- Studying and reflecting upon the scriptural truths.

Maintaining such contacts with the higher values of life is called **'Satsang'** (Which in Sanskrit means 'Good Company'). Satsang helps us to stabilize our sense of detachment, and with detachment disappears our deluded vision of the world. Satsang, in our present-day convention, is considered a gathering of devotees, who sing bhajans and dance, in the praise of their chosen Deity. However, Satsang is also keeping a good company of scriptures, people, activities and visiting holy places, so as to allow our mind an environment, which provides a constant and consistent stimuli of higher values. Satsang helps our mind to stabilize our sense of detachment, and with detachment disappears our deluded vision of the world. We can think of Satsang as a fortress we build around ourselves to protect us against the temptations that we encounter in our daily lives. Many things, events and people will try to pull us away from the spiritual path. The chances are good that despite our knowledge and determination to stay on the path, we will be lured away from it through the influence of people with lower goals. Therefore, for the spiritual seeker, to seek out the company of the good is of paramount importance. As a result of the influence of Satsang, the mind develops the capacity to withdraw from the usual fields of attractions in the world and to find the calm atmosphere of dispassion.

Another source of extreme attachment is the physical body, for we share a common weakness to pamper it. The body has no doubt its part to play both in material and spiritual progress, but to spend an entire lifetime merely beautifying it and meeting its endless demands is, besides being quite out of proportion to the returns gained, detrimental to our progress. The body assumes a special glory as long as life exists, but as soon as the breath leaves it, those near and dear to us are even repelled by its sight. This shows that the respect the body does enjoy during its life is not because of the physical structure itself; any glory it has is lent to it by the life principle pulsating in it.

Spiritual students must develop a new relationship to the body and its worldly enjoyments. The right attitude would be to play in the world as in a field of sport and to consider secular activities as hobbies–all the while maintaining a constant vision of the ultimate goal of human existence, that is, realization of one's Self. However, many of us allow ourselves to be entangled with life's activities, ever postponing our deeper spiritual practice.

In childhood, we waste our days in play. Our fascination is with toys and games. In youth, we consume our time with pursuits of lust and passion. Although our attachment to toys and games has fallen away, we labeled our time and energy by courting the objects of our love. In the middle years of our life, we are busy aggrandising for ourselves, and our family material goods labeled "mine" and "ours." In old age, our mind is riled with agitations, being constantly worried about one thing or another.

Thus, at every stage of our lives, we are constantly preoccupied with one demand or another, finding neither the time nor the inclination to turn towards the Divinity (one's own supreme nature). In life, we cannot expect to be completely free of worldly entanglements; to wait for such a time before we undertake the spiritual path is absurd. It is like waiting for the waves to calm down in the ocean before deciding to take a swim in it. Therefore, if we as spiritual students are to make any progress in our path, (material or spiritual), we must cultivate mental dispassion for the enchantments of the particular state of life in which we find ourselves.

Six Mental Qualities (षड्-संम्पत्ति- Shad-Sampati)

In Vivekachudamani, Adi Sankaracharya outlines four qualifications of the fit student of Vedanta. (1) Discrimination (विवेक-Viveka), (2) Detachment (वैराग्य-Vairagya), (3) Six Mental Qualities (षड्-संम्पत्ति-Shad-Sampati) and (4) Burning desire for liberation (मुमुक्षुत्व-Mumukshutva). The four qualifications are those determining factors in a seeker that can ensure success. The degree to which the four are present in a seeker, to that degree his success in spiritual (as well as material life) endeavors is assured. The first two, we have already discussed. Next are the six mental qualities that help the seeker gain control of the mind. These are (1) Calmness (सम-Sama), (2) Self-control (दम-Dama), (3) Self-withdrawal (उपरति-Uparati); (4) Forbearance (तितिक्षा-Titiksha), (5) Faith (श्रद्धा-Sraddha) and (6) Tranquility and poise (समाधान-Samadhan).

Calmness is a condition experienced by the mind when it does not function in worldly activities but is quietly contemplating on the supreme goal. On the other hand, **Self-control** is a discipline concerned with the outer fields of activities, the discipline of controlling the sense organs. To withdraw the mental rays that shoot out through the sense organs for the perception of their respective objects of pleasure and to absorb those rays within the sense organs is self-control. When one has gained a degree of proficiency in calmness and self-control, **Self-withdrawal** automatically takes place. In Self-withdrawal, the seeker's mental condition is such that it is no longer affected by disturbances created by external objects.

When we first learn of these requirements of a spiritual student, we may find them very delicate, difficult, and distressing feats, but in fact the more we practice them, the more we understand that these qualities describe the state of mind of everyone who is trying to execute any great work. Even on a material plane, we find that these mental qualities are essential for a person who wants success in his activities. In successful business people, we can observe a certain amount of self-control within and without, as well as Self-withdrawal, at least while they are at the desk. However, the spiritual seeker needs a subtlety a million times greater than the materialist.

The fourth psychological quality of the mind indicating spiritual stamina is **forbearance**. Meek surrender and silent suffering are glorified in all religions of the world. Even to bring about a revolution in the outer world, the revolutionaries are called upon to make silent sacrifices. How much more essential, then, is forbearance for the inner revolution of an individual who is trying to free himself from his psychological and intellectual confinements. This capacity of the mind to accommodate and forbear cheerfully all vicissitudes of life and patiently ignore any obstacles is Penance or Titiksha.

Unfortunately, many people indulge in acts of perversion in the name of Tapascharya or Titiksha. They persecute themselves physically and mentally in the name of spiritual seeking, and as a result of their Self-persecution, all they gain in the end is a crooked, ugly, deformed mind. Discarding one's cloths or starving oneself to a skinny existence, denying the body its bare necessities or giving unnecessary pain to the mind, running away from life, or preserving oneself on an inhuman diet in solitary caves, living an animal's life exposed to a brutal climate or breaking the body in an effort to make it endure more discomforts–none of these is true Tapascharya, Penance or Titiksha. True forbearance is the result of the mind being governed by an intellectual conviction the divine goal of life is fulfilled through Self-realization; when that conviction is firm, the mind cooperates and faces all difficulties and obstacles to reach the goal. Such a firm person alone is fit for realizing the pure Self. If one has any doubt whether they are able to, capable of, or cut out for Tapascharya, Penance, Titiksha, or true forbearance discussed here, all one has to do is to recall and remember a time, amongst several occasions in their lives, when they have undergone such an experience and demonstrated their latent ability of forbearance without complaint. Every time you have aimed to secure higher grades in your academic examinations, or undertaken the responsibilities of a project, got involved in the responsibilities of a social function or the wedding of a daughter or son, just recall the enormous difficulties and challenges, physical, mental, and intellectual, you encountered on your way. Haven't you endured all such challenges with a smile on your face and came out the other end with a sense of accomplishment and satisfaction. This happened only due to the meek surrender of your mind to the goal that you have committed yourself to. As soon as one surrenders oneself to a higher purpose in life, the inherent and latent capacities in us get invoked effortlessly.

Since every situation, of its own nature, must keep on changing, it would be foolish to get upset at every change. It is wisdom to suffer adversities meekly, with the comfort and consolation of the knowledge of their finite nature. It is the attitude of the wise to go through life, in joy and sorrow, in success and in failure, with the constant awareness– "**Even this will pass away.**"

Strong Faith (श्रद्धा-Sraddha) in one's ideal is the fifth quality of a spiritual aspirant. Sraddha is not blind faith, as it is often misunderstood by those who have not carefully analyzed it. Adi Sankaracharya is very clear in his definition of **Sraddha** as a healthy attempt to gain a clear intellectual appreciation of the secret significance underlying the worlds of the scriptures and the teacher. The scriptures give us, through the technique of suggestion, as clear a description of the infinite Truth as is possible through finite sounds and words. Being beyond the mind, pure Consciousness cannot be defined by words; therefore, the supreme goal of human evolution can only be indicated by the scriptures. An honest and sincere effort on the part of the student is absolutely necessary if the words indicating the Truth are to be correctly interpreted, understood, and made use of. This capacity to realize the words of the scriptures in all their suggestiveness is called Sraddha.

The last of the six great qualities is Tranquility and Poise (समाधान-Samadhan). In Sankaracharya's definition, **Samadhan** is a state of poise and tranquility that the mind gains when it is trained to revel continuously in the concept of a perfect idea.

When we are on the ground, our neighbors may be a nuisance to us. We may even argue over the boundaries of our property. But when we take off in a plane, these bickering seem to have no meaning. From those heights, 'my property' and 'their property' seem to merge into one unbroken expanse. In an aerial view of the world, there are no mental agitations because in that vision of oneness, the differences of opinion about boundary lines pale into insignificance.

Similarly, when a spiritual aspirant raises himself into the greater ambits of spiritual vision, his mind can no longer entertain any agitations at the ordinary levels of likes and dislikes. This inner poise, gained as a result of constant contemplation of the supreme Reality, is called **Samadhan**. These six mental qualities are essential in the psychological makeup of a fully evolved seeker, who alone can walk the last lap of the journey with success.

Burning Desire for Liberation (मुमुक्षुत्व-Mumukshutva)

The six mental qualities cannot bear fruit unless they grow in a heart watered by discrimination and detachment and plowed with an intense desire for liberation (Mumukshutva). When an individual develops his subtle discrimination enough to recognise the depth of life's weaknesses, he develops a pressing urgency for liberation.

Once a seeker asked his Guru about the meaning of Mumukshutva. Without a word, the master took the student by the hand and led him to the nearby river. There, he grabbed the student by the neck and pushed his head into the water, holding it immersed for many seconds. When he finally released his hold on the student and the student grabbed frantically for some gulps of air, the teacher said, "When you want to realize God as much you just yearned to get a breath of air, you will have a burning desire for liberation."

Mumukshutva is not an idle enthusiasm to gain an unknown goal through some mysterious intervention of a God or a teacher. The seeker must be clear about the goal and the various techniques and paths by which he can attain it. The inner revolution of turning the mind's attention away from the external world to discover the divine depths of one's inner nature cannot be accomplished as a half-hearted hobby. It can only be the result of a lifelong dedication and a full-time endeavor. A seeker who is ready to live every moment of his life in diligent pursuit of the Real is a **Mumukshu**, one consumed by a burning desire for liberation.

Self-unfoldment must come to express itself in your own heart. As long as it is loaded with base urges, motives and schemes, the Self-shackled heart cannot 'take-off' from its fields of sorrow and restlessness into the cloudless sky of spiritual freedom. Break those shackles by cultivating the four qualifications and the six mental qualities of a sincere spiritual seeker and make the mind-intellect vehicle light enough for the take-off into the heights of meditative bliss.

Meditation (एकाग्र ध्यान- Aikagrah Dhyana)

It is not enough to strive to understand the sacred texts, which any professor can; nor merely to feel the Truth, which any person without vision can. Understanding is developed through the study of the scriptures, and feelings for God are increased by devotion. Yet, study alone will never take us to the Truth. Nor is feeling the Truth sufficient for us to realize it. Alone, neither way is enough for realizing the Truth because the Truth lies beyond the mind. To make Truth our own, we must apprehend it directly in our own experience. It is in the seat of meditation that we learn to use the mind to rise beyond the mind–and realize the Truth as our own innermost Self.

The knowledge of Vedanta we have newly gained may not bless us yet because the mind that absorbed the teaching is still the old mind, filled with its old habits. In order to reap the blessings of our spiritual search we need to create a new habit in the mind, the habit of seeing our identity in the pure Self, not in the body, mind, or intellect. Again and again, we must cut our identification with the not-Self. The various paths prescribed by the great masters of the past help us in developing that habit. But in addition to following those paths–as we act without selfish desire (Karma-yoga), learn to be devoted to the Lord (Bhakti yoga), and study the scripture (Gyan yoga)–we must consciously turn the mind away from extroverted pursuits to contemplate upon the essentially blissful nature of the Self.

The mind learns to accept new habits of thinking through the practice of meditation. In meditation, the mind dwells only on one thought, a thought that reminds us of the Lord and our own pure and limitless nature.

Preparing the Mind (Japa)

Meditation is the subject of human activities and requires that our minds be fully prepared for it through the various methods of purification prescribed by the masters. The time taken for medication is a small part of the day, while the rest of the day is employed in various activities. These activities have an influence on our meditation. If, for instance, our activities are selfish and greedy, then agitations will disturb the mind in its attempts at meditation. In contrast, disciplined and selfless actions purify the mind and make it peaceful–and ready for meditation. Thus, in order to become effective meditators, we must organize our day's activities in such a way as to prepare in the inner personality a conducive atmosphere for meditation.

Even after having prepared the mind through various methods of purification, the masters still do not advise us to dive straight into meditation but urge us to prepare the mind first by chanting the Lord's name. New students of Vedanta, in their initial eagerness, may wonder why they should take up any sadhana at all other than pure meditation. It is natural for seekers to question the importance of preparatory techniques such as Japa, the repetition of a divine name. In responding to such a query, the masters answer to this impatience of the student that in Japa, the mind is given a word symbol of the Divine (a Mantra) to chant silently to itself, to the exclusion of all other thoughts. When the mind is constantly chanting a chosen mantra, it reaches a state of single-point attention, the beginning stage of meditation. Thus, Japa is a training for the mind that prepares a student for meditation by bringing the mind to attend to a single-point focus. Without that initial preparation, the student's attempt at meditation will very likely end in dismal failure. In fact, Japa properly done can bring a more sustained single pointedness of the mind than all the hasty attempts at meditation. A mind seasoned with Japa is like prepared food that is ready for consumption after a few short seconds of warming on the fire. A japa-conditioned mind can soar to unimaginable heights in meditation in a very short time.

The logic behind a Japa is simple. We cannot say a word without a thought form rising up immediately in the mind, nor can we have a thought form without its corresponding name. Try this! Can you repeat the word *Bottle* without its form appearing in your mind? Try it. Can you say the word *Shirt* and not have the image of a garment appear in your mind's eye? This close connection between the name and the form constitutes the underlying principle of the technique called Japa. As soon as we chant our chosen name of the Lord (a mantra), an association with Him automatically rises up in the mind.

Another important principle employed in the technique of Japa is the fact that attachment is caused by repetition of thought. Thoughts running continuously towards an object create an attachment to it. When our thought flow towards an object increases, our attachment to it also increases; and when we reduce our thought flow towards an object, our attachment diminishes. Then when the thought flow towards an object is completely expelled from the mind, no attachment remains at all. Thus, by continuous repletion of the name of the Lord, we get attached to Him, with a consequent detachment from the outer world of objects.

If you are a beginner at meditation, you will experience a challenge and some difficulty in keeping mind in your control which will keep running away in all directions. Do not worry about it at all. Let your mind do what it does and just silently observe it. The mind tends to drift away repeatedly from the point of concentration, even while chanting a mantra. To prevent such digression and to maintain concentration, you can apply certain external aids, such as the fragrance of flowers or incense or the sound of bells or any other aid that works for you. If the mind still runs away, try again and again, to bring it back to the point of concentration.

If subjective disturbances continue to plague you, keep your eyes open and even chant your mantra out loud until the disturbances disappear and the mind gains relative poise and concentration. You can apply the same treatment when sleep tries to overcome you during Japa.

If you are still unable to maintain your concentration in spite of these efforts, you may be overstepping your present capacity to concentrate. If so, practice concentration upon a larger field. For instance, to begin with, study the scriptures or stories about the various divine incarnations during the allotted meditation time. Thus, through study, you can develop the art of maintaining one consistent thought, that of the Divine. Later, you can introduce forms or pictures of divine beings to help you channel your thoughts in one direction. When you find yourself successful at this stage, choose to concentrate on one feature of the Lord's form, such as His face; still later, narrow your point of concentration down to Lord's smile. Thus, stage by stage, you learn to converge your thoughts to single-pointed focus. When you reach sufficient concentration, close your eyes again and practice chanting your mantra in the mind.

A mind that still remains unsteady may at times respond to persuasion. You can try to draw the attention of the mind to the profits of concentration and the supreme benefits to be achieved through meditation. Some minds may not react to persuasion but are curious by nature. In such cases, kindle the curiosity of the mind by introducing it to investigate the mystery of the unknown Self within. When this also fails, sometimes a little punishment is in order. You can threaten the uncooperative mind with fasting or a cold bath. Once you have enunciated your threat, do not fail to carry the promised punishment out if the mind persists in disobeying you, however, be careful not to carry out this punishment too far, and use it only as a last recourse.

Yet another practical way of controlling a rambling mind is to let the intellect witness the pranks of the mind, just as though it were a disobedient child. After trying all the means of controlling such a child, an intelligent mother tries the method of disinterestedly witnessing his mischievous deeds. The child invariably feels uneasy at her silent approach and quietly returns to her care. Similarly, when the mind realizes that the intellect is watching it, it becomes Self-conscious and ashamed, and returns to the control of the intellect.

The final and the last stage of contemplative practice is meditation (Dhyana). When the seeker has succeeded in keeping his single-pointed concentration for a prolonged period of time, he is ready to enter the state of thoughtlessness (samadhi).

As long as the mind is engaged in chanting the Lord's name, the mind and intellect are still active. As you step up the concentrated spell of chanting and then suddenly stop to experience the silence of the mind, there is now neither the mind nor the intellect. That moment of dynamic silence is the peace inherent in your pure Self. In its purest form, meditation at this juncture is a point at which the meditator (the experiencer, the subject), meditated (experienced, the object) and the meditation (experience) all merge into one.

The Self in each one of us is the supreme Consciousness that pervades all of life. It is like the sun reflected in a pool of water. When the water in the pool is disturbed, the sun's reflection is not seen; when it is steady and calm, the reflection becomes visible. Similarly, pure Consciousness is reflected in the 'thought pool,' the mind. If agitations exist in the mind, the reflection of Consciousness cannot be seen. However, when agitations cease and the mind becomes peaceful and calm, the Self reveals Itself. At this point, the meditator reaches the state called samadhi, which literally means 'tranquil mind.'

As we have already seen, the Self is known in three states: the waking, the dream, and the deep sleep states. These states of consciousness can be represented in the three sounds that comprise AUM: A, U, and M. The sound A represents the waking state; the sound U represents the dream state; and the sound M represents the deep-sleep state. The waking state is superimposed on the A sound because it is the first of the three states of consciousness, and the sound A is the first letter of the alphabets, in any language. The dream state occurs between the waking state and the deep-sleep-states and is thus second among the three states of consciousness. Since U is the second between A and M, it is used to represent the middle state, the dream state. The sound M represents deep sleep in that it is the closing sound of a syllable, just as deep sleep is the final state of the mind at rest.

A short, pregnant silence is inevitable between two successive utterings of AUM. This silence represents yet another state, the fourth, called **Turiya** in Sanskrit. This is the state of perfect bliss when the individual-self recognises its identity with the supreme. In fact, the silence of Turiya is the very substratum upon which the three sounds A-U-M are built. And when the sounds are no longer uttered, what remains is pure, undisturbed silence. We may consider, therefore, that the three sounds emerge out of silence, exist in silence, and merge back into silence again. Similarly, pure Consciousness remains ever present. The three states of consciousness (waking, dream, and deep sleep) emerge out of Consciousness, exist in Consciousness, and finally merge back into Consciousness. When we transcend these three states, we realize the pure Self.

Self-realization is often described as occurring in two stages. In the initial stage of realization, the last trace of individuality lingers only to experience Godhood. This state is called Savikalpa Samadhi (सविकल्प समाधि). The second stage of realization is called Nirvikalpa Samadhi (निर्विकल्प समाधि). In this stage, the last trace of individuality, which had previously claimed realization, itself merges with the Infinite. What remains thereafter is only Brahman, the one supreme Reality.

Nirvikalpa Samadhi is recognized as one of the highest states of consciousness, and the second stage of samadhi. In Sanatan traditions, samadhi is regarded as the pinnacle of all spiritual and intellectual activity, in addition to being a precondition for attaining moksha. In yoga, Samadhi is considered to be the final limb of Patanjali's eightfold path, a state in which individual and universal consciousness unite.

The state prior to Nirvikalpa Samadhi is Savikalpa Samadhi, in which meditative absorption occurs and one's experience of time and space alters. In Savikalpa Samadhi, thoughts still exist, but they do not affect the practitioner, whereas in Nirvikalpa Samadhi, mental activity merges with the Self. As such, it is a state of total absorption, in which it is not possible to perceive any distinction between the knower (experiencer), the act of knowing (the experience) and the object known (experienced).

In Nirvikalpa Samadhi, the Ego and samskaras (mental or emotional impressions, that is Vasanas) dissolve, leaving behind only pure consciousness. It is considered to be a state of being at one with the Divine, in which Jivatma and Paramatma merge. It has been described as a state of oneness, limitless bliss, or true ecstasy, but those who have documented it find it difficult to describe since it is a state beyond the capacity and capability of the instruments of knowing (BMI).

Nirvikalpa Samadhi occurs spontaneously, and therefore cannot be practiced in itself. In order to reach this state, one must first practice, in addition to Bahiranga Sadhanas, the eight limbs as prescribed by Patanjali's Yoga Sutras, mentioned earlier in this book e.g.

1. Five social observances called **Yamas (यम)**, which include Ahimsa (non-violence), Sat (truthfulness), Asteya (non-stealing), Brahmacharya (self-control) and Aparigraha (non-possessiveness).

2. Five moral observances called **Niyamas (नियम)** including Saucha (purity), Santosha (contentment), Tapas (Self-discipline), Svadhyaya (Study of the Self), Ishvarapranidhana (devotion or surrender).

3. **Yogasana (योगासन)**- a discipline to maintain a healthy body. The difference between yoga and yogasana is that yogasana only lays emphasis on the physical side of the discipline while yoga also gives importance to the mental and spiritual aspects.

4. **Pranayama (प्राणायाम)** - Breathing techniques as a means of controlling prana (vital life force energy).

5. **Pratyahara (प्रत्यहार)**- Withdrawal of the senses.

6. **Dharana (धारण)**–Concentration.

7. **Dhyana (ध्यान)**–Meditation.

8. **Samadhi (समाधि)**- Enlightenment or bliss.

Through repeated practice of meditation, the mind learns to abide in the blissful silence of the Self and own up the knowledge it has assumed through study. When the extroverted mind disappears in the silence of the pure Self, the merger is complete. As the great Vedantin Sri Sankaracharya describes it, the merger is as water mixing with water, light combining with light, and space merging with space. In each of these examples, the merger not only creates a homogeneity, but also leaves not a trace of recognition of the separateness that existed before the merger. Similarly, in meditation, the identity of the individuality is lost in the experience of the Self, which is one with Brahman, unlimited Consciousness.

Care in Meditation: Regularity and sincerity are the secret of success in meditation. Go slowly; allow the momentum of meditation to lift you into it. Evolution is not a matter of hurrying. Meditation is not a question of dashing into divine silence; let it come to you. We can never dash into sleep, can we? We prepare ourselves for sleep and then invoke it. Sleep comes in its own rhythm and envelops us.

Everything in nature is slow and steady–except for earthquakes and storms, which are destructive. Opening of a flower, the germination of a seed, the growth of a tree, the sunrise and the moonrise, the high tide, and the low tide–all are slow processes, though they are precisely timed. If you sit near the sea and watch, you will find how slowly and steadily the waves rise and fall; how rhythmic it all is. There are no jerks. In the same way, you cannot dash into the presence of the Lord. You cannot force your entry. If silence does not easily envelop you during meditation, do not despair. Spiritual life is meant for the imperfect, not the perfect. The seeker who condemns himself for his imperfections is a fool. He does not know what he is doing. He is unintelligently meditating upon his own negative qualities and imperfections, and therefore his imperfections become more and more pronounced. Instead, surrender your imperfections to the Lord.

When we offer fruits and flowers to our spiritual teacher, we are symbolically surrendering our imperfections to him. Flowers are the source of fragrance, and that fragrance is symbolic of our vasanas. When we offer flowers, we are symbolically offering up our vasanas. When we offer fruits, we are symbolically offering fruits of our actions. By thus offering up the vasanas that block us from the Divine and by surrendering our attachment to the results of our actions symbolized by the fruit, we are making ourselves available for the Lord to cure us of our imperfections. This attempt at surrendering leads to the highest mood of meditation. An emotional person who surrenders to the beloved Lord of his heart reaches the same mood of meditation as the intellectual one, who after he has understood that the Consciousness illumines everything is his own pure Self, blissful serenity within.

By thus surrendering the bundle of your futile memories of the past and your worries about the future at His feet, rest in a mood of cheer. Rich in a faith born of understanding, learn to smile away your sorrows. Be unaffected by the play of Sattva, Rajas, and Tamas in you. With such a cheerful mind, you can transform the subtle equipment within you and prepare it for the meditative flight. Meditation should not be ordered by the clock on the wall or the position of the sun in the sky. Instead, it should depend upon the cheer and vigor in the mind.

Never give up. Strive on. Regularity and sincerity will take you to your goal. Spiritual unfoldment is reserved for the wise heroes.

17

Appendix 1

Reflective Practice

Dharam Sevak Course, Chinmaya Garden, Coimbatore, Tamil Nadu, India

25th July, 2016, 5:25 AM to 12:30 PM

As soon as Swamini Vimalananda Ji ordered us to spend 7 hours in isolation in a room with no connectivity with the outside world, to reflect upon and meditate, my inner voice ordered me to grab the opportunity and to put myself forward. I wanted to be the first one to go in so that my experience is protected from unwanted information and the experience of others. My wish was granted, and I commenced my solitude at 5:25 AM the next morning in a room so appropriately named **'Guru Samarpan.'**

I had woken up at 4:00 AM in the morning and finished my morning ablutions or *nitya karma* by 4:30 AM. Just before I met the *sadhika*, who would guide me to the room, I read a few pages of the book *Meditation and Life* by Pujya Gurudev Swami Chinmayananda Saraswati ji and received his blessing. Gurudev's blessings were so powerful that I found myself sitting in front of his smiling photo in the solitude room to continue my meditation, reflection, and contemplation.

A few pages that I managed to read on meditation were effective enough to give me strength and confidence to introspect and look within. Gurudev's blessing came as assurance to me as if Gurudev was saying to me, "Young man, remember those pages that you read in my book this morning. This is nothing new for you, you have done this before, you have been on this path for some time, not only since you became involved with my mission, but long before. You have commenced this journey of meditation and contemplation, so continue on this path and you shall reach your destination."

Some of the words that I was able to retain from his book were, "Bringing oneself to the point where one could be an honest, sincere, and conscious observer of one's own inner vanities, weaknesses and animalistic instinct and negative impulses, is the most difficult task in the process of meditation. However, if you have brought yourself to this point, the forward journey, that is identifying and replacing your negative and animalistic thoughts and impulses with the positive and divine thoughts, is not difficult at all. In fact, it is an automatic process, almost seamless, it just happens."

He advised me to recount a few of my recent successes where I have been able to hunt down my long-standing bad and unhealthy addictive habits and have successfully replaced them with positive, healthy, and divine thoughts. This was his way of giving me strength and courage by helping me to recognise and hold on to my inner mental strength which has been at play in identifying and eradicating the under mentioned demonic values and habits. Gurudev, I realized, wanted me to have full realization of the workings of my *antahkaran* and to fully appreciate how body, mind, and intellect functions and have full awareness of it so that I could remain in control and command of my inner strength.

As I walked in the room and heard sounds of Rajeshwari locking the room behind me, my mind started to push out threats and fears. Several

'What ifs' and questions sprung forth. But as soon as I surrendered myself, I experienced complete calmness. I closed my eyes, and my thoughts became directed and streamed forth. My life story, like a movie, started to roll out in front of me. The reflective account presented in Appendix 2, was written as a result of achieving a meditative state of mind.

18

Appendix 2

Here, I would like to give an account of my reflection on a quick scan of my life, and enlist a few of recent successes through the process of contemplation and meditation:

1. **Smoking**

On August 9, 2013, I received a phone call from a friend who gave me the sad news of her father who was taken seriously ill and was admitted in the hospital. He was diagnosed with lung cancer.

This was one of the many such news items which I had received in the past without getting even slightly affected. However, at this point in my life, Gurudev had already blessed me with the art of contemplation and meditation. So naturally, this training came handy, and I captured this thought and pondered over it. I started to ask myself questions: Why did this information come to me when even my wife could have received this information? Is God giving me a message through this news? Is this an indication for me to take charge of my health and design the future health of my body? Is God prompting me to pick up a fight with my bad habits? Is this God's way of showing His kindness and mercy on me and protecting me from future health calamities? Does He have a bigger and better plan for me in store?

Gurudev's wisdom and confidence proved right once again and I immediately took a resolve, within a few seconds of the news, to quit smoking. And I did. I went around the house and collected all my stock and threw it in the bin. From that day onwards, I have not touched a cigarette let alone smoking one. I celebrated its 10th anniversary on August 9, 2022.

It's worth mentioning here that it wasn't my first attempt at giving up smoking. I have been smoking cigarettes since the age of 17, when I was in secondary school. Since then, there have been several attempts at giving up smoking. There have been several greater motivational factors, both negative as well as positive, but none of these worked. I had given up smoking on several occasions but had failed time and again.

Since the victory over my smoking addiction, I have won a few more wars, but haven't made note of specific dates of these subsequent victories. This day is not less than a festival for me to celebrate and to remind myself of the victory of inner strength over my **Vyasanasur** (**व्यसनासुर**). I celebrate it like how Dussehra is celebrated to remind us of the victory of good over evil personified through Rama over Ravana.

This victory became a fountain of inspiration and boosted my confidence. It helped me to carry on tackling other addictive habits head on, for example, alcohol consumption, food addiction, being overweight, including some serious health conditions like diabetes, high cholesterol levels, respiratory difficulties. A perfectly unhealthy body, an unkempt, dirty, and untidy temple where the altar of my Divine Lord could not be established, let alone His *Pran Prathista*. So, this temple had to be cleaned thoroughly, so that the Divine could shine through me.

2. **Weight Loss and Other Health Conditions:**

In August 2014, I had my regular GP appointment with regards to diabetes. Shockingly, I weighed 130 Kgs on the scale, when my doctor undertook my health measurements. I returned home in shock and disgust. This horrible and disgusting thought of excessive weight and declining health seriously affected me and disturbed my peace of mind.

I was adamant that something must be done quickly, before it was too late. But what, I wasn't sure.

At the dinner table, in September 2014 in India, I noticed concern in my brother-in-law's eyes who is an Orthopedic Consultant. I asked for his advice and that conversation with him resulted in an appointment with a Bariatric Consultant. The latter advised me to consider 'Sleeve Gastrostomy,' one of the few surgical options, to address my weight problem along with other health conditions. The surgeon was ready to operate on me if I gave him the go ahead.

Though I was tempted to take his offer, I wanted to involve Kshama (my wife) in this big decision. Kshama was supportive of the idea, which led me to further consultations with some other friends from the medical field, including my GP. Their advice was clear and unanimous and had a balanced view of benefits and risks associated with any surgical procedure. The only worrying factor was that I have never been to a hospital in my entire life. This added a bit of anxiety and fear of going under the knife.

However, my mental strength again came to assist me and helped me to pull the string tight on the bow of my resolve and shoot the arrow of my decision at the target of good health and positive values. The arrow did hit the bull's eye. On December 30, 2014, I was operated upon in a reputed hospital in Delhi by a well experienced surgeon. After post-operative observations, I was discharged from the hospital on January 2, 2015 with some advice on post-operative care, lifestyle changes and dietary plan for the next 5 months to receive the best possible health benefits.

I was pleasantly surprised to notice a sharp drop in my weight within the first 6 days. I recorded a loss of 8 kilograms of weight on my first follow up appointment on January 5, 2015. Though a dramatic and quick weight loss was anticipated, it wasn't fully comprehended by my mind.

This acknowledgement of sharp weight loss of 1.5 kilograms per day was a welcome sign, which no doubt strengthened my resolve to diligently follow dietary advice. Consequently, I ended up losing 25 kilograms in the first 2 months and another 28 kilograms in the next 3. Along with losing a total of 53 kilograms in 5 months, positive signs of other health benefits began to manifest. First good news was delivered by my GP when he confirmed that my blood sugar level came down to normal limits for a non-diabetic at the end of 3 months of surgery. However, I was advised to continue with metformin, until I was medically declared non-diabetic.

In July/August, 2015, when I went back to India, a full body scan showed very positive and encouraging results on all counts. My heart condition improved, my LDL level came down to normal, my cholesterol level normalized, I had already stopped snoring and experienced sound sleep patterns. I experienced a surge in my energy levels and consequently, became quite active in my daily life. Most people around me, family and friends, were able to notice a continued drastic transformation in my health and body. I, too, was pleased to witness the work of God and the glory of Gurudev's blessings.

The miraculous and quick change in my body weight and shape has its snowball effect. I became greedy and started to pick on other weaknesses in me. More than greed, it was my faith (श्रद्धा) in the blessings of God and *Guru Parampara* that increased many folds. My confidence started to grow and consequently, I decided to quit alcohol, followed by consumption of meat and non-vegetarian products. Though I was just a social drinker, I still decided to quit that too.

3. Rejecting Meat and Non-vegetarian Food

Most important to note here is the fact that I was becoming increasingly aware, over the years, of my inner strengths and capabilities. My abilities to focus on my thoughts and my meditative capabilities were becoming better. For example, I was watching a TV serial *Siya Ke Ram*, wherein

Sita, upon Trijata's inquisition, was explaining what makes *Sattvic, Rajasic or Tamasic* food and its relationship with one's body, mind and intellect. Having received this information in my BMI, I used the same channel of thinking and analysis that was used at the time of quitting smoking on August 9, 2013, and a similar resolution was taken. On June 29, 2016, I took a decision not to consume meat or non-vegetarian products anymore. I got up and collected all the meat products from the fridge and threw them in the bin.

The above account of my resolutions, consequent achievements and resulting dividends and profits, are undoubtedly the **Prasad** (प्रसाद) from God and the blessings of *Guru* lineage, without which nothing would have been possible.

Having read the above account of achievements and transition from Hell to Heaven, it is very likely that the readers might form a perception that I have a strong personality and will power which they lack and hence, it may not be possible for them to achieve what I did. Believe me, it has nothing to do with a strong personality. It's to do with knowledge gained and practicing the following clarification.

"It should not be difficult at all to drop the false identification once one has intellectually comprehended the real identity. In fact, it is an almost effortless, natural, and automatic occurrence. It happens itself rather than requiring a conscious and deliberate attempt to detach. It is a process of sublimation rather than suppression of desires. When the seeker's attention is fixed on the real and the higher purposes or desires, the lower impulses, and desires, prompted by the unreal, effortlessly dissolve."

19

About The Author

Anupam Srivastava is a Leadership Enhancer, Transformation Mentor, Social Worker, Counsellor, Mind Coach, Thinker and Spiritual Seeker. He has mastered the science of transforming people into fully functional individuals and integrating them into the full scope of life including professional activities. His conviction in the inherent capacities of people, depth of his knowledge, practice and experience in transformational work and his insight into modern psychology and the wealth of old Indian wisdom ensures that the human capital benefits as well as secure their fuller engagement in productive and economic activities.

Social Worker & Counsellor

Anupam is a United Kingdom based social work and counseling practitioner who has worked extensively with a wide range of people over 37 years. As a practitioner, he worked extensively with dysfunctional children & families, including child protection, and looked after children. Assuming various roles and responsibilities in his career as a practitioner, practice educator, trainer, mentor, and coach, he not only taught but also trained hundreds of students, professionals, and volunteers in translating theory into practice. His talent and expertise lie in his ability to recognize and identify psychological barriers to learning and make the transformational journey a pleasant experience for his students and mentees.

Conceiving, Building and Succeeding

Founding Director of Acorn Fostering Services (UK) and Enabling World (India), Anupam's mission of transformational work with people has now been translated into Insight Life Coaching Services in India.

Anupam has an innate talent of 'conceiving, building and succeeding' on business ideas. His journey of transforming ideas into success stories commenced way back in 1992, when he associated himself with a direct selling business and achieved an unmatched feat of generating a huge turnover without selling a single product while still working full time at job. Remarkably, his success was propelled by his sheer ability to enhance and train people under him for better performance.

This was one of the reasons he was invited to join the management board of the Asian Counseling Services–a huge platform catering to a wider community in the UK. Anupam wrote the counseling skills training programme using his vast domain knowledge, got it nationally accredited, and trained hundreds of counselors. He was instrumental in redesigning and reshaping the organization and its service delivery in line with the ethical and professional standards prescribed by the British Association of Counselling and Psychotherapy (BACP).

With a vast body of related work experience under his belt, Anupam then set out to start his own private foster care agency–Acorn Fostering Service Ltd - in Leicester, UK, in the year 2003. It turned out to be a big success story and is thriving in the UK till date.

Transformational Mentor

Anupam is skilled in the science of transforming people into highly functional individuals, be they school students who undergo tremendous academic improvement as well as overall personality development, or CEOs and directors who witness better employee response in their organizations.

He strives to bridge the chasm between the contemporary world and spirituality and relate the wisdom encapsulated concepts of spirituality in day-to-day situations of modern life. He has worked extensively with students in India through his Performance Enhancement Programs in the last few years to bring about a change in the learning process. Most of these students have produced tangible results in the form of thumping academic success without putting themselves under tremendous pressure as is the trend these days.

Mind Coach

This is one of the first few steps Anupam has taken in his bid to contribute to nation-building as a Mind Coach. He is bringing his extensive professional experience and expertise, both in business management as well as in the field of professional counseling practice, to set up nationwide Counseling Services in India which are based on global standards and ethical framework.

He has already started on this path by developing four path-breaking wellness programmes that cater to every stratum of the society. With his **Employee Wellbeing** programme, Anupam aims to counter employee related challenges faced by India Inc, by looking after the mental and emotional health of working professionals. The **Academic Wellbeing** programme is a collaborative proposal to work in partnership with academic institutions in India to help young people of all ages to have an opportunity to express their concerns and challenges in a safe environment and build their Self-worth. With his **Ayush Wellbeing** programme, Anupam proposes to work in partnership with health professionals, organizations, and institutions to make a range of nonpharmacological interventions available to patients and their families. The **Emotional Wellbeing** programme aims to increase the acceptability of counseling as an important therapy among the Indian population, and to make confidential, culturally sensitive, and affordable services available to the citizens.

Spiritual Seeker

Anupam was neither satisfied nor convinced with the ritualistic format of religion. His inquisitive disposition convinced him that there was more than what meets the eyes when it comes to systemized religion. His 39+ years' journey of spiritual exploration that started at the age of 20 opened him to the study of scriptures and works of many masters. He found his spiritual *Guru* in Late Swami Chinmayananda Saraswati of Chinmaya Mission whose highly intellectual, logical, scientific, and rational interpretations, of various Upanishads, Bhagavad Gita, and several translations in English of Adi Shankaracharya's *Granths* and commentaries, appealed to his own scientific temperament and helped him draw parallels between Objective Science of Modern Psychology and Subjective Science of Spirituality.

Contact the Author

Anupam Srivastava

https://insightlcs.com/profile/index.html

kshamanupam@gmail.com

+91 9811684618

+44 7973278937

20

References

General References From the Books by Swami Chinmayananda Saraswati:

- The Holy Gita
- Vivekachudamani
- Self-Unfoldment
- Meditation and Life
- Chandogya Upanishad
- Svetasvatara Upanishad
- Mandukya Upanishad

Web References

The Meaning of Life According to Hinduism

https://u.osu.edu/group5/2014/10/12/the-meaning-of-life-according-to-hinduism/comment-page-1

Gita Chapter 7 - Verse 17 - 7.17 tesam jnani - Slokam

https://shlokam.org/bhagavad-gita/7-17

https://www.britannica.com › topic › Ganesha

https://en.wikipedia.org › wiki › Vishnu_Purana

https://www.ekhartyoga.com › Blog

https://www.enjoycommunitywellness.com › 2019/11/24

Hinduism - Wikipedia

https://en.wikipedia.org › wiki › Hinduism

https://en.wikipedia.org › wiki › God_in_Hinduism

Historicity of the Ramayana - Wikipedia

https://en.wikipedia.org › wiki › Historicity_of_the_Ra...

Brahma - Wikipedia

https://en.wikipedia.org › wiki › Brahma

Hanuman - Wikipedia

https://en.wikipedia.org › wiki › Hanuman

Hanuman | Hindu mythology - Encyclopedia Britannica

https://www.britannica.com › topic › Hanuman

https://www.academia.edu › Who_Hanuman

https://www.britannica.com › ... › Spirituality

Shiva - Wikipedia

https://en.wikipedia.org › wiki › Shiva

Shiva | Definition, Forms, God, Symbols, Meaning, & Facts

https://www.britannica.com › topic › Shiva

Ten Thousand Names of Shiva, Shiva Dasa Sahasranama

https://ramanisblog.in › 2016/11/24 › ten-thousand-na...

Tridevi - Wikipedia

https://en.wikipedia.org › wiki › *Tridevi*

Tridevi - the three supreme Goddess in Hinduism - Hindu FAQS

https://www.hindufaqs.com › Hindu FAQs

What is the OM Symbol ☐ Meaning and How to Chant it

https://www.yogitimes.com › article › what-is-om-symb...

The Aum Symbol - History And Meaning

https://symbolsarchive.com › aum-symbol-history-mea...

You Write. We Publish.

To publish your own book, contact us.

We publish poetry collections, short story collections, novellas and novels.

contact@thewriteorder.com

Instagram- thewriteorder

www.facebook.com/thewriteorder

www.ingramcontent.com/pod-product-compliance
Lightning Source LLC
LaVergne TN
LVHW091627070526
838199LV00044B/965